Mastering

Java

MACMILLAN MASTER SERIES

Accounting
Advanced English Language
Advanced Pure Mathematics
Arabic
Banking
Basic Management
Biology
British Politics
Business Administration
Business Communication
Business Law
C Programming
C++ Programming
Catering Theory
Chemistry
COBOL Programming
Communication
Databases
Economic and Social History
Economics
Electrical Engineering
Electronic and Electrical Calculations
Electronics
English as a Foreign Language
English Grammar
English Language
English Literature
French
French 2
German
German 2

Global Information Systems
Human Biology
Internet
Italian
Italian 2
Java
Manufacturing
Marketing
Mathematics
Mathematics for Electrical and
   Electronic Engineering
Microsoft Office
Modern British History
Modern European History
Modern World History
Pascal and Delphi Programming
Philosophy
Photography
Physics
Psychology
Science
Shakespeare
Social Welfare
Sociology
Spanish
Spanish 2
Statistics
Study Skills
Visual Basic
World Religions

Macmillan Master Series
Series Standing Order ISBN 0–333–69343–4
(outside North America only)

You can receive future titles in this series as they are published by placing a standing order.
Please contact your bookseller or, in case of difficulty, write to us at the address below with
your name and address, the title of the series and the ISBN quoted above.

Customer Services Department, Macmillan Distribution Ltd
Houndmills, Basingstoke, Hampshire RG21 6XS, England

Mastering

Java

William Buchanan, BSc, CEng, PhD
Senior Lecturer
Department of Electrical and Electronic Engineering
Napier University
Edinburgh

Series Editor
William Buchanan

MACMILLAN

This book is dedicated to my beautiful wife.

Microsoft, Windows 95, Windows NT are trademarks of Microsoft
Corporation.

Published 1998 by
MACMILLAN PRESS LTD
Houndmills, Basingstoke, Hampshire RG21 6XS
and London
Companies and representatives
throughout the world

ISBN 0–333–73008–9

A catalogue record for this book is available
from the British Library.

This book is printed on paper suitable for recycling and
made from fully managed and sustained forest sources.

10	9	8	7	6	5	4	3	2	1
07	06	05	04	03	02	01	00	99	98

Typeset by W. Buchanan in Great Britain

Printed and bound in Great Britain by
Biddles Ltd, Guildford and King's Lynn

Contents

Preface

Java is one of the fastest growing development languages and has the great advantage that is was developed after the Internet and WWW were created. It is by no means an easy language to learn, but it is relatively easy to create graphics and windows-based programs.

If I were to personally rate the top-ten advantages of Java I would rate them as:

1. Direct WWW/Internet support. Java contains direct support for most of the Internet, such as HTTP, Socket programming, and so on.
2. Runs in a client/server environment. Where the program is run on a server and sends the results to the client.
3. Produces applets which are platform-independent. This allows applets to be run on a PC, a Mac, a Sun workstation, an HP workstation or any other computer which has a browser which support Java applets.
4. It is event-driven rather than procedural-driven. This means that it supports events, such as keypresses, mouse actions, and so on. These make the program more responsive and easier to design. Many programming languages are procedural-based where the code is run in a sequential manner.
5. It has direct support for windows, buttons, menus, and so on. Many software compilers have non-standard add-ons for the support of these objects, which can lead to compiler dependence. Microsoft Windows, though, now has a standard library called Win32 which gives support to C++, Delphi and Visual Basic.
6. Direct support for bit-mapped graphics. Most languages, such as C++ and Pascal, have graphics support as an add-on to the basic language. This again leads to compiler dependence. Microsoft Windows, though, now has a standard library called Win32 which gives support to C++, Delphi and Visual Basic.
7. It is totally object-oriented. Programs are produced by defining classes which are operated on by methods. An instance of a class is known is an object.
8. It produces either stand-alone programs which are run with an interpreter, or applets which run within browsers.
9. It is based on C and C++, but with many enhancements. It also gets rid of many of the difficult areas of C/C++ programming, such as pointers, strings and the lack of strong data type checking.

10. It is freely available over the Internet and it is easy to upgrade and to add to.

This book is intended as an introduction to Java and is practical in its approach. I feel the best way of learning the language is to use practical examples. Many of the chapters also contain project work which is intended to give readers some practical work which requires a degree of thought, planning and testing.

Further information and source code can be found on the WWW page:

```
http://www.eece.napier.ac.uk/~bill_b/java.html
```

Help from myself can be sought using the email address:

```
w.buchanan@napier.ac.uk
```

I would personally like to thank Suzannah Tipple, Isobel Munday and Christopher Glennie at Macmillan for their hard work and their continued support for the Mastering IT and Computing series. I would also like to thank Olivier Sagner for his excellent researching of Java Sockets. Finally, I would like to thank my family, Julie, Billy, Jamie and David for their love and understanding.

I hope that students, tutors and professionals will find Java as stimulating as I found it when writing this book. Related, and forthcoming, books in this series include: Mastering the Internet, Mastering Intranets, Mastering Global Information Systems, Mastering Network Operating Systems (Windows NT, NetWare and UNIX), Mastering Pascal and Delphi, and Mastering C++. Potential, and existing, authors who are interested in writing in this series should contact either myself or one to the Acquisition Editor at Macmillan.

Dr William Buchanan.

1 Introduction to Java

1.1 Introduction

Java 1.0 was first released in 1995 and was quickly adopted as it fitted well with Internet-based programming. It was followed by Java 1.1 which gave faster interpretation of Java applets and included many new features. This book documents the basic features of Java 1.0 and the enhancements that have been made in Java 1.1.

It is a general-purpose, concurrent, class-based, object-oriented language and has been designed to be relatively simple to built complex applications. Java is developed from C and C++, but some parts of C++ have been dropped and others added.

Java has the great advantage over conventional software languages in that it produces code which is computer hardware independent. This is because the compiled code (called bytecodes) is interpreted by the WWW browser. Unfortunately this leads to slower execution, but, as much of the time in a graphical user interface program is spent updating the graphics display, then the overhead is, as far as the user is concerned, not a great one.

The other advantages that Java has over conventional software languages include:

- It is a more dynamic language than C/C++ and Pascal, and was designed to adapt to an evolving environment. It is extremely easy to add new methods and extra libraries without affecting existing applets and programs. It is also useful in Internet applications as it supports most of the standard compressed image, audio and video formats.
- It has networking facilities built into it. This provides support for TCP/IP sockets, URLs, IP addresses and datagrams.
- While Java is based on C and C++ it avoids some of the difficult areas of C/C++ code (such as pointers and parameter passing).
- It supports client/server applications where the Java applet runs on the server and the client receives the updated graphics information. In the most extreme case the client can simply be a graphics terminal which runs Java applets over a network. The small 'black-box' networked computer is one of the founding principles of Java, and it is hoped in the future that small

1

Java-based computers could replace the complex PC/workstation for general purpose applications, like accessing the Internet or playing network games. This 'black-box' computer concept is illustrated in Figure 1.1.

Most existing Web browsers are enabled for Java applets (such as Internet Explorer 3.0 and Netscape 2.0 and later versions). Figure 1.2 shows how Java applets are created. First the source code is produced with an editor, next a Java compiler compiles the Java source code into bytecode (normally appending the file name with .class). An HTML page is then constructed which has the reference to the applet. After this a Java-enabled browser or applet viewer can then be used to run the applet.

The Java Development Kit (JDK) is available, free, from Sun Microsystems from the WWW site http://www.javasoft.com. This can be used to compile Java applets and standalone programs. There are versions for Windows NT/95, Apple Mac and UNIX-based systems with many sample applets.

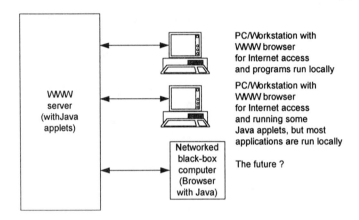

Figure 1.1 Internet accessing

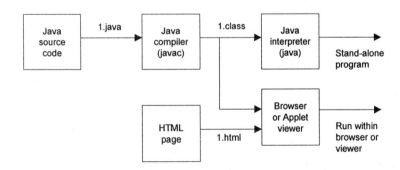

Figure 1.2 Constructing Java applets and standalone programs

Table 1.1 shows the main files used in the PC version and Figure 1.3 shows the directory structure of the JDK tools. The Java compiler, Java interpreter and applet viewer programs are stored in the `bin` directory. On the PC, this directory is normally set up in the PATH directory, so that the Java compiler can be called while the user is in another directory. The following is a typical setup (assuming that the home directory is c: *javahome*):

```
PATH=C:\WINDOWS;C:\WINDOWS\COMMAND;C:\javahome\BIN
CLASSPATH=C:\javahome\LIB;.;C:\javahome
```

Table 1.1 JDK programs

File	Description
javac.exe	Java compiler
java.exe	Java interpreter
appletViewer.exe	Applet viewer for testing and running applets
classes.zip	It is needed by the compiler and interpreter
javap.exe	Java class disassembler
javadoc.exe	Java document generator
javah.exe	C Header and Stub File Generator
jar.exe	Java Archive Tool which combines class files and other resources into a single jar file.
jbd.exe	Java debugger

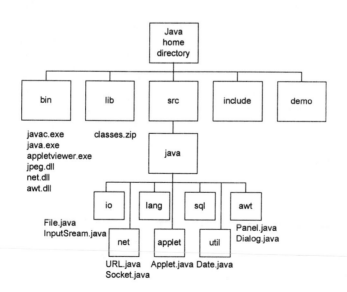

Figure 1.3 Sample directory structure of JDK for a PC-based system

The `lib` directory contains the `classes.zip` file which is a zipped-up version of the Java class files. These class files are stored in the directories below the `src/java` directory. For example, the `io` classes (such as `File.java` and `InputStream.java`) are used for input/output in Java, the `awt` classes (such as `Panel.java` and `Dialog.java`) are used to create and maintain windows. These and other classes will be discussed later.

The `include` directory contains header files for integrating C/C++ programs with Java applets and the `demo` directory contains some sample Java applets.

1.2   Standalone programs

A Java program can be run as a standalone program or as an applet. A standalone program allows the Java program to be run without a browser and is normally used when testing the Java applet. The method of output to the screen is:

```
System.out.println("message");
```

which prints a message (`message`) to the display. This type of debugging is messy as these statements need to be manually inserted in the program. It is likely that later versions of the JDK toolkit will contain a run-time debugger which will allow developers to view the execution of the program.

To run a standalone program the `java.exe` program is used and the user adds output statements with the `System.out.println()` method. Note that there is no output to the main graphics applet screen with this method.

Java program 1.1 gives a simple example of a standalone program. The `public static void main(Strings[] args)` defines the main method. Sample run 1.1 shows how the Java program is created (with `edit`) and then compiled (with `javac.exe`), and then finally run (with `java.exe`).

📖 Java program 1.1
```
public class chap1_01
{
  public static void main(String[] args)
    {
    int i;
      i=10;
      System.out.println("This is an example of the ");
      System.out.println("output from the standalone");
      System.out.println("program");
      System.out.println("The value of i is " + i);
  }
}
```

```
C:\DOCS\notes\java>edit chap1_01.java
C:\DOCS\notes\java>javac chap1_01.java
C:\DOCS\notes\java>java chap1_01
This is an example of the
output from the standalone
program
The value of i is 10
```

The process of developing a standalone Java program is:

- Create a Java program. This is the main Java program file and is created by a text editor (such as edit in a PC-based system). These files are given the .java file extension. In Sample run 1.1 the file created is chap1_01.java.
- Compile program to a class file. This is created by the Java compiler (javac.exe) when there is a successful compilation. By default, the file produced has the same filename as the source file and the .class file extension. In Sample run 1.1 the file created is chap1_01.class.
- Run program with the Java interpreter. The Java interpreter (java.exe) reads from the class file (which contains the bytecode) and gives the required output.

1.3   Comments

Java supports single line comments with a double slash (//) or multi-line comments which are defined between a /* and a */. The single line comment makes everything on the line after the double slash a comment. A few examples are:

```
PI=3.14157;      // Sets the value of pi
area=PI*r*r      // Area is PI times the square of the radius
/* No more comments   */
```

1.4   Java reserved words

Like any programming language, Java has various reserved words which cannot be used as a variable name. These are given next:

```
abstract      boolean      break        byte         case          cast
catch         char         class        cons         continue      default
do            double       else         extends      final         finally
float         for          future       generic      goto          if
implements    import       inner        instanceof   in            interface
long          native       new          null         operator      outer
package       private      protected    public       rest          return
short         static       super        switch       synchronized  this
throw         throws       transient    try          var           unsigned
virtual       void         volatile     while
```

1.5 Numbers and representations

1.5.1 Exponent representation

Relatively large or small numbers can be represented in exponent format. Table 1.2 gives some examples of this format.

Table 1.2 Exponent format conversions.

Value (or PHYSICAL CONSTANT)	Exponent format
0.000 000 001	1e-9
1 234 320	1.23432e6
1 000 000 000 000	1e12
0.023	2.3e-2
0.943230	9.4323e-1
CHARGE OF ELECTRON	1.602e-19
MASS OF ELECTRON	9.109e-31
PERMITTIVITY OF FREE SPACE	8.854e-12
SPEED OF LIGHT	2.998e8

1.5.2 Hexadecimal and octal numbers

Hexadecimal numbers are useful for representing binary values and are represented in Java with a preceding 0x (a zero and an 'x'). To convert a binary value to hexadecimal the value is organised in groups of 4 bits. Then each of the 4-bit groups is represented as a hexadecimal value. For example:

```
0100 1101 1100 1111
```

is represented by:

```
0x4DCF
```

in Java. An octal value has a preceding 0 (zero) value. Program 1.2 shows a simple Java program which has two integer variables (val1 and val2). These are given a value of 34h and 20o. It can be seen in Sample run 1.2 that the output of the program prints the equivalent decimal value.

📖 **Java program 1.2**
```
public class chap1_02
{
 public static void main (String args[])
 {
 int val1=0x34,val2=020;

   System.out.println(" Val1 is "+val1+" Val2 is "+val2);
 }
}
```

💻 **Sample run 1.2**
```
C:\java\src\chap1>edit chap1_02.java
C:\java\src\chap1>javac chap1_02.java
C:\java\src\chap1>java chap1_02
 Val1 is 52 Val2 is 16
```

1.6 Data types

Variables within a program can be stored as either boolean values, numbers or as characters. For example, the resistance of a copper wire would be stored as a number (a real value), whether it exists or not (as a boolean value) and the name of a component (such as "R1") would be stored as characters.

An integer is any value without a decimal point. Its range depends on the number of bytes used to store it. A floating-point value is any number and can include a decimal point. This value is always in a signed format. Again, the range depends on the number of bytes used.

Integers either take up 1, 2, 4 or 8 bytes in memory for a byte, short, int and long, respectively. These are all represented in 2's complement notation and thus can store positive and negative integer values. Table 1.3 gives some typical ranges for data types.

Table 1.3 Typical ranges for data types

Type	Storage (bytes)	Range
boolean	1-bit	True or False
byte	1	−128 to 127
short	2	−32 768 to 32 767
int	4	−2 147 483 648 to 2 147 483 647
long	8	2 223 372 036 854 775 808 to −2 223 372 036 854 775 809
char	2	16-bit unsigned integers representing Unicode characters.
float	4	$\pm3.4\times10^{-38}$ to $\pm3.4\times10^{38}$
double	8	$\pm1.7\times10^{-308}$ to $\pm1.7\times10^{308}$

1.7 Characters and strings

Typically, characters are stored using either ASCII or EBCDIC codes. ASCII is an acronym for American Standard Code for Information Interchange and EBCDIC for Extended Binary Coded Decimal Interchange Code. Table 1.4 gives a full listing of the ASCII character set.

ASCII characters from decimal 0 to 32 are non-printing characters that are used either to format the output or to control the hardware. Program 1.3 displays an ASCII character for an entered decimal value. The `print()` method displays the ASCII character. Test run 1.3 shows a sample run (note that some of the displayed characters are non-printing).

Table 1.4 ASCII character set

Hex	Char	Hex	Char	Hex	Char	Hex	Char	Hex	Char	Hex	Char	Hex	Char	Hex	Char
00	NUL	10	DLE	20	SP	30	0	40	@	50	P	60	'	70	p
01	SOH	11	DC1	21	!	31	1	41	A	51	Q	61	a	71	q
02	STX	12	DC2	22	"	32	2	42	B	52	R	62	b	72	r
03	ETX	13	DC3	23	#	33	3	43	C	53	S	63	c	73	s
04	EOT	14	DC4	24	$	34	4	44	D	54	T	64	d	74	t
05	ENQ	15	NAK	25	%	35	5	45	E	55	U	65	e	75	u
06	ACK	16	SYN	26	&	36	6	46	F	56	V	66	f	76	v
07	BEL	17	ETB	27	'	37	7	47	G	57	W	67	g	77	w
08	BS	18	CAN	28	(	38	8	48	H	58	X	68	h	78	x
09	HT	19	EM	29	)	39	9	49	I	59	Y	69	i	79	y
0A	NL	1A	SUB	2A	*	3A	:	4A	J	5A	Z	6A	j	7A	z
0B	VT	1B	ESC	2B	+	3B	;	4B	K	5B	[	6B	k	7B	{
0C	FF	1C	FS	2C	,	3C	<	4C	L	5C	\	6C	l	7C		
0D	CR	1D	GS	2D	-	3D	=	4D	M	5D	]	6D	m	7D	}
0E	SO	1E	RS	2E	.	3E	>	4E	N	5E	^	6E	n	7E	~
0F	SI	1F	US	2F	/	3F	?	4F	O	5F	-	6F	o	7F	DEL

📖 Java program 1.3

```
public class chap1_03
{
 public static void main (String args[])
 {
 char ch;
     for (ch=0;ch<256;ch++)
        System.out.print(" " + ch); // print from 0 to 255
 }
}
```

💻 Sample run 1.3

```
□ □ □ □ □ □
□ □ □ □ □ □ □ □ □ □   □ □ -   ! " # $ % & ' ( ) * + , - .
/ 0 1 2 3 4 5 6 7 8 9 : ; < = > ? @ A B C D E F G H I J K L M N
O P Q R S T U V W X Y Z [ \ ] ^ _ ` a b c d e f g h i j k l m n
o p q r s t u v w x y z { | } ~ □ □ □ , f „ … † ‡ ^ ‰ Š ‹ Œ □ □
□ □ ` ' " " • - — ~ ™ š › œ □ □ Ÿ   ¡ ¢ £ ¤ ¥ ¦ § ¨ © ª « ¬ - ®
¯ ° ± ² ³ ´ µ ¶ · ¸ ¹ º » ¼ ½ ¾ ¿ À Á Â Ã Ä Å Æ Ç È É Ê Ë Ì Í Î
Ï Ð Ñ Ò Ó Ô Õ Ö × Ø Ù Ú Û Ü Ý Þ ß à á â ã ä å æ ç è é ê ë ì í î
ï ð ñ ò ó ô õ ö ÷ ø ù ú û ü ý þ ÿ
```

Characters of type `char` are stored as 2-byte Unicode characters (0x0000 to 0xFFFF). This allows for internationalisation of the character set. The characters from 0 to 255 (0x0000 to 0x00FF) are standard extended ASCII character set (ISO8859-1, or Latin-1), where the characters are stored as the binary digits associated with the character. For example, the ASCII code for the character 'A' is 65 decimal (0x41); the binary storage for this character is thus 0100 0001. Some examples of ASCII codes are given in Table 1.5.

Table 1.5 Examples of ASCII characters

Decimal	Hex	Binary	Character
32	0x20	0010 0000	SPACE
65	0x41	0100 0001	'A'
66	0x42	0100 0010	'B'
90	0x5A	0101 1010	'Z'
97	0x61	0110 0001	'a'
122	0x7A	0111 1010	'z'
7	0x07	0000 0111	Ring the bell
8	0x08	0000 1000	Perform a backspace

The `println()` method sends a formatted string to the standard output (the display). This string can include special control characters, such as new lines ('\n'), backspaces ('\b') and tabspaces ('\t'); these are listed in Table 1.6.

The `println()` method writes a string of text to the standard output and at the end of the text a new line is automatically appended, whereas the `print()` method does not append the output with a new line.

Table 1.6 Special control (or escape sequence) characters

Characters	Function
\"	Double quotes (")
\'	Single quote (')
\\	Backslash (\ )
\unnnn	Unicode character in hexadecimal code, e.g. \u041 gives '!'
\0nn	Unicode character in octal code, e.g. \041 gives '!'
\b	Backspace (move back one space)
\f	Form-feed
\n	New line (line-feed)
\r	Carriage return
\t	Horizontal tab spacing

Special control characters use a backslash to inform the program to escape from the way they would be normally be interpreted. The carriage return ('\r') is used to return the current character pointer on the display back to the start of the line (on many displays this is the leftmost side of the screen). A form-feed control character ('\f') is used to feed line printers on a single sheet and the horizontal tab ('\t') feeds the current character position forward one tab space.

Quotes enclose a single character, for example 'a', whereas inverted commas enclose a string of characters, such as "Mastering Java". Java has a special String object (string). Java program 1.4 shows an example of declaring two strings (name1 and name2) and Sample run 1.4 shows a sample run. The '\"' character is used to display inverted commas and the backspace character has been used to delete an extra character in the displayed string. The BELL character is displayed with the '\007' and '\u0007' escape sequence characters. Other escape characters used include the horizontal tab ('\t') and the new line character ('\n').

Strings can be easily concatenated using the '+' operator. For example to build a string of two strings (with a space in-between) then following can be implemented:

```
String name1, name2, name3;

    name3=name1+" " + name2;
```

📖 Java program 1.4
```
public class chap1_04
{

 public static void main (String args[])
 {

 String name1="Bill", name2="Buchanan";

     System.out.println("Ring the bell 3 times \u0007\007\007");
     System.out.print("\"My name is Bill\"\n");
     System.out.println("\t\"Buchh\banan\"");

     System.out.println(name1 + " " + name2);

 }
}
```

🖥 Sample run 1.4
```
C:\java\src\chap1>java chap1_04
Ring the bell 3 times
"My name is Bill"
        "Buchanan"
Bill Buchanan
```

1.8 Declaration of variables

A program uses variables to store data. Before a program can use a variable, its name and its data type must first be declared. A comma groups variables of the same data type. For example, if a program requires integer variables num_steps and bit_mask, floating-point variables resistor1 and resistor2, and two character variables char1 and char2, then the following declarations can be made:

```
int      num_steps,bit_mask;
float    resistor1,resistor2;
char     char1,char2;
```

Program 1.5 is a simple program that determines the equivalent parallel resistance of two resistors of 1000 and 500 Ω connected in parallel. It contains three floating-point declarations for the variables resistor1, resistor2 and eq_resistance.

📖 Java program 1.5
```
public class chap1_05
{
  public static void main (String args[])
  {
  float resistor1, resistor2, equ_resistance;

      resistor1=1500;
      resistor2=500;
      equ_resistance=1/(1/resistor1+1/resistor2);
      System.out.println("Equ. resistance is "+equ_resistance);
  }
}
```

It is also possible to assign an initial value to a variable at the point in the program at which it is declared. This is known as variable initialisation. Program 1.6 gives an example of this with the declared variables resistor1 and resistor2 initialised with 1000.0 and 500.0, respectively. Sample run 1.5 gives an example run.

📖 Java program 1.6
```
public class chap1_06
{
  public static void main (String args[])
  {
  float resistor1=1500, resistor2=500, equ_resistance;

      equ_resistance=1/(1/resistor1+1/resistor2);
      System.out.println("Equ. resistance is "+equ_resistance);
  }
}
```

```
C:\jdk1.1.6\src\chap1>edit chap1_03.java
C:\jdk1.1.6\src\chap1>javac chap1_03.java
C:\jdk1.1.6\src\chap1>java chap1_03
Equ. resistance is 375.0
```

1.9   Java operators

Java has a rich set of operators, of which there are four main types:

- Arithmetic
- Logical
- Bitwise
- Relational

1.9.1 Arithmetic

Arithmetic operators operate on numerical values. The basic arithmetic operations are add (+), subtract (-), multiply (*), divide (/) and modulus division (%). Modulus division gives the remainder of an integer division. The following gives the basic syntax of two operands with an arithmetic operator.

```
operand operator operand
```

The assignment operator (=) is used when a variable 'takes on the value' of an operation. Other short-handed operators are used with it, including add equals (+=), minus equals (-=), multiplied equals (*=), divide equals (/=) and modulus equals (%=). The following examples illustrate their uses.

Statement	Equivalent
x+=3.0;	x=x+3.0;
voltage/=sqrt(2);	voltage=voltage/sqrt(2);
bit_mask *=2;	bit_mask=bit_mask*2;
screen_val%=22+1;	screen_val=screen_val%22+1;

In many applications it is necessary to increment or decrement a variable by 1. For this purpose Java has two special operators; ++ for increment and -- for decrement. These can either precede or follow the variable. If they precede, then a pre-increment/decrement is conducted, whereas if they follow it, a post-increment/decrement is conducted. The following examples show their usage.

Statement	Equivalent
`no_values--;`	`no_values=no_values-1;`
`i--;`	`i=i-1;`
`screen_ptr++;`	`screen_ptr=screen_ptr+1;`

When the following example code is executed the values of `i`, `j`, `k`, `y` and `z` will be 10, 12, 13, 10 and 10, respectively. The statement `z=--i` decrements `i` and assigns this value to `z` (a pre-increment), while `y=i++` assigns the value of `i` to `y` and then increments `i` (a post-increment).

```
i=10;  j=11;   k=12;
y=i++;      /*    assign i to y then increment i        */
z=--i;      /*    decrement i then assign it to z       */
j++;        /*    increment j                           */
++k;        /*    increment k                           */
```

Table 1.7 summarises the arithmetic operators.

Table 1.7 Arithmetic operators

Operator	Operation	Example
−	subtraction or minus	5-4→1
+	addition	4+2→6
*	multiplication	4*3→12
/	division	4/2→2
%	modulus	13%3→1
+=	add equals	x += 2 is equivalent to x=x+2
-=	minus equals	x -= 2 is equivalent to x=x-2
/=	divide equals	x /= y is equivalent to x=x/y
*=	multiplied equals	x *= 32 is equivalent to x=x*32
=	assignment	x = 1
++	increment	Count++ is equivalent to Count=Count+1
--	decrement	Sec-- is equivalent to Sec=Sec-1

1.9.2 Relationship

The relationship operators determine whether the result of a comparison is TRUE or FALSE. These operators are greater than (>), greater than or equal to (>=), less than (<), less than or equal to (<=), equal to (==) and not equal to (!=). Table 1.8 lists the relationship operators.

1.9.3 Logical (TRUE or FALSE)

A logical operation is one in which a decision is made as to whether the operation performed is TRUE or FALSE. If required, several relationship operations can be grouped together to give the required functionality. Java assumes that a numerical value of 0 (zero) is FALSE and that any other value is TRUE. Table 1.9 lists the logical operators.

Logical AND operation will only yield a TRUE if all the operands are TRUE. Table 1.10 gives the result of the AND (&&) operator for the operation Operand1 && Operand2. The logical OR operation yields a TRUE if any one of the operands is TRUE. Table 1.10 gives the logical results of the OR (||) operator for the statement Operand1 || Operand2.

Table 1.8 Relationship operators

Operator	Function	Example	TRUE Condition
>	greater than	(b>a)	when b is greater than a
>=	greater than or equal	(a>=4)	when a is greater than or equal to 4
<	less than	(c<f)	when c is less than f
<=	less than or equal	(x<=4)	when x is less than or equal to 4
==	equal to	(x==2)	when x is equal to 2
!=	not equal to	(y!=x)	when y is not equal to x

Table 1.9 Logical operators

Operator	Function	Example	TRUE condition
&&	AND	((x==1) && (y<2))	when x is equal to 1 *and* y is less than 2
||	OR	((a!=b) || (a>0))	when a is not equal to b *or* a is greater than 0
!	NOT	(!(a>0))	when a is *not* greater than 0

Table 1.11 gives the logical result of the NOT (!) operator for the statement `!Operand`.

Table 1.10 AND and OR logical truth table

Operand1	Operand2	AND	OR
FALSE	FALSE	FALSE	FALSE
FALSE	TRUE	FALSE	TRUE
TRUE	FALSE	FALSE	TRUE
TRUE	TRUE	TRUE	TRUE

Table 1.11 NOT logical truth table

Operand	Result
FALSE	TRUE
TRUE	FALSE

For example, if `a` has the value 1 and `b` is also 1, then the following relationship statements would apply:

Statement	Result
`(a==1) && (b==1)`	TRUE
`(a>1) && (b==1)`	FALSE
`(a==10) || (b==1)`	TRUE
`!(a==12)`	TRUE

Java program 1.7 shows a Java program which proves the above table and Sample run 1.6 shows a sample run.

Java program 1.7

```java
public class chap1_07
{
 public static void main (String args[])
 {
 int a=1,b=1;

     if ((a==1) && (b==1)) System.out.println("TRUE");
     else System.out.println("FALSE");
     if ((a>1) && (b==1)) System.out.println("TRUE");
     else System.out.println("FALSE");
     if ((a==10) || (b==1)) System.out.println("TRUE");
     else System.out.println("FALSE");
     if (!(a==10)) System.out.println("TRUE");
     else System.out.println("FALSE");

 }

}
```

```
C:\java\src\chap1>java chap1_07
TRUE
FALSE
TRUE
TRUE
```

1.9.4 Bitwise

The bitwise operators are similar to the logical operators but they should not be confused as their operation differs. Bitwise operators operate directly on the individual bits of an operand(s), whereas logical operators determine whether a condition is TRUE or FALSE.

Numerical values are stored as bit patterns in either an unsigned integer format, signed integer (2's complement) or floating-point notation (an exponent and mantissa). Characters are normally stored as ASCII characters.

The basic bitwise operations are AND (&), OR (|), 1's complement or bitwise inversion (~), XOR (^), shift left (<<), shift right with sign (>>) and right shift without sign (>>>). Table 1.12 gives the results of the AND, OR and XOR bitwise operation on two bits *Bit1* and *Bit2*.

Table 1.12 Bitwise AND truth table

Bit1	Bit2	AND	OR	XOR
0	0	0	0	0
0	1	0	1	1
1	0	0	1	1
1	1	1	1	0

Table 1.13 gives the truth table for the NOT (~) bitwise operator on a single bit.

Table 1.13 Bitwise NOT truth table

Bit	Result
0	1
1	0

The bitwise operators operate on each of the individual bits of the operands. For example, if two decimal integers 58 and 41 (assuming 8-bit unsigned binary values) are operated on using the AND, OR and EX-OR bitwise operators, then the following applies.

	AND	OR	EX-OR
58	00111010b	00111010b	00111010b
41	00101001b	00101001b	00101001b
Result	00101000b	00111011b	00010011b

The results of these bitwise operations are as follows:

```
58 & 41 = 40        (that is, 00101000b)
58 | 41 = 59        (that is, 00111011b)
58 ^ 41 = 19        (that is, 00010011b)
```

Java program 1.8 shows a program which tests these operations and Sample run 1.7 shows a test run.

The 1's complement operator operates on a single operand. For example, if an operand has the value of 17 (00010001b) then the 1's complement of this, in binary, will be 11101110b.

📖 Java program 1.8

```
public class chap1_08
{
 public static void main (String args[])
 {
 int a=58,b=41,val;
        val=a&b; System.out.println("AND "+ val);
        val=a|b; System.out.println("OR "+ val);
        val=a^b; System.out.println("X-OR "+ val);
 }
}
```

💻 **Sample run 1.7**
```
C:\java\src\chap1>java chap1_08
AND 40
OR 59
X-OR 19
```

To perform bit shifts, the <<, >> and >>> operators are used. These operators shift the bits in the operand by a given number defined by a value given on the right-hand side of the operation. The left-shift operator (<<) shifts the bits of the operand to the left and zeros fill the result on the right. The right-shift operator (>>) shifts the bits of the operand to the right and zeros fill the result if the integer is positive; otherwise it will fill with 1s. The right shift with sign (>>>) shifts the bits and ignores the sign flag; it thus treats signed integers as unsigned integers. The standard format for the three shift operators is:

```
operand >> no_of_bit_shift_positions
operand << no_of_bit_shift_positions
operand >>> no_of_bit_shift_positions
```

For example, if y = 59 (00111011), then y >> 3 will equate to 7 (00000111) and y<<2 to 236 (11101100). Table 1.14 gives a summary of the basic bitwise operators.

Table 1.14 Bitwise operators

Operator	Function	Example
&	AND	c = A & B
|	OR	f = z | y
^	XOR	h = 5 ^ f
~	1's complement	x = ~y
>>	shift right	x = y >> 1
<<	shift left	y = y << 2

The following examples use shortened forms of the bitwise operators:

`i<<=2` equivalent to `i=i<<2` *shift bits of i 2 positions to the left*

`time |= 32` equivalent to `time=time | 32` *OR bits of time with 32 decimal*

`bitval^=22` equivalent to `bitval=bitval^22` *bitval is EX-ORed with 22*

1.10 Precedence

There are several rules for dealing with operators:

- Two operators, apart from the assignment, should never be placed side by side. For example, x * % 3 is invalid.
- Groupings are formed with parentheses; anything within parentheses will be evaluated first. Nested parentheses can also be used to set priorities.
- A priority level or precedence exists for operators. Operators with a higher precedence are evaluated first; if two operators have the same precedence, then the operator on the left-hand side is evaluated first. The priority levels for operators are as follows:

HIGHEST PRIORITY

() [] .	primary
! ~ ++ -- -	unary
* / %	multiply
+ -	additive
<< >> >>>	shift
< > <= >=	relation
== !=	equality
&	

^			bitwise
|			
&&			logical
||			
=	+=	-=	assignment

LOWEST PRIORITY

The assignment operator has the lowest precedence. The following example shows how operators are prioritised in a statement (=> shows the steps in determining the result):

```
23 + 5 % 3 / 2 << 1     =>
23 + 2 / 2 << 1         =>
23 + 1 << 1             =>
23 + 2                  => 25
```

1.11 Data type conversion

A variable's data type can be changed temporarily using a technique known as casting or coercion. The cast modifier precedes the operand and the data type is defined in parentheses. Typical modifiers are (float), (int), (char) and (double). In Program 1.9 two integers b and c are divided and the result is assigned to a. Since b and c are both integers, the operator is an integer division. The result will thus be 1, as an integer division is performed. Sample run 1.8 shows a sample run.

📖 Java program 1.9

```
public class chap1_09
{
 public static void main (String args[])
 {
 int    b,c;
 float  val;
        b=6; c=11;
        val = c / b;
        System.out.println("Result is "+ val);
 }
}
```

💻 **Sample run 1.8**
```
C:\java\src\chap1>java chap1_09
Result is 1
```

Program 1.10 performs a floating-point division as the variable c has been recast or coerced to a float. Sample run 1.9 shows a sample run.

Java program 1.10

```
public class chap1_10
{
 public static void main (String args[])
 {
 int    b,c;
 float  val;
        b=6; c=11;
        val = (float) c / b;
        System.out.println("Result is "+ val);
 }
}
```

Sample run 1.9

```
C:\java\src\chap1>java chap1_10
Result is 1.8333334
```

1.12 Exercises

1.12.1 Determine the octal, decimal and hexadecimal ASCII codes for the following:

- ESC (Escape)
- DEL (Delete)
- '~' (tilde)
- '_' (underscore)
- NULL (Null character)

1.12.2 What special characters does Java use for the following:

- A new line
- A horizontal tab space
- An inverted comma (')
- Double inverted commas (")

1.12.3 Java Program 1.11 allows answers in this question to be checked by replacing the 0x34 value with the required value.

Java program 1.11

```
public class chap1_11
{
 public static void main (String args[])
 {
 int val1=0x34;
```

```
      System.out.println(" Val1 is "+val1);
   }
}
```

Complete the following table, giving the equivalent decimal, hexa-decimal or octal numbers.

Hexadecimal	Octal	Decimal
0x12		
0xA1		
0x1f0		
	013	
	027	
	0206	

1.12.4 Program 1.12 can be used to test results in this question. Replace the equation given in bold type with the required statement. Determine the results of the following:

(i)   21 % 4 % 2 * 3 + 2
(ii)   25 + 5 % 2 * 4 - 1
(iii)   3 * 3 * 7 % 2
(iv)   (7 + 4) % 4 * 2
(v)   25 % 3

📖 Java program 1.12
```
public class chap1_12
{
 public static void main (String args[])
 {
 int val1;

   val1=21 % 4 % 2 * 3 + 2;
    System.out.println(" Val1 is "+val1);
 }
}
```

1.12.5 Program 1.13 can be used to test results in this question. Replace the equations given in bold type with the required statement. Assuming x=14 and y=8, determine the results of the following:

(i)   x % y + 2
(ii)   x++
(iii)   --x
(iv)   x & y
(v)   x | y

```
(vi)      4 * (x + y * 2)
(vii)     x << 3
(viii)    y >> 1
```

📖 **Java program 1.13**

```
public class chap1_13
{
 public static void main (String args[])
 {
 int x=14, y=8, z;

    z= x % y + 2;
    System.out.println(" x is "+ x);
    System.out.println(" y is "+ y);
    System.out.println(" z is "+ z);
 }
}
```

1.12.6   Using a Java program determine the results of the following:

```
(i)      0x32 + 011
(ii)     0x31 & 044
(iii)    0x4B | 013
(iv)     011 * 0x31
(v)      ~32
(vi)     0xAA - 055
(vii)    0xFF + 0x10
(viii)   !(0xCF)
(ix)     ~(032)
```

1.12.7   Assuming x=1 and y=2, determine whether each of the following will result in a TRUE or a FALSE. Answers can be tested using the template of Program 1.14.

```
(i)      ((x==1) && (y!=2))
(ii)     ((x!=1) || (y==2))
(iii)    (!(x==2))
(iv)     (!((x==1) && (y==2)))
(v)      ((x>0) && (y<2))
(vi)     (x<=1)
(vii)    ((y>1) || (x==1))
```

📖 **Java program 1.14**

```
public class chap1_14
{
 public static void main (String args[])
 {
 int x=1, y=2;
```

```
        if ((x==1) && (y!=2)) System.out.println("TRUE");
        else System.out.println("FALSE");
  }
}
```

1.12.8   Modify Java program 1.3 so that it displays the whole range of Unicode characters (Hint the loop should go from 0x0000 to 0xffff).

2 Java Selection

2.1 Selection statements

2.1.1 *if...else*

A decision is made with the `if` statement. It logically determines whether a conditional expression is TRUE or FALSE. For a TRUE, the program executes one block of code; a FALSE causes the execution of another (if any). The keyword `else` identifies the FALSE block. In Java, braces ({ }) are used to define the start and end of the block.

Relationship operators, include:

- Greater than (>)
- Less than (<)
- Greater than or equal to (>=)

- Less than or equal to (<=)
- Equal to (==)
- Not equal to (!=)

These operations yield a TRUE or FALSE from their operation. Logical statements (&&, ||, !) can then group these together to give the required functionality. These are:

- AND (&&)
- OR (||)

- NOT (!)

If the operation is not a relationship, such as bitwise or an arithmetic operation, then any non-zero value is TRUE and a zero is FALSE. The following is an example syntax of the `if` statement. If the statement block has only one statement then the braces ({ }) can be excluded.

```
if (expression)
{
    statement block
}
```

The following is an example format with an `else` extension.

```
if (expression)
{
    statement block1
```

```
}
else
{
    statement block2
}
```

It is possible to nest if..else statements to give a required functionality. In the next example, *statement block1* is executed if expression1 is TRUE. If it is FALSE then the program checks the next expression. If this is TRUE the program executes *statement block2*, else it checks the next expression, and so on. If all expressions are FALSE then the program executes the final else statement block, in this case, *statement block4*:

```
if (expression1)
{
    statement block1
}
else if (expression2)
{
    statement block2
}
else if (expression3)
{
    statement block3
}
else
{
    statement block4
}
```

Figure 2.1 shows a diagrammatic representation of this example statement.

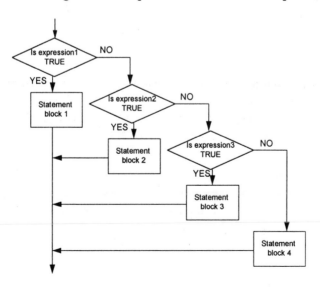

Figure 2.1 Structure of the compound if statement

Java program 2.1 gives an example of a program which uses the if...else statement. In this case the variable `col` is tested for its value. When it matches a value from 0 to 6 the equivalent colour code is displayed. If it is not between 0 and 6 then the default message is displayed (`"Not Defined Yet!"`). Sample run 2.1 shows a sample run.

📖 **Java program 2.1**

```
public class chap2_01
{
   public static void main (String args[])
   {
   int col;
      col=4;
      if (col==0) System.out.println("BLACK");
      else if (col==1) System.out.println("BROWN");
      else if (col==2) System.out.println("RED");
      else if (col==3) System.out.println("ORANGE");
      else if (col==4) System.out.println("YELLOW");
      else if (col==5) System.out.println("GREEN");
      else System.out.println("Not Defined Yet!");

   }
}
```

💻 **Sample run 2.1**

```
C:\java\src\chap2> edit chap2_01.java
C:\java\src\chap2> javac chap2_01.java
C:\java\src\chap2> java chap2_01
YELLOW
```

Some mathematical problems require the solution of a quadratic equation. The standard form is:

$$ax^2 + bx + c = 0$$

The solution of x in this equation is given by:

$$x_{1,2} = \frac{-b \pm \sqrt{b^2 - 4ac}}{2a}$$

This can yield three possible types of results:

1. if $b^2=4ac$, there will be a single real root ($x=-b/2a$)
2. else, if $b^2>4ac$, there will be two real roots:

$$x_1 = \frac{-b + \sqrt{b^2 - 4ac}}{2a}, \qquad x_2 = \frac{-b - \sqrt{b^2 - 4ac}}{2a}$$

3. else, the roots will be complex:

$$x_1 = \frac{-b}{2a} + j\frac{\sqrt{4ac - b^2}}{2a}, \qquad x_2 = \frac{-b}{2a} - j\frac{\sqrt{4ac - b^2}}{2a}$$

Program 2.2 determines the roots of a quadratic equation. In this program the if..else statement is used to determine if the roots are real, complex or singular. The value passed to the square-root function (sqrt()) should be tested to determine if it is negative. If it is, it may cause the program to terminate as the square root of a negative number cannot be calculated (it is numerically invalid). The program may also terminate if a is zero as this causes a divide by zero error (the trap for this error is left as a tutorial question). To use the sqrt() method the import java.lang.Math; line must be included in the program (this will be discussed in more detail, later).

📖 Java program 2.2

```
import java.lang.Math;   // required for the sqrt() method

public class chap2_02
{
   public static void main (String args[])
   {
   double a,b,c,root1,root2,real,imag;

      a=1; b=2; c=1;
      System.out.println("a, b and c are "+a+ " "+b+" "+c);
      if (b*b==4*a*c)
      {
         root1=-b/(2*a);
         System.out.println("Single root of "+root1);
      }
      else if (b*b>4*a*c)
      {
         root1=(-b+Math.sqrt(b*b-4*a*c))/(2*a);
         root2=(-b-Math.sqrt(b*b-4*a*c))/(2*a);
         System.out.println("Real roots of "+root1+ " " +root2);
      }
      else
      {
         real=-b/(2*a);
         imag=Math.sqrt(4*a*c-b*b)/(2*a);
         System.out.println("Real roots of "+real+ "+/-j "+imag);
      }
   }
}
```

Three sample runs 2.2, 2.3 and 2.4 test each of the three types of roots that occur. In Sample run 2.2 the roots of the equation are real. In Sample run 2.3 the roots are complex, i.e. in the form x+jy. In Sample run 2.4 the result is a singular root.

```
C:\java\src\chap2>java chap2_02
a, b and c are 1.0 1.0 -2.0
Real roots of 1.0 -2.0
```

```
C:\java\src\chap2>java chap2_02
a, b and c are 2.0 2.0 4.0
Real roots of -0.5+/-j 1.3228756555322954
```

```
C:\java\src\chap2>java chap2_02
a, b and c are 1.0 2.0 1.0
Single root of -1.0
```

2.1.2 switch

The switch statement is used when there is a multiple decision to be made. It is normally used to replace the if statement when there are many routes of execution the program execution can take. The syntax of switch is as follows.

```
switch (expression)
{
   case const1: statement(s) : break;
   case const2: statement(s) ; break;
   :             :
   default:      statement(s) ; break;
}
```

The switch statement checks the expression against each of the constants in sequence (the constant must be an integer or character data type). When a match is found the statement(s) associated with the constant is (are) executed. The execution carries on to all other statements until a break is encountered or to the end of switch, whichever is sooner. If the break is omitted, the execution continues until the end of switch. If none of the constants matches the switch expression a set of statements associated with the default condition (default:) is executed. The data type of the switch constants can be either byte, char, short, int or long.

Java program 2.3 is the equivalent of Java program 2.1 but using a switch statement. Sample run 2.5 shows a sample run.

📖 Java program 2.3

```
import java.lang.Math;

public class chap2_03
{
   public static void main (String args[])
   {
```

```
    int col;
    col=4;
    switch (col)
    {
    case 0:    System.out.println("BLACK");    break;
    case 1:    System.out.println("BROWN");    break;
    case 2:    System.out.println("RED");      break;
    case 3:    System.out.println("ORANGE");   break;
    case 4:    System.out.println("YELLOW");   break;
    case 5:    System.out.println("GREEN");    break;
    default:   System.out.println("Not defined yet!");
    }
  }
}
```

🖥 **Sample run 2.5**
```
C:\java\src\chap2>java chap2_03
YELLOW
```

2.2 Exercises

2.2.1 Modify Java program 2.1 and also program 2.3 so that they display all of the resistor colour codes. The complete table is:

0	BLACK	1	BROWN	2	RED
3	ORANGE	4	YELLOW	5	GREEN
6	BLUE	7	VIOLET	8	GREY
9	WHITE				

2.2.2 Write a program which determines if an entered integer value is exactly divisible by 4. For example, the following outline code can be used to determine if a value is exactly divisible by 2:

📖 Java program 2.4
```
public class chap2_04
{
    public static void main (String args[])
    {
    int val;

    val=3;

    if ((val % 2)==0)
        System.out.println("Value is even");
    else
        System.out.println("Value is odd");
    }
}
```

2.2.3 Modify the program developed in Exercise 2.2.2 so that it determines if the entered value is exactly divisible by 10.

2.2.4 Write a program which determines if an entered integer value is exactly divisible by 3 and 4. The following outline code can be used to determine if a value is exactly divisible by 2 and 3:

```
if (((val % 2)==0) && ((val % 3)==0))
    System.out.println("Value is even");
else
    System.out.println("Value is odd");
```

2.2.5 Modify the program developed in Exercise 2.2.4 (using the || operator) so that it displays if the value is exactly divisible by 3 or 4.

2.2.6 Test Program 2.2 for its results when a is equal to zero. What is the result? What do you think NaN means?

2.2.7 Modify Program 2.2 so that it does not give an incorrect value when a is zero. Note that, when a is zero, there is a single root of:

$$x = -\frac{c}{b}$$

Use it to complete Table 2.2. Note that if a is 0 then the root will be −c/b.

Table 2.1 Roots of a quadratic equation

Equation	Root(s)
$x^2 + 21x - 72 = 0$	
$5x^2 + 2x + 1 = 0$	
$25x^2 - 30x + 9 = 0$	
$6x^2 + 9x - 20 = 0$	

Table 2.2 Root of a quadratic equation

Equation	Root
$0x^2 + 4x - 2 = 0$	
$0x^2 + 6x + 6 = 0$	

3 Java Loops

3.1 Loops

3.1.1 for()

Many tasks within a program are repetitive, such as prompting for data, counting values, and so on. The `for` loop allows the execution of a block of code for a given control function. The following is an example format; if there is only one statement in the block then the braces can be omitted. Figure 3.1 shows a flow chart representation of this statement.

```
for (starting condition; test condition; operation)
{
     statement block
}
```

where :

starting condition	–	the starting value for the loop;
test condition	–	if test condition is TRUE the loop will continue execution;
operation	–	the operation conducted at the end of the loop.

Displaying ASCII characters

Program 3.1 displays ASCII characters for entered start and end decimal values. Sample run 3.1 displays the ASCII characters from decimal 40 (' (') to 50 ('2'). The type conversion (char) is used to convert an integer to a char.

📖 Java program 3.1
```
public class chap3_01
{
   public static void main (String args[])
   {
   int start,end,ch;
      start=40; end=50;
      for (ch=start;ch<=end;ch++)
          System.out.println((int)ch+" "+(char)ch);
   }
}
```

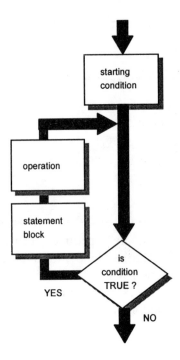

Figure 3.1 Flow chart representation of the for statement

```
C:\java\src\chap2>java chap3_01
40 (
41 )
42 *
43 +
44 ,
45 -
46 .
47 /
48 0
49 1
50 2
```

Simulation of a mathematical equation

The program in this section will simulate the results of the equation:

$$y = 3x^2 - 12x - 1$$

for values of x from 0 to 100 in steps of 10. Program 3.2 gives a Java program which implements this. Test run 3.2 shows a sample run of the program. It can be seen that the value of x varies from 0 to 100, in steps of 10.

Java program 3.2

```java
public class chap3_02
{
   public static void main (String args[])
   {
   double x,y;
      System.out.println("X    Y");
      for (x=0;x<=100;x+=10)
      {
            y=3*(x*x)-12*x-1;
            System.out.println(x+" "+y);
      }
   }
}
```

Sample run 3.2

```
C:\java\src\chap2>java chap3_02
X    Y
0.0 -1.0
10.0 179.0
20.0 959.0
30.0 2339.0
40.0 4319.0
50.0 6899.0
60.0 10079.0
70.0 13859.0
80.0 18239.0
90.0 23219.0
100.0 28799.0
```

Boolean logic

Program 3.3 is an example of how a Boolean logic function can be analysed and a truth table generated. The `for` loop generates all the required binary permutations for a truth table. The Boolean function used is:

$$Z = \overline{(A.B) + C}$$

A schematic of this equation is given in Figure 3.2. Test run 3.3 shows a sample run. The above equation is implemented in Java with:

```java
z=~((a & b) | c)          // not ( (a and b) or c)
```

and as z is a 16-bit integer then to just show the first bit of the value then the following bit mask is used:

```java
z=~((a & b) | c) & 1;  // mask-off least-significant bit
```

which will only display the least-significant bit of the operation.

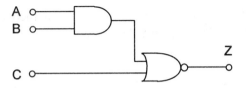

Figure 3.2 Digital circuit

📖 Java program 3.3

```
public class chap3_03
{
    public static void main (String args[])
    {
    int a,b,c,z;

        System.out.println("A B C Z");

        for (a=0;a<=1;a++)
        for (b=0;b<=1;b++)
        for (c=0;c<=1;c++)
        {
            z=~((a & b) | c) & 1;
            System.out.println(a + " "+b +" "+ c +" "+ z);
        }
    }
}
```

💻 Sample run 3.3

```
C:\java\src\chap2>java chap3_03
A B C Z
0 0 0 1
0 0 1 0
0 1 0 1
0 1 1 0
1 0 0 1
1 0 1 0
1 1 0 0
1 1 1 0
```

3.1.2 while( )

The while() statement allows a block of code to be executed while a specified condition is TRUE. It checks the condition at the start of the block; if this is TRUE the block is executed, else it will exit the loop. The syntax is:

```
while (condition)
{
    :         :
    statement block
    :         :
}
```

If the statement block contains a single statement then the braces may be omitted (although it does no harm to keep them).

3.1.3 do...while()

The do...while() statement is similar in its operation to while() except that it tests the condition at the bottom of the loop. This allows *statement block* to be executed at least once. The syntax is:

```
do
{
        statement block
} while (condition);
```

As with for() and while() loops the braces are optional. The do...while() loop requires a semicolon at the end of the loop, whereas the while() does not.

Figure 3.3 shows a flow chart representation of the do...while() and the while() loops. In both loops a TRUE condition will cause the statement block to be repeated.

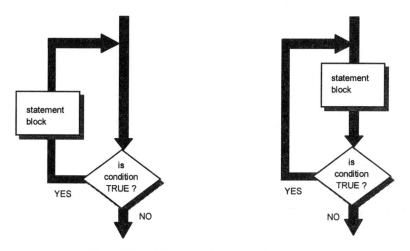

Figure 3.3 while() and do...while() loops

3.1.4 Conversion from decimal to octal

Octal numbers uses base eight. To convert a decimal value to an octal number the decimal value is divided by 8 recursively and each remainder noted. The first remainder gives the least significant digit and the final remainder the most significant digit. For example, the following shows the octal equivalent of the decimal number 55:

```
8 | 55
      6  r 7  <<< LSD (least significant digit)
      0  r 6  <<< MSD (most significant digit)
```

Thus the decimal value 55 is equivalent to 67o (where the o represents octal). Program 3.4 shows a program which determines an octal value for an entered decimal value. Unfortunately, it displays the least significant digit first and the most significant digit last, thus the displayed value must be read in reverse. Test run 3.4 shows a sample run.

📖 Java program 3.4

```
public class chap3_04
{
    public static void main (String args[])
    {
    int val,remainder;

        val=55;
        System.out.println("Conversion to octal (in reverse)");
        do
        {
            remainder=val % 8;    // find remainder with modulus
            System.out.print(remainder);
            val=val / 8;
        } while (val>0);
    }
}
```

💻 Sample run 3.4

```
Conversion to octal (in reverse)
76
```

3.2   Exercises

3.2.1   Write a program which prints all the characters from '0' (zero) to 'z' in sequence using a for loop.

3.2.2   Enter Program 3.1 and use it to complete Table 3.1.

3.2.3   Write a program which lists the square of the values from 1 to 10. A sample run in shown in Sample run 3.5.

3.2.4   Write a program which displays the squares, cubes and fourth powers of the first 10 integers. A sample run in shown in Sample run 3.6.

Table 3.1 ASCII characters

Value	Character
34	
35	
36	
37	
38	
64	
65	
66	
67	
68	
69	
70	

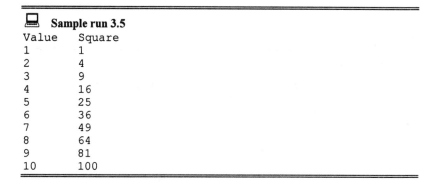

Sample run 3.5

```
Value    Square
1        1
2        4
3        9
4        16
5        25
6        36
7        49
8        64
9        81
10       100
```

Sample run 3.6

```
Number   Square   Cube   Fourth
--------------------------
1        1        1      1
2        4        8      16
3        9        27     81
      etc
```

3.2.5 Write a program which displays the *y* values in the formulas given below and with the given *x* steps.

Equation	Range of *x*
(i) $y = 4x + 1$	0 to 50 in steps of 5
(ii) $y = \sqrt{x} - 1$	1 to 10 in steps of 0.5
(iii) $y = 5x^2 + 3x - 2$	−5 to 5 in steps of 0.5

A sample run in shown in Sample run 3.7.

3.2.6   Java program 3.5 gives a program which displays the sine of a number from 0° to 90° in steps of 10° and Sample run 3.8 gives a sample run. Modify it so that it determines the cosine of an angle from 0° to 90° in steps of 10°. (Hint: use cos() method instead of sin().)

📖 Java program 3.5
```java
import java.lang.Math;

public class chap3_05
{
   public static void main (String args[])
   {
   double val;

      System.out.println("Val\tSine");
      for (val=0;val<=90;val+=10)
      {
         System.out.println(val+"\t"+
      Math.sin(val*3.14/180)); // convert to radians
      }
   }
}
```

3.2.7   Modify Program 3.3 so that it determines the truth table for the following Boolean equation:

$$Z = \overline{(A + B).C}$$

Table 3.1 Truth table

A	B	C	Z
0	0	0	
0	0	1	
0	1	0	
0	1	1	
1	0	0	
1	0	1	
1	1	0	
1	1	1	

6.4.8 Write a program to convert from decimal to binary (base 2). A sample run is shown in Sample run 3.9 with a value of 42. Hint: Modify Program 3.4 so that the operator value is 2 rather that 8.

Sample run 3.9
```
The value in binary is (in reverse) 0100001
```

6.4.9 Write a program to convert from decimal to hexadecimal (base 16). A sample run for a value of 42 is shown in Sample run 3.10. Program 3.6 shows a sample outline of the program.

Sample run 3.10
```
The value in hex is (in reverse) A2
```

📖 Java program 3.6

```java
public class chap3_06
{
   public static void main (String args[])
   {
   int val, remain;

      val=55;
      System.out.println("Conversion to hex (in reverse)");
      do
      {
         remain=val % 16;    // find remainder with modulus
         if (remain<10) System.out.print(remainder);
         else if (remain==10) System.out.print('A');
         else if (remain==11) System.out.print('B');
                etc
         val=val / 16;
      } while (val>0);
   }
}
```

4 Java Objects and Classes

4.1 Introduction

C++ added object-oriented programming onto C. This allows the language to contain non object-oriented code and object-oriented code. Java differs in that it is completely object-oriented. This chapter discusses the main parts of object-oriented design, that is:

- Classes. This is a collection of data and methods that operate on the data.
- Objects. This is a created instance of a class which contains its own class data.
- Methods. These are used to operate on objects and are equivalent to procedures (in Pascal) and functions (in C).
- Constructors. These are used to initialise an instance of a class.
- Method overloading. These are used to define a method which has different parameters passed to it.
- Garbage collection. This is used to clean-up unused objects.

4.2 Classes

Classes are a general form of structures, which are common in many languages. They basically gather together data members, and in object-oriented design, they also include methods (known as functions in C and procedures in Pascal) which operate on the class. Everything within Java is contained within classes.

In C a program is normally split into modules named functions. Typically these functions have parameters passed to them or from them. In Java these functions are named methods and operate within classes. Java program 4.1 includes a `circle` class which contains two methods:

- `public float area(double r)`. In which the value of `r` is passed into the method and the return value is equal to πr^2 (`return(3.14159*r*r)`). The preceding `public double` defines that this method can be accessed from another class (public) and the double defines that the return type is of type double.

- public float circum(double r). In which the value of r is passed into the method and the return value is equal to 2πr (return(2*3.14159*r)). The preceding public double defines that this method can be accessed from another class (public) and the double defines that the return type is of type double.

In defining a new class the program automatically defines a new data type (in Program 4.1 this new data type is named Circle). An instance of a class must first be created, thus for the Circle it can be achieved with:

```
Circle cir;
```

this does not create a Circle object, it only refers to it. Next the object can be created with the new keyword with:

```
cir = new Circle();
```

These two lines can be merged together into a single line with:

```
Circle cir = new Circle();
```

which creates an instance of a Circle and assigns a variable to it. The methods can then be used to operate on the object. For example to apply the area() method:

```
val=cir.area(10);
```

can be used. This passes the value of 10 into the radius variable in the area() method and the return value will be put into the val variable. Sample run 4.1 shows a sample run.

📖 Java program 4.1

```
public class chap4_01
{
   public static void main(String[] args)
   {
      Circle cir=new Circle();
      System.out.println("Area is "+cir.area(10));
      System.out.println("Circumference is "+cir.circum(10));
   }
}
class Circle        // class is named Circle
{
   public double circum(double radius)
   {
```

```
        return(2*3.14159*radius);            // 2πr
    }
    public double area(double radius)
    {
        return(3.14159*radius*radius);       // πr²
    }
}
```

The data and methods within a class can either be:

- Private. These are variables (or methods) which can only be used within the class and have a preceding `private` keyword. By default variables (the members of the class) and methods are private (restricted).
- Public. These are variables (or methods) which can be accessed from other classes and have a preceding `public` keyword.

It is obvious that all classes must have a public content so that they can be accessed by external functions. In Program 4.2 the `Circle` class has three public parts:

- The methods `area()` and `circum()`, which determine the area and circumference of a circle.
- The `Circle` class variable `radius`.

Once the `Circle` class has been declared then the class variable `radius` can be accessed from outside the `Circle` class using:

```
cir.radius=10;
```

which sets the class variable (`radius`) to a value of 10. The methods then do not need to be passed the value of radius as it is now set within the class (and will stay defined until either a new value is set or the class is deleted).

📖 Java program 4.2
```
public class chap4_02
{
    public static void main(String[] args)
    {
    Circle cir=new Circle();
        cir.radius=10;
        System.out.println("Area is "+c.area());
        System.out.println("Circumference is "+c.circum());
```

```
    }
}
class Circle
{
public float radius;

    public double circum()
    {
        return(2*3.14159*radius);
    }
    public double area()
    {
        return(3.14159*radius*radius);
    }
}
```

Many instances of a class can be initiated and each will have their own settings for their class variables. For example, in Program 4.3, two instances of the Circle class have been declared (cir1 and cir2). These are circle objects. The first circle object (cir1) has a radius of 15 and the second (cir2) has a radius of 10. Sample run 4.2 shows a sample run.

📖 Java program 4.3
```
public class chap4_03
{
    public static void main(String[] args)
    {
    Circle cir1, cir2;

        cir1=new Circle();
        cir2=new Circle();

        cir1.radius=15;
        cir2.radius=10;


        System.out.println("Area1 is "+cir1.area());
        System.out.println("Area2 is "+cir2.area());

    }
}
class Circle
{
public float radius;

    public double circum()
    {
        return(2*3.14159*radius);
    }
    public double area()
    {
        return(3.14159*radius*radius);
    }
}
```

```
C:\java\src\chap4>java chap4_03
Area1 is 706.85775
Area2 is 314.159
```

4.3   Constructors

A constructors allows for the initialisation of a class. It is a special initialisation function that is automatically called whenever a class is declared. The constructor always has the same name as the class name, and no data types are defined for the argument list or the return type. Normally a constructor is used to initialise a class.

Program 4.4 has a class which is named Circle. The constructor for this class is Circle(). Sample run 4.3 shows a sample run. It can be seen that initially when the program is run the message "Constructing a circle" is displayed when the object is created.

📖 Java program 4.4

```
public class chap4_04
{
   public static void main(String[] args)
   {
   Circle c1,c2;
   double area1,area2;
      c1=new Circle();   c2=new Circle();

      c1.radius=15;      area1=c1.area();
      c2.radius=10;      area2=c2.area();
      System.out.println("Area1 is "+area1);
      System.out.println("Area2 is "+area2);
   }
}
class Circle
{
public float radius;

   public Circle()    // constructor called when object created
   {
      System.out.println("Constructing a circle");
   }
   public double circum()
   {
      return(2*3.14159*radius);
   }
   public double area()
   {
      return(3.14159*radius*radius);
   }
}
```

```
C:\java\src\chap4>java chap4_04
Constructing a circle
Constructing a circle
Area1 is 706.85775
Area2 is 314.159
```

C++ has also a destructor which is a member of a function and is automatically called when the class is destroyed. It has the same name as the class name but is preceded by a tilde (~). Normally a destructor is used to clean-up when the class is destroyed. Java normally has no need for destructors as it implements a technique known as garbage collection which gets rids of objects which are no longer needed. If a final clear-up is required then the `finalize()` method can be used. This is called just before the garbage collection. For example:

```
class Circle
{
   public Circle()    // constructor called when object created
   {
     System.out.println("Constructing a circle");
   }
   public finalize()    // called when object deleted
   {
     System.out.println("Goodbye. I'm out with the trash");
   }

   public double circum()
   {
     return(2*3.14159*radius);
   }
   public double area()
   {
     return(3.14159*radius*radius);
   }
}
```

4.4   Method overloading

Often the programmer requires to call a method in a number of ways but wants the same name for the different implementations. Java allows this with method overloading. With overloading the programmer defines a number of methods, each of which has the same name but which are called with a different argument list or return type. The compiler then automatically decides which one should be called. For example in Java Program 4.5 the programmer has defined two square methods named `sqr()` and two for `max()`, which is a maximum method. The data type of the argument passed is of a different type for each of the methods, that is, either an `int` or a `double`. The return type is also different. The data type of the parameters passed to these methods is tested by the compiler and it then determines which of the methods it requires to use. Sample run 4.4 shows a sample run.

📖 Java program 4.5

```java
public class chap4_05
{
    public static void main(String[] args)
    {
    MyMath m;
    int val1=4;
    double val2=4.1;

        m=new MyMath();

        System.out.println("Sqr(4)="+m.sqr(val1));
        System.out.println("Sqr(4.1)="+m.sqr(val2));
        System.out.println("Maximum (3,4)="+m.max(3,4));
        System.out.println("Maximum (3.0,4.0)="+m.max(3.0,4.0));
    }
}
class MyMath
{
    public int sqr(int val)
    {
        return(val*val);
    }
    public double sqr(double val)
    {
        return(val*val);
    }
    public int max(int a, int b)
    {
        if (a>b) return(a);
        else return(b);
    }
    public double max(double a, double b)
    {
        if (a>b) return(a);
        else return(b);
    }
}
```

⌨ **Sample run 4.4**

```
C:\java\src\chap4>java chap4_05
Sqr(4)=16
Sqr(4.1)=16.81
Maximum (3,4)=4
Maximum (3.0,4.0)=4.0
```

The argument list of the overloaded function does not have to have the same number of arguments for each of the overloaded functions. Program 4.6 shows an example of an overloaded method which has a different number of arguments for each of the function calls. In this case the max() function can either be called with two integer values or by passing an array to it. Arrays will be covered later.

📖 Java program 4.6

```java
public class chap4_06
{
   public static void main(String[] args)
   {
   MyMath  m;
   int     val1=4, arr[]={1,5,-3,10,4}; // array has 5 elements
   double  val2=4.1;

      m=new MyMath();

      System.out.println("Sqr(4)="+m.sqr(val1));
      System.out.println("Sqr(4.1)="+m.sqr(val2));
      System.out.println("Maximum (3,4)="+m.max(3,4));
      System.out.println("Maximum (array)="+m.max(arr));
   }
}

class MyMath
{
   public int sqr(int val)
   {
      return(val*val);
   }
   public double sqr(double val)
   {
      return(val*val);
   }
   public int max(int a, int b)
   {
      if (a>b) return(a);
      else return(b);
   }
   public int max(int a[])
   {
   int i,max;
      max=a[0];                    // set max to first element
      for (i=1;i<a.length;i++)     //a.length returns array size
         if (max<a[i]) max=a[i];
      return(max);
   }
}
```

💻 **Sample run 4.5**
```
C:\java\src\chap4>java chap4_06
Sqr(4)=16
Sqr(4.1)=16.81
Maximum (3,4)=4
Maximum (array)=10
```

4.5 Static methods

Declaring an object to get access to the methods in the MyMath class is obviously not efficient as every declaration creates a new object. If we just want access to the methods in a class then the methods within the class are declared as static methods. The methods are then accessed by preceding the method with the class name. Static methods are associated with a class and not an object, thus there is no need to create an object with them. Thus in Program 4.7 the methods are accessed by:

```
val=MyMath.sqr(val1);   val=MyMath.max(3,4);
val=MyMath.max(arr);
```

Sample run 4.6 shows a sample run.

📖 Java program 4.7
```
public class chap4_07
{
   public static void main(String[] args)
   {
   int     val1=4, arr[]={1,5,-3,10,4};   // array has 5 elements
   double  val2=4.1;
      System.out.println("Sqr(val1) "+MyMath.sqr(val1));
      System.out.println("Sqr(arr) "+MyMath.sqr(val2));
      System.out.println("Max(3.0,4.0) "+MyMath.max(3,4));
      System.out.println("Max(arr) "+MyMath.max(arr));
   }
}
class MyMath
{
   public static int sqr(int val)
   {
      return(val*val);
   }
   public static double sqr(double val)
   {
      return(val*val);
   }
   public static int max(int a, int b)
   {
      if (a>b) return(a);
      else return(b);
   }
   public static int max(int a[])
   {
   int i,max;
      max=a[0];                          // set max to first element
      for (i=1;i<a.length;i++)   //a.length returns array size
         if (max<a[i]) max=a[i];
      return(max);
   }
}
```

```
C:\java\src\chap4>java chap4_06
Sqr(val1) 16
Sqr(arr) 16.81
Max(3.0,4.0) 4
Max(arr) 10
```

4.6   Constants

Classes can contain constants which are defined as `public static` class variables. Such as:

```
class MyMath
{
   public static final double E = 2.7182818284590452354;
   public static final double PI = 3.14159265358979323846;
   public int sqr(int val)
   {
      return(val*val);
   }
   public double sqr(double val)
   {
      return(val*val);
   }
}
```

In this case the value of π is referenced by:

```
omega=2*MyMath.PI*f
```

The static class variables are declared as final so that they cannot be modified when an object is declared. Thus the following is INVALID:

```
MyMath.PI=10.1;
```

Program 4.8 shows a sample program and Sample run 4.7 shows a sample run.

📖 **Java program 4.8**

```
public class chap4_08
{
   public static void main(String[] args)
   {
      System.out.println("PI is "+m.PI);
      System.out.println("E is ="+m.E);
   }
}
class MyMath
{
```

```
public static final double E = 2.7182818284590452354;
public static final double PI = 3.14159265358979323846;
public static int sqr(int val)
{
    return(val*val);
}
public static double sqr(double val)
{
    return(val*val);
}
public static int max(int a, int b)
{
    if (a>b) return(a);
    else return(b);
}
public static int max(int a[])
{
int i,max;

    max=a[0];                    // set max to first element
    for (i=1;i<a.length;i++)     //a.length returns array size
       if (max<a[i]) max=a[i];
    return(max);

}
}
```

Sample run 4.7
```
C:\java\src\chap4>java chap_08
PI is 3.141592653589793
E is =2.718281828459045
```

4.7   Garbage collection

Most programming languages have a technique which allows memory to be
freed once a variable or an object is not being used any more. C++ uses the
free function to free the memory allocated to a variable or object. This is a
very efficient technique but many programmers forget to free up memory once
an object is not required. This leads to programs which tend to eat up memory.

Java does not have a method to release memory, but instead uses a garbage
collection process which gets rid of objects which are no longer needed. The
Java interpreter keeps a track of the objects that have been allocated and
which variables are used with which objects. Then when an object is not used
the interpreter deletes the object. The garbage collector runs as a low-priority
process and picks up objects which need to be deleted. Thus it allows the programmer to develop programs which do not need to worry about the deletion
of objects.

4.8.1 Create a `Rectangle` class which contains the variables `base` and `height`. The class has the associated method called `area()`, which determines the area from one-half of the base times the height. The following is an outline of a usage of the class:

```
Rectangle rec1;
double area;

rect1=new Rectangle();

rect1.base=15;
rect1.height=15;
area=rect1.area();
```

Modify the program so that it creates several instances of rectangles.

4.8.2 Add the following methods to the `MyMath` class (Program 4.7):

(i)
```
min(int a, int b);   // returns minimum of two values
min(double a, double b); // returns minimum of two values
min(int a[]); // return minimum of an integer array
min(double a[];// return minimum of a double array
```

(ii)
```
mean(int a, int b);   // returns mean of two values
mean(double a, double b);// returns mean of two values
mean(int a[]); // return mean of an integer array
mean(double a[];// return mean of a double array
```

(iii)
```
isodd(int a);   // returns true if value is odd, else false
iseven(int a);   // returns true if value is even, else false
```

(iv)
```
fact(int a);   // returns factorial of the value
```

(v)
```
stdev(int a[]);   // returns standard deviation
stdev(double a[]);// returns standard deviation
```

The formulas which can be used to determine the mean ($\bar{x}$), standard deviation (σ) and factorial ($n!$) are:

$$Mean = \bar{x} = \frac{1}{N}\sum_{i=1}^{N} x_i \qquad Stdev = \sigma = \sqrt{\frac{1}{N}\sum_{i=1}^{N}\left(x_i - \bar{x}\right)^2}$$

$$n! = n \times (n-1) \times (n-2)....2 \times 1$$

4.8.3 Write a program with a `Line` class with separate methods which determine the gradient of a straight line (m) and the point at which a straight line cuts the y-axis (c). The entered parameters are two points on the line, that is, (x_1, y_1) and (x_2, y_2). From this program complete Table 4.1 (the first row has already been completed).

Table 4.1 Straight line calculations

x_1	y_1	x_2	y_2	m	c
3	3	4	5	2	−3
−1	5	0	−1		
100	50	−10	−10		
−1	−1	1	3		

Formulas to calculate these values are:

$$m = \frac{y_2 - y_1}{x_2 - x_1} \qquad c = y_1 - mx_1$$

4.8.4   Write a program which determines the magnitude and angle of a complex number (in the form $x+iy$, or $x+jy$). The program should use methods to determine each of the values. Complete Table 4.2 using the program (the first row has already been completed), where:

$$mag = \sqrt{x^2 + y^2} \qquad angle = \tan^{-1}\left(\frac{y}{x}\right)$$

Table 4.2 Complex number calculation

x	y	*Mag.*	*Angle(°)*
10	10	14.142	45
−10	5		
100	50		
−1	−1		

4.8.5   The sine function can be calculated, from first principles, with:

$$\sin(x) = x - \frac{x^3}{3!} + \frac{x^5}{5!} - \frac{x^7}{7!} + \frac{x^9}{9!} - \ldots$$

where the value of x is in radians. Java program 4.9 determines the sine function using the above formula, where the series is stopped when an individual term in the equation is less than 1×10^{-6}. It also uses a factorial method (fact) and a standard method from the Math class (pow), which will be covered in the next chapter. Sample run 4.8 shows a sample run.

📖 Java program 4.9

```
import java.lang.Math;  // required for the pow() method

public class chap4_09
{
```

```
public static void main(String[] args)
{

    System.out.println("Sin(1.2) is "+MyMath.sin(1.2));
}
}
class MyMath
{
public static double sin(double x)
{
double val, term;
int n, sign;

    sign=1;
    val=x;
    n=3;
    do
    {
        term=Math.pow(x,n)/fact(n);
        n=n+2;
        sign=-sign;
        val=val+sign*term;

    } while (term>1e-6);
    return(val);
}

public static long fact(long n)
{
    long i, result;

    result=1;
    for (i=2;i<=n;i++)
        result=result*i;
    return(result);
}
}
```

⌨ **Sample run 4.8**
```
C:\java\src\chap4>java chap04_12
Sin(1.2) is 0.9320390842607376
```

Using Program 4.9 as a basis, add a method for a cosine function. It can be calculated, from first principles, with:

$$\cos(x) = 1 - \frac{x^2}{2!} + \frac{x^4}{4!} - \frac{x^6}{6!} + \frac{x^8}{8!} - \ldots$$

The error in the function should be less than 1×10^{-6}.

4.8.6 Add a mathematical method which determines the exponential of a value using the first principles formula:

$$e^x = 1 + \frac{x}{1!} + \frac{x^2}{2!} + \frac{x^3}{3!} + \frac{x^4}{4!} + \ldots$$

5 Java Class Libraries and Arrays

5.1 Package statements

The `package` statement defines that the classes within a Java file are part of a given package. The full name of a class is:

package . classFilename

The fully qualified name for a method is:

package . classFilename . method_name ()

Each class file with the same package name is stored in the same directory. For example, the `java.applet` package contains several files, such as:

```
applet.java          appletcontent.java
appletstub.java      audioclip.java
```

Each has a first line of:

```
package java.applet;
```

and the fully classified names of the class files are:

```
java.applet.applet          java.applet.appletcontent
java.applet.appletstub      java.applet.audioclip
```

These can be interpreted as in the `java/applet` directory. An example listing from the class library given in Sample run 5.1.

Normally when a Java class is being developed it is not part of a package as it is contained in the current directory.

⌨ **Sample run 5.1**
```
java/
java/lang/
java/lang/Object.class
java/lang/Exception.class
java/lang/Integer.class
```

The main packages are:

```
java.applet          java.awt              java.awt.datatransfer
java.awt.event       java.awt.image        java.awt.peer
java.beans           java.io               java.lang
java.lang            java.lang.reflect     java.math
java.net             java.rmi              java.rmi.dgc
java.rmi.registry    java.rmi.server       java.security
java.security.acl    java.security.interfaces java.sql
java.text            java.util             java.utils.zip
```

5.2   Import statements

The `import` statement allows previously written code to be included in the applet. This code is stored in class libraries (or packages), which are compiled Java code. For the JDK tools, the Java source code for these libraries is stored in the `src/java` directory.

For example a Java program which uses maths methods will begin with:

```
import java.lang.Math;
```

This includes the `math` class libraries (which is in the `java.lang` package). The default Java class libraries are stored in the `classes.zip` file in the `lib` directory. This file is in a compressed form and should not be unzipped before it is used. The following is an outline of the file.

```
Searching ZIP: CLASSES.ZIP
Testing: java/
Testing: java/lang/
Testing: java/lang/Object.class
Testing: java/lang/Exception.class
Testing: java/lang/Integer.class
    ::             ::
Testing: java/lang/Win32Process.class
Testing: java/io/
Testing: java/io/FilterOutputStream.class
Testing: java/io/OutputStream.class
    ::             ::
Testing: java/io/StreamTenizer.class
Testing: java/util/
Testing: java/util/Hashtable.class
Testing: java/util/Enumeration.class
    ::             ::
Testing: java/util/Stack.class
Testing: java/awt/
Testing: java/awt/Toolkit.class
Testing: java/awt/peer/
Testing: java/awt/peer/WindowPeer.class
    ::             ::
Testing: java/awt/peer/DialogPeer.class
Testing: java/awt/Image.class
Testing: java/awt/MenuItem.class
```

```
Testing: java/awt/MenuComponent.class
Testing: java/awt/image/
   ::            ::
   ::            ::
Testing: java/awt/ImageMediaEntry.class
Testing: java/awt/AWTException.class
Testing: java/net/
Testing: java/net/URL.class
Testing: java/net/URLStreamHandlerFactory.class
   ::            ::
Testing: java/net/URLEncoder.class
Testing: java/applet/
Testing: java/applet/Applet.class
Testing: java/applet/AppletContext.class
Testing: java/applet/AudioClip.class
Testing: java/applet/AppletStub.class
```

The other form of the `import` statement is:

```
import package.*;
```

which will import all the classes within the specified package. Table 5.1 lists the main class libraries and some sample libraries.

It can be seen that upgrading the Java compiler is simple, as all that is required is to replace the class libraries with new ones. For example, if the basic language is upgraded then `java.lang.*` files is simply replaced with a new version. The user can also easily add new class libraries to the standard ones. A complete listing of the classes is given in Appendix D.

Table 5.1 Class libraries

Class libraries	Description	Example libraries
java.lang.*	Java language	java.lang.Class java.lang.Number java.lang.Process java.lang.String
java.io.*	I/O routines	java.io.InputStream java.io.OutputStream
java.util.*	Utilities	java.util.BitSet java.util.Dictionary
java.awt.*	Windows, menus and graphics	java.awt.Point java.awt.Polygon java.awt.MenuComponent java.awt.MenuBar java.awt.MenuItem
java.net.*	Networking (such as sockets, URLs, ftp, telnet and HTTP)	java.net.ServerSocket java.net.Socket java.net.SocketImpl
java.applet.*	Code required to run an applet	java.applet.AppletContext java.applet.AppletStub java.applet.AudioClip

5.3 Mathematical operations

Java has a basic set of mathematics methods which are defined in the `java.lang.Math` class library. Table 5.2 outlines these methods. An example of a method in this library is `abs()` which can be used to return the absolute value of either a `double`, an `int` or a `long` value. Java automatically picks the required format and the return data type will be of the same data type of the value to be operated on.

As the functions are part of the `Math` class they are preceded with the `Math.` class method. For example:

```
val2=Math.sqrt(val1);
val3=Math.abs(val2);
z=Math.min(x,y);
```

Java stand-alone program 5.1 shows a few examples of mathematical operations and Sample run 5.2 shows a sample compilation and run session.

Table 5.2 Methods defined in `java.lang.Math`

Method	Description
`double` **abs**`(double a)`	Returns the absolute double value of a.
`float` **abs**`(float a)`	Returns the absolute float value of a.
`int` **abs**`(int a)`	Returns the absolute integer value of a.
`long` **abs**`(long a)`	Returns the absolute long value of a.
`double` **acos**`(double a)`	Returns the arc cosine of a, in the range of 0.0 through `Pi`.
`double` **asin**`(double a)`	Returns the arc sine of a, in the range of `Pi`/2 through `Pi`/2.
`double` **atan**`(double a)`	Returns the arc tangent of a, in the range of $-$`Pi`/2 through `Pi`/2.
`double` **atan2**`(double a, double b)`	Converts rectangular co-ordinates (a, b) to polar (r, theta).
`double` **ceil**`(double a)`	Returns the 'ceiling' or smallest whole number greater than or equal to a.
`double` **cos**`(double a)`	Returns the trigonometric cosine of an angle.
`double` **exp**`(double a)`	Returns the exponential number e (2.718...) raised to the power of a.

Table 5.2 Methods defined in `java.lang.Math` (continued)

`double floor( double a)`	Returns the 'floor' or largest whole number less than or equal to a.
`double IEEEremainder(` `double f1, double f2)`	Returns the remainder of f1 divided by f2 as defined by IEEE 754.
`double log(double a)`	Returns the natural logarithm (base e) of a.
`double max(double a,` `double b)`	Takes two `double` values, a and b, and returns the greater.
`double max(float a,` `float b)`	Takes two `float` values, a and b, and returns the greater number of the two.
`int max(int a, int b)`	Takes two `int` values, a and b, and returns the greater number.
`long max(long a,long b)`	Takes two long values, a and b, and returns the greater.
`double min(double a,` `double b)`	Takes two double values, a and b, and returns the smallest.
`float min(float a,` `float b)`	Takes two float values, a and b, and returns the smallest.
`int min(int a, int b)`	Takes two integer values, a and b, and returns the smallest number.
`long min(long a,` `long b)`	Takes two long values, a and b, and returns the smallest number of the two.
`double pow(double a,` `double b)`	Returns the number a raised to the power of b.
`double random()`	Generates a random number between 0.0 and 1.0.
`double rint(double b)`	Converts a double value into an integral value in double format.
`long round(double a)`	Rounds off a double value by first adding 0.5 to it and then returning the largest integer that is less than or equal to this new value.
`int round(float a)`	Rounds off a float value by first adding 0.5 to it and then returning the largest integer that is less than or equal to this new value.
`double sin(double a)`	Returns the trigonometric sine of a.
`double sqrt(double a)`	Returns the square root of a.
`double tan(double a)`	Returns the trigonometric tangent of an angle.

📖 Java program 5.1

```
import java.lang.Math;
public class chap5_01
{
    public static void main(String[] args)
    {
    double x,y,z;
    int i;
        i=10;
        y=Math.log(10.0);
        x=Math.pow(3.0,4.0);
        z=Math.random(); // random number from 0 to 1
        System.out.println("Value of i is " + i);
        System.out.println("Value of log(10) is " + y);
        System.out.println("Value of 3^4 is " + x);
        System.out.println("A random number is " + z);
        System.out.println("Square root of 2 is " + Math.sqrt(2));
    }
}
```

🖥 Sample run 5.2

```
C:\DOCS\notes\INTER\java>javac chap05_1.java
C:\DOCS\notes\INTER\java>java chap05_1
Value of i is 10
Value of log(10) is 2.30259
Value of 3^4 is 81
A random number is 0.0810851
Square root of 2 is 1.41421
```

Java has also two predefined mathematical constants. These are:

- Pi is equivalent to 3.14159265358979323846
- E is equivalent to 2.7182818284590452354

5.4 Arrays

An array stores more than one value, of a common data type, under a collective name. Each value has a unique slot and is referenced using an indexing technique. For example a circuit with five resistor components could be declared within a program with five simple float declarations. If these resistor variables were required to be passed into a method then all five values would have to be passed through the parameter list. A neater way uses arrays to store all of the values under a common name (in this case R). Then a single array variable can then be passed into any method that uses it.

The declaration of an array specifies the data type, the array name and the number of elements in the array in brackets ([]). The following gives the standard format for an array declaration.

```
        data_type array_name[];
```

The array is then created using the `new` keyword. For example, to declare an integer array named `new_arr` with 200 elements then the following is used:

```
int new_arr[];

    new_arr=new int[200];
```

or, in a single statement, with:

```
int new_arr[]=new int[200];
```

Java program 5.2 gives an example of this type of declaration where an array (`arr`) is filled with 20 random numbers.

Figure 5.1 shows that the first element of the array is indexed 0 and the last element as `size-1`. The compiler allocates memory for the first element `array_name[0]` to the last array element `array_name[size-1]`. The number of bytes allocated in memory will be the number of elements in the array multiplied by the number of bytes used to store the data type of the array.

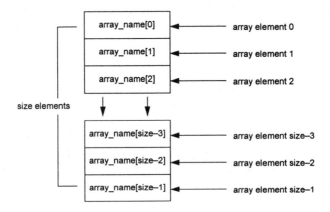

Figure 5.1 Array elements

📖 Java program 5.2

```
public class chap5_02
{
    public static void main(String[] args)
    {
        double arr[]=new double[20];
        int   i;

        for (i=0;i<20;i++)   arr[i]=Math.random();
        for (i=0;i<20;i++)   System.out.println(arr[i]);
    }
}
```

```
C:\java\src\chap5>java chap5_02
0.6075765411193292
0.7524300612559963
0.8100796233691735
0.45045015538577704
0.32390753542869755
0.34033464565015836
0.5079716192482706
0.6426253967106341
0.7691175624480434
0.6475110502592946
0.1416366173783874
0.21181433233783153
0.21758072702009412
0.24203490620407764
0.7587570097412505
0.4470154908107362
0.19823448357551965
0.7340429664182364
0.7402367706819387
0.8975606689180567
```

Another way to create and initialise an array is to define the elements within the array within curly brackets ({ }). Each element in the array is separated by a comma. The size of the array is then equal to the number of elements in the array. For example:

```
int     arr1[]={-3, 4, 10, 100, 30, 22};
String  menus[]={"File", "Edit", "View", "Insert", "Help"};
```

A particular problem in most programming languages (such as C and Pascal) exists when accessing array elements which do not exist, especially by accessing an array element which is greater than the maximum size of the array. Java overcomes this by being able to determine the size of the array. This is done with the length field. For example, the previous example can be modified with:

```
for (i=0;i<arr.length;i++)    arr[i]=Math.random();
for (i=0;i<arr.length;i++)    System.out.println(arr[i]);
```

Java program 5.3 gives an example of an array of strings. In this case the array contains the names of playing cards. When run the program displays five random playing cards. Sample run 5.4 shows a sample run.

📖 Java program 5.3

```
public class chap5_03
{
    public static void main(String[] args)
    {
    int cards,pick;
    String    Card[]={"Ace","King","Queen","Jack","10",
```

```
                       "9", "8", "7", "6", "5", "4", "3", "2"};
      for (cards=0;cards<5;cards++)
      {
          pick=(int)Math.round((Card.length)*Math.random());
          System.out.print(Card[pick] + " ");
      }
   }
}
```

```
Ace   10   King   2   3
```

Multi-dimensional arrays are declared in a similar manner. For example an array with 3 rows and 4 columns is declared with either of the following:

```
int arr[][]=new int[3][4];
```

or if the initial values are known with:

```
int arr[][]= { {1,2,3,4}, {5,6,7,8}, {9,10,11,12} } ;
```

where `arr[0][0]` is equal to 1, `arr[1][0]` is equal to 5, `arr[2][3]` is equal to 12, and so on. This is proved with Java program 5.4 and Sample run 5.5.

📖 Java program 5.4
```
public class chap5_04
{
    public static void main(String[] args)
    {
    int    row,col;
    int    arr[][]={ {1,2,3,4},{5,6,7,8}, {9,10,11,12} };

    for (row=0;row<3;row++)
       for (col=0;col<4;col++)
           System.out.println("Arr["+row+"]["+col+"]="+arr[row][col]);
    }
}
```

```
C:\java\src\chap5>java chap5_05
Arr[0][0]=1
Arr[0][1]=2
Arr[0][2]=3
Arr[0][3]=4
Arr[1][0]=5
Arr[1][1]=6
Arr[1][2]=7
Arr[1][3]=8
Arr[2][0]=9
Arr[2][1]=10
Arr[2][2]=11
Arr[2][3]=12
```

5.5.1   The `classes.zip` file contains all of the standard Java class libraries (a partial listing is shown in Sample run 5.1). Locate this file and determine the following:

(i)   The location of the file.
(ii)   The size of the file.
(iii)   The class directories within it.
(iv)   Some of the classes within it.

5.5.2   Using the methods in Java program 4.9 and the method developed in Exercise 4.8.5, and the standard sine and cosine library methods, write a program which determines the error between the standard library methods and the developed methods. From this, complete Table 5.3.

Table 5.3 Sine and cosine results

Value	Standard cosine function	Developed cosine function	Standard sine function	Developed sine function
2	−0.41614683		0.9092974	
−0.5				
1				
−1				

5.5.3   Compare the result from the exponential method developed in Exercise 4.8.6 with the standard `Math.exp()` library method.

5.5.4   Write a program, using arrays, with a method that returns the smallest value in an array. Refer to Program 4.6 for an outline of the program. Use method overloading to create one for an integer array and another for a double array.

5.5.5   Java program 5.5 can be used to arrange the values in an array in descending order and Sample run 5.6 shows a sample run. Explain its operation.

📖 Java program 5.5

```
public class chap5_05
{
    public static void main(String[] args)
    {
    int array[]={1,4,7,3,-1,4};
    Array Arr = new Array();

        Arr.a=array;
        Arr.show();
```

```
                Arr.descend();
                Arr.show();
        }
}
class Array
{
int a[];

    public void show()
    {
    int i;
        for (i=0;i<a.length;i++)
            System.out.println("Val "+i+" "+a[i]);
    }
    public void descend()
    {
    int i,j,temp;
        for (i=0;i<a.length-1;i++)
            for (j=i+1;j<a.length;j++)
                if (a[i]<a[j]) // swap values in array
                {
                    temp=a[i];
                    a[i]=a[j];
                    a[j]=temp;
                }
    }
}
```

🖥 **Sample run 5.6**

```
C:\java\src\chap4>java chap04_13
Val 0 1
Val 1 4
Val 2 7
Val 3 3
Val 4 -1
Val 5 4
Val 0 7
Val 1 4
Val 2 4
Val 3 3
Val 4 1
Val 5 -1
```

5.5.6   Write a method that arranges an array in ascending values.

5.5.7   Write a program which fills a two-dimensional array with five rows and four columns. Each row should be filled with the row number, the row number squared, the row number cubed and the row number to the fourth power. Thus the array will contain:

1	1	1	1
2	4	8	16
3	8	27	81
4	16	64	256
5	25	125	625

Rewrite the program using a method to fill the array and another one to display its contents.

The results in soccer matches between four nations are:

Scotland	3	France	3
Germany	2	Spain	0
Spain	1	Scotland	1
France	1	Germany	1
Scotland	1	Germany	2
Spain	2	France	0

The resulting league table (assuming 3 points for a win and 1 point for a draw) is:

	Played	Won	Draw	Lost	GoalsFor	GoalsAgainst	Pts
Germany	3	2	1	0	5	2	7
Spain	3	1	1	1	3	3	4
Scotland	3	0	1	2	5	6	2
France	3	1	1	2	4	6	2

Write a Java program which stores the team names, their associated points (Pts), their goals for and against, the games they have won, drawn and lost, and the number of games they have played. The program will then sort the teams into their respective league positions. Java program 5.6 shows how the league can be set up and how it can be sorted using the points values. Unfortunately it does not take into account goal difference (which is used to sort the position when the points are the same). The rules for the sort should be:

1. The team with the highest number of points has the highest position.
2. If two teams have the same number of points then the team with the higher goal difference (goals for minus goal against) has the higher position.
3. If two teams have the same number of points and they have the same goal difference then the team with the higher number of goals scored has the higher position.
4. If two teams have identical points, goals scored and goals against then the teams are arranged alphabetically.

 Java program 5.6

```
public class chap5_06
{
```

```
    public static void main(String[] args)
    {
        String names[]={"France","Scotland", "Germany","Spain"};
        int pts[]={2,2,7,4};

        League league = new League();

        league.name=names;
        league.pts=pts;

        league.show();
        league.sort();
        league.show();
    }
}
class League
{
String    name[];
int       pts[];


    public void show()
    {
        int i;
        System.out.println("Name   Pts");

        for (i=0;i<pts.length;i++)
        {
            System.out.println(name[i]+" "+pts[i]);
        }
    }

    public void sort()
    {
    int       i,j,temp;
    String    tempstr;

        for (i=0;i<pts.length-1;i++)
            for (j=i+1;j<pts.length;j++)
                if (pts[i]<pts[j])
                {
                    temp=pts[i];
                    pts[i]=pts[j];
                    pts[j]=temp;
                    tempstr=name[i];
                    name[i]=name[j];
                    name[j]=tempstr;
                }
    }
}
```

```
C:\java\src\chap4>java chap04_05
Name       Pts
France     2
Scotland   2
Germany    7
Spain      4
Name       Pts
Germany    7
Spain      4
France     2
Scotland   2
```

6 Java Applets

6.1 Introduction

As has been previously discussed a Java program can either be run as an applet within a WWW browser (such as Microsoft Internet Explorer or Netscape Communicator) or can be interpreted as a standalone program. The basic code within each program is almost the same and they can be easily converted from one to the other (typically a Java program will be run through an interpreter to test its results and then converted to run as an applet).

6.2 Applet tag

An applet is called from within an HTML script with the APPLET tag, such as:

```
<applet code="Test.class" width=200 height=300></applet>
```

which loads an applet called Test.class and sets the applet size to 200 pixels wide and 300 pixels high. Table 6.1 discusses some optional parameters.

Table 6.1 Other applet HTML parameters

Applet parameters	Description
CODEBASE=*codebaseURL*	Specifies the directory (*codebaseURL*) that contains the applet's code.
CODE=*appletFile*	Specifies the name of the file (*appletFile*) of the compiled applet.
ALT=*alternateText*	Specifies the alternative text that is displayed if the browser cannot run the Java applet.
NAME=*appletInstanceName*	Specifies a name for the applet instance (*appletInstanceName*). This makes it possible for applets on the same page to find each other.

Table 6.1 Other applet HTML parameters (cont.)

Applet parameters	Description
WIDTH=*pixels* HEIGHT=*pixels*	Specifies the initial width and height (in *pixels*) of the applet.
ALIGN=*alignment*	Specifies the *alignment* of the applet. Possible values are: left, right, top, texttop, middle, absmiddle, baseline, bottom and absbottom.
VSPACE=*pixels* HSPACE=*pixels*	Specifies the number of *pixels* above and below the applet (VSPACE) and on each side of the applet (HSPACE).

6.2.1 Applet viewer

A useful part of the JDK tools is an applet viewer which is used to test applets before they are run within the browser. The applet viewer on the PC version is AppletViewer.exe and the supplied argument is the HTML file that contains the applet tag(s). It then runs all the associated applets in separate windows.

6.3   Creating an applet

Java applet 6.1 shows a simple Java applet which displays two lines of text and HTML script 6.1 shows how the applet integrates into an HTML script.

First the Java applet (j1.java) is created. In this case the edit program is used. The directory listing below shows that the files created are chap6_01. java and chap6_01.html (note that Windows NT/95 displays the 8.3 file-name format on the left-hand side of the directory listing and the long file-name on the right-hand side).

📖 **Java applet 6.1** (chap6_01.java)

```
import java.awt.*;
import java.applet.*;

public class chap6_01 extends Applet
{
  public void paint(Graphics g)
  {
    g.drawString("This is my first Java",5,25);
    g.drawString("applet.....",5,45);
  }
}
```

📖 **HTML script 6.1** (chap6_01.html)

```
<HTML><TITLE>First Applet</TITLE>
<APPLET CODE=chap6_01.class WIDTH=200
HEIGHT=200></APPLET></HTML>
```

```
C:\java\src\chap6> edit chap6_01.java
C:\java\src\chap6> edit chap6_01.html
C:\java\src\chap6> dir
CHAP6_~1 HTM        111   14/05/98   18:40 chap6_01.html
CHAP6_~1 JAV        228   13/05/98   22:35 chap6_01.java
```

Next the Java applet is compiled using the `javac.exe` program. It can be seen from the listing that, if there are no errors, the compiled file is named `chap6_01.class`. This can then be used, with the HTML file, to run as an applet.

◻️ **Sample run 6.2**
```
C:\java\src\chap6> javac chap6_01.java
C:\java\src\chap6> dir
CHAP6_~1 HTM        111   14/05/98   18:40 chap6_01.html
CHAP6_~1 JAV        228   14/05/98   18:43 chap6_01.java
CHAP6_~1 CLA        460   14/05/98   18:43 chap6_01.class
C:\java\src\chap6> appletviewer chap6_01.html
```

6.4 Applet basics

Java applet 6.1 recaps the previous Java applet. This section analyses the main parts of this Java applet.

📖 **Java applet 6.1** (chap6_01.java)
```
import java.awt.*;
import java.applet.*;
public class chap6_01 extends Applet
{
  public void paint(Graphics g)
  {
   g.drawString("This is my first Java",5,25);
   g.drawString("applet.....",5,45);
  }
}
```

6.4.1 Applet class

The start of the applet code is defined in the form:

```
public class chap6_01 extends Applet
```

which informs the Java compiler to create an applet named `chap6_01` that extends the existing Applet class. The `public` keyword at the start of the statement allows the Java browser to run the applet, while if it is omitted the browser cannot access the applet.

The `class` keyword is used to creating a class object named `chap6_01` that extends the applet class. After this the applet is defined between the left and right braces (grouping symbols).

6.4.2 Applet methods

Methods allow Java applets to be split into smaller sub-tasks (just as C uses functions). These methods have the advantage that:

- They allow code to be reused.
- They allow for top-level design.
- They make applet debugging easier as each method can be tested in isolation to the rest of the applet.

A method has the `public` keyword, followed by the return value (if any) and the name of the method. After this the parameters passed to the method are defined within rounded brackets. Recapping from the previous example:

```
public void paint(Graphics g)
{
    g.drawString("This is my first Java",5,25);
    g.drawString("applet.....",5,45);
}
```

This method has the `public` keyword which allows any user to execute the method. The `void` type defines that there is nothing returned from this method and the name of the method is `paint()`. The parameter passed into the method is `g` which has the data type of `Graphics`. Within the `paint()` method the `drawString()` method is called. This method is defined in `java.awt.Graphics` class library (this library has been included with the `import java.awt.*` statement. The definition for this method is:

```
public abstract void drawString(String str, int x, int y)
```

which draws a string of characters using the current font and colour. The x,y position is the starting point of the baseline of the string (`str`).

It should be noted that Java is case sensitive and the names given must be referred to in the case that they are defined as.

6.5 The paint() object

The `paint()` object is the object that is called whenever the applet is redrawn. It will thus be called whenever the applet is run and then it is called whenever the applet is redisplayed.

Java applet 6.2 shows how a `for()` loop can be used to display the square and cube of the values from 0 to 9. Notice that the final value of `i` within the `for()` loop is 9 because the end condition is `i<10` (while `i` is less than 10).

📖 **Java applet 6.2** (chap6_02.java)

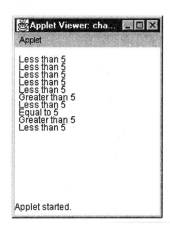

```
import java.awt.*;
import java.applet.*;
public class chap6_02 extends Applet
{
  public void paint(Graphics g)
  {
  int    i;

    g.drawString("Value Square Cube",5,10);
    for (i=0;i<10;i++)
    {
      g.drawString(""+ i,5,20+10*i);
      g.drawString(""+ i*i ,45,20+10*i);
      g.drawString(""+ i*i*i,85,20+10*i);
    }
  }
}
```

📖 **HTML script 6.2** (chap6_02.html)

```
<HTML> <TITLE>First Applet</TITLE>
<APPLET CODE=chap6_02.class WIDTH=200
HEIGHT=200></APPLET></HTML>
```

Java applet 6.3 uses a `for()` loop and the `if()` statement to test if a value is less than, equal to or greater than 5. The loop is used to repeat the test 10 times.

📖 **Java applet 6.3** (chap6_03.java)

```
import java.awt.*;
import java.applet.*;
import java.lang.Math;
public class chap6_03 extends Applet
{
  public void paint(Graphics g)
  {
    int      i,x;
    double   val;
    for (i=0;i<10;i++)
    {
      val=Math.random();

      x=(int)(val*10.0);
  // Convert value between 0 and 10

    if (x<5)
      g.drawString("Less than 5",5,20+i*10);
    else if (x==5)
      g.drawString("Equal to 5",5,20+i*10);
    else
      g.drawString("Greater than 5",5,20+i*10);
    }
  }
}
```

📖 **HTML script 6.3** (chap6_03.html)

```
<HTML>
<TITLE>First Applet</TITLE>
<APPLET CODE=chap6_03.class WIDTH=200 HEIGHT=200>
</APPLET></HTML>
```

The random() method is used to generate a value between 0 and 1, the returned value is then multiplied by 10 so as to convert into a value between 0 and 10. Then it is converted to an integer using the data type modifier (int). The if() statement is then used to test the value.

6.6   Exercises

6.6.1   Write a Java applet which displays the following table of powers.

```
Value        Square      Cube      Fourth power
1            1           1         1
2            4           8         16
3            9           27        81
4            16          64        256
5            25          125       625
6            36          216       1296
```

6.6.2   Write a Java applet which displays the following table of square root values from 1 to 15.

```
Value      Square root
1          1
2          1.414214
3          1.732051
4          2
5          2.236068
6          2.44949
7          2.645751
8          2.828427
9          3
10         3.162278
11         3.316625
12         3.464102
13         3.605551
14         3.741657
15         3.872983
```

6.6.3   Write a Java applet which display 20 random numbers from between 0 and 20.

6.6.4 Convert the following exercises so that they run within an applet:

    (i)   Exercise 4.8.3.
    (ii)   Exercise 5.5.5.
    (iii)   Exercise 5.5.6.
    (iv)   Project at the end of Chapter 5.
    (v)   Exercise 4.8.5.

6.6.5 Write a Java applet that simulates the rolling of two dice. A sample output is:

    Dice 1: 3
    Dice 2: 5
    Total: 8

6.6.6 Using a Java applet determine the results of the following:

    (i) $\sqrt{11.23}$
    (ii) $\tan^{-1}(0.5)$ (Hint: use `atan()`)
    (iii) $\sin(2.1)$
    (iv) $4^{2.1}$
    (v) $12.43^{-2.5}$
    (vi) e^{-3}

6.7 Project

Write a Java applet which contains all the cards in a deck. It will then give the deck a shuffle and display the cards in the deck. Java program 6.4 shows an outline of a program but does not contain all of the cards in the deck. Sample run 6.3 shows a sample run of the program. Implement the following:

(i)   Convert the program to an applet.
(ii) Add the rest of the card to the deck.
(iii) Increase the number of shuffles.
(iv) Add suits to the deck.

📖 **Java program 6.4** (`chap6_04.java`)

```
import java.lang.Math;

public class chap6_04
{
```

```
      public static void main(String[] args)
      {
      String names[]={"Ace","King", "Queen","Jack", "10"};

          Cards card = new Cards();

          card.name=names;
          card.nshuffle=20; // 20 shuffles of cards

          System.out.println("Before shuffle");
          card.show();
          card.shuffle();
          System.out.println("After shuffle");
          card.show();
      }
}
class Cards
{
String    name[];
int       nshuffle;

    public void show()
    {
    int i;
        for (i=0;i<name.length;i++)
        {
            System.out.println(name[i]);
        }
    }

    public void shuffle()
    { .
    int i, pos1, pos2;
    String tempstr;

        for (i=0;i<nshuffle;i++)
        {
            pos1=(int) ((name.length)*Math.random());
            pos2=(int) ((name.length)*Math.random());
            tempstr=name[pos1];
            name[pos1]=name[pos2];
            name[pos2]=tempstr;
        }
    }
}
```

⌨ **Sample run 6.3**

```
Before shuffle
Ace
King
Queen
Jack
10
After shuffle
King
10
Jack
Queen
Ace
```

7 Java Mouse and Keyboard Methods

7.1 Introduction

The previous chapters have discussed the Java programming language. This chapter investigates event-driven programs. Traditional methods of programming involve writing a program which flows from one part to the next in a linear manner. Most programs are designed using a top-down structured design, where the task is split into a number of sub-modules, these are then called when they are required. This means that it is relatively difficult to interrupt the operation of a certain part of a program to do another activity, such as updating the graphics display.

In general Java is event-driven where the execution of a program is not predefined and its execution is triggered by events, such as a mouse click, a keyboard press, and so on. The main events are:

- Initialisation and exit methods (`init()`, `start()`, `stop()` and `destroy()`).
- Repainting and resizing (`paint()`).
- Mouse events (`mouseUp()`, `mouseDown()` and `mouseDrag()` for Java 1.0, and `mousePressed()`, `mouseReleased()` and `mouseDragged()` for Java 1.1).
- Keyboard events (`keyUp()` and `keyDown()` for Java 1.0, and `keyPressed()` and `keyReleased()` for Java 1.1).

7.2 Java 1.0 and Java 1.1

There has been a big change between Java 1.0 and Java 1.1. The main change is to greatly improve the architecture of the AWT, which helps in compatibility. Java 1.0 programs will work with most browsers, but only upgraded browsers will work with Java 1.1. The main reasons to upgrade though are:

- Java 1.1 adds new features.
- Faster architecture with more robust implementations of the AWT.
- Support for older facilities will be phased out.

7.2.1 Deprecation

Older facilitates which are contained with Java 1.0 and are still supported Java 1.1, but the Java compiler gives a deprecation warning. This warning means that the facility will eventually be phased-out. The warning is in the form of:

```
C:\jdk1.1.6\src\chap7>javac chap7_01.java
Note: chap7_01.java uses a deprecated API.   Recompile with "-
deprecation" for details.
1 warning
```

The full details on the deprecation can be found by using the –deprecation flag. For example:

```
C:\jdk1.1.6\src\chap7>javac -deprecation chap7_01.java
chap7_01.java:9: Note: The method boolean mouseUp(java.awt.
Event, int, int) in class java.awt.Component has been depre-
cated, and class chap7_01 (which is not deprecated) overrides
it.

    public boolean mouseUp(Event event,
                  ^
Note: chap7_01.java uses a deprecated API.   Please consult the
documentation for a better alternative.
1 warning
```

7.3   Initialisation and exit methods

Java applets have various reserved methods which are called when various events occur. Table 7.1 shows typical initialisation methods and their events, and Figure 7.1 illustrates how they are called.

Table 7.1 Java initialisation and exit methods

Method	Description
public void **init**()	This method is called each time the applet is started. It is typically used to add user-interface components.
public void **stop**()	This method is called when the user moves away from the page on which the applet resides. It is thus typically used to stop processing while the user is not

accessing the applet. Typically it is used to stop animation or audio files, or mathematical processing. The `start()` method normally restarts the processing.

`public void` **`paint`**`(Graphics g)`	This method is called when the applet is first called and whenever the user resizes or moves the windows.
`public void` **`destroy()`**	This method is called when the applet is stopped and is normally used to release associated resources, such as freeing memory, closing files, and so on.

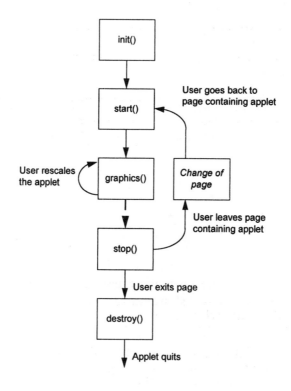

Figure 7.1 Java initialisation and exit methods

Java applet 7.1 gives an example using the `init()` and `start()` methods. The variable i is declared within the applet and it is set to a value of 5 in the `init()` method. The `start()` method then adds 6 onto this value. After this the `paint()` method is called so that it displays the value of i (which should equal 11).

📖 Java applet 7.1 (chap7_01.java)

```java
import java.awt.*;
import java.applet.*;

public class chap7_01 extends Applet
{
int      i;

  public void init()
  {
    i=5;
  }
  public void start()
  {
    i=i+6;
  }
  public void paint(Graphics g)
  {
   g.drawString("The value of i is "
          + i,5,25);
  }
}
```

Applet Viewer: cha...
Applet

The value of i is 11

Applet started.

📖 HTML script 7.1 (chap7_01.html)

```html
<HTML>
<TITLE>Applet</TITLE>
<APPLET CODE=chap7_01.class WIDTH=200
HEIGHT=200>
</APPLET></HTML>
```

7.4   Mouse events in Java 1.0

Most Java applets require some user interaction, normally with the mouse or from the keyboard. A mouse operation causes mouse events. The six basic mouse events which are supported in Java 1.0 are:

- `mouseUp(Event evt, int x, int y)`
- `mouseDown(Event evt, int x, int y)`
- `mouseDrag(Event evt, int x, int y)`
- `mouseEnter(Event evt, int x, int y)`
- `mouseExit(Event evt, int x, int y)`
- `mouseMove(Event evt, int x, int y)`

Java applet 7.2 uses three mouse events to display the current mouse cursor. Each of the methods must return a true value to identify that the event has been handled successfully (the return type is of data type boolean thus the return could only be a true or a false). In the example applet, on moving the mouse cursor with the left mouse key pressed down the `mouseDrag()` method is automatically called. The x and y co-ordinate of the cursor is stored in the x and y variable when the event occurs. This is used in the methods to build a message string (in the case of the drag event the string name is Mouse-DragMsg).

The mouseEnter() method is called when the mouse enters the component, mouseExit() is called when the mouse exits the component and mouse-Move() when the mouse moves (the mouse button is up).

📖 Java applet 7.2 (chap7_02.java)

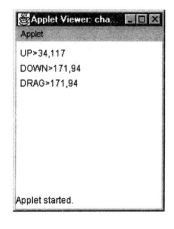

```java
import java.awt.*;
import java.applet.*;
public class chap7_02 extends Applet
{
String  MouseDownMsg=null;
String  MouseUpMsg=null;
String  MouseDragMsg=null;

  public boolean mouseUp(Event event,
    int x, int y)
  {
    MouseUpMsg = "UP>" +x + "," + y;
    repaint();   // call paint()
    return(true);
  }
  public boolean mouseDown(Event event,
    int x, int y)
  {
    MouseDownMsg = "DOWN>" +x + "," + y;
    repaint();   // call paint()
    return(true);
  }

  public boolean mouseDrag(Event event,
    int x, int y)
  {
    MouseDragMsg = "DRAG>" +x + "," + y;
    repaint();   // call paint()
    return(true);
  }

  public void paint(Graphics g)
  {
    if (MouseUpMsg !=null)
      g.drawString(MouseUpMsg,5,20);
    if (MouseDownMsg !=null)
      g.drawString(MouseDownMsg,5,40);
    if (MouseDragMsg !=null)
      g.drawString(MouseDragMsg,5,60);
  }
}
```

📖 HTML script 7.2 (chap7_02.html)

```html
<HTML>
<TITLE>Applet</TITLE>
<APPLET CODE=chap7_02.class WIDTH=200
HEIGHT=200>
</APPLET></HTML>
```

7.5 Mouse event handling in Java 1.1

Java 1.1 has changed the event handling. In its place is the concept of listeners. Each listener receivers notification about the types of events that it is interested in. For mouse handling the two listeners are:

- MouseListener. This has the associated methods of:
  - mousePressed() which is equivalent to mouseDown() in Java 1.0
  - mouseReleased() which is equivalent to mouseUp() in Java 1.0
  - mouseEntered() which is equivalent to mouseEnter() in Java 1.0
  - mouseExited() which is equivalent to mouseExit() in Java 1.0
  - mouseClicked()
- MouseMotionListener. This has the associated methods of:
  - mouseDragged() which is equivalent to mouseDrag() in Java 1.0
  - mouseMoved() which is equivalent to mouseMove() in Java 1.0

7.5.1 Mouse methods

The arguments passed to the methods have also changed, in that there are no x and y integers passed, and there is no return from them. Their syntax is as follows:

```
public void mousePressed(MouseEvent event) {};
public void mouseReleased(MouseEvent event) {};
public void mouseClicked(MouseEvent event) {};
public void mouseExited(MouseEvent event) {};
public void mouseEntered(MouseEvent event) {};
public void mouseDragged(MouseEvent event) {};
public void mouseMoved(MouseEvent event) {};
```

The x and y co-ordinates of the mouse event can be found by accessing the getX() and getY() methods of the event, such as:

```
x=event.getX();    y=event.getY();
```

7.5.2 Event class

The other main change to the Java program is to add the java.awt.event package, with:

```
import java.awt.event.*;
```

7.5.3 Class declaration

The class declaration is changed so that the appropriate listener is defined. If both mouse listeners are required then the class declaration is as follows:

```
public class class_name extends Applet
   implements MouseListener, MouseMotionListener
```

7.5.4 Defining components that generate events

The components which generate events must be defined. In the case of a
mouse event these are added as:

```
this.addMouseListener(this);
   this.addMouseMotionListener(this);
```

7.5.5 Updated Java program

Java applet 7.3 gives the updated Java program with Java 1.1 updates.

📖 Java applet 7.3 (chap7_03.java)

```
import java.awt.*;
import java.applet.*;
import java.awt.event.*;

public class chap7_02 extends Applet
implements MouseListener, MouseMotionListener
{
String  MouseDownMsg=null;
String  MouseUpMsg=null;
String  MouseDragMsg=null;

  public void init()
  {
       this.addMouseListener(this);
       this.addMouseMotionListener(this);
  }

  public void paint(Graphics g)
  {
    if (MouseUpMsg !=null)  g.drawString(MouseUpMsg,5,20);
    if (MouseDownMsg !=null) g.drawString(MouseDownMsg,5,40);
    if (MouseDragMsg !=null) g.drawString(MouseDragMsg,5,60);
  }

  public void mousePressed(MouseEvent event)
  {
    MouseUpMsg = "UP>" +event.getX() + "," + event.getY();
    repaint();    // call paint()
  }
  public void mouseReleased(MouseEvent event)
  {
    MouseDownMsg = "DOWN>" +event.getX() + "," + event.getY();
    repaint();    // call paint()
  }
  public void mouseClicked(MouseEvent event) {};
  public void mouseExited(MouseEvent event) {};
  public void mouseEntered(MouseEvent event) {};

   public void mouseDragged(MouseEvent event)
   {
    MouseDragMsg = "DRAG>" +event.getX() + "," + event.getY();
    repaint();    // call paint()
   }
  public void mouseMoved(MouseEvent event) {};
}
```

In many applets the user is prompted to select an object using the mouse. To achieve this the x and y position of the event is tested to determine if the cursor is within the defined area. Java applet 7.4 is a program which allows the user to press the mouse button on the applet screen. The applet then uses the mouse events to determine if the cursor is within a given area of the screen (in this case between 10,10 and 100,50). If the user is within this defined area then the message displayed is HIT, else it is MISS. The graphics method g.drawRect(x1,y1,x2,y2) draws a rectangle from (x1,y1) to (x2,y2).

📖 **Java applet 7.4** (chap7_04.java)

```java
import java.awt.*;
import java.applet.*;
public class chap7_04 extends Applet
{
String  Msg=null;
int     x_start,y_start,x_end,y_end;

  public void init()
  {
    x_start=10;   y_start=10;
    x_end=100;    y_end=50;
  }

  public boolean mouseUp(Event event,
   int x, int y)
  {
    if ((x>x_start) && (x<x_end) &&
          (y>y_start) && (y<y_end))
              Msg = "HIT";
    else Msg="MISS";
    repaint();   // call paint()
    return(true);
  }

  public boolean mouseDown(Event event,
   int x, int y)
  {
    if ((x>x_start) && (x<x_end) &&
          (y>y_start) && (y<y_end))
              Msg = "HIT";
    else Msg="MISS";
    repaint();   // call paint()
    return(true);
  }

  public void paint(Graphics g)
  {

  g.drawRect(x_start,y_start,x_end,y_end);
    g.drawString("Hit",30,30);
    if (Msg !=null)
      g.drawString("HIT OR MISS: "
        + Msg,5,80);
  }
}
```

HTML script 7.3 (chap7_04.html)

```
<HTML>
<TITLE>Applet</TITLE>
<APPLET CODE=j8.class WIDTH=200 HEIGHT=200>
</APPLET></HTML>
```

Java applet 7.5 gives the updated Java program with Java 1.1 updates.

Java applet 7.5 (chap7_05.java)

```
import java.awt.*;
import java.applet.*;
import java.awt.event.*;

public class chap7_05 extends Applet implements MouseListener
{
String  Msg=null;
int     x_start,y_start,x_end,y_end;

  public void init()
  {
    x_start=10;    y_start=10;
    x_end=100;     y_end=50;
    this.addMouseListener(this);
  }

  public void mousePressed(MouseEvent event)
  {
    int x,y;
    x=event.getX(); y=event.getY();

    if ((x>x_start) && (x<x_end) && (y>y_start) && (y<y_end))
              Msg = "HIT";
    else Msg="MISS";
    repaint();    // call paint()
  }

  public void mouseReleased(MouseEvent event)
  {
    int x,y;
    x=event.getX();  y=event.getY();
    if ((x>x_start) && (x<x_end) && (y>y_start) && (y<y_end))
              Msg = "HIT";
    else Msg="MISS";
    repaint();    // call paint()
  }
  public void mouseEntered(MouseEvent event) {};
  public void mouseExited(MouseEvent event) {};
  public void mouseClicked(MouseEvent event) {};

  public void paint(Graphics g)
  {

  g.drawRect(x_start,y_start,x_end,y_end);
    g.drawString("Hit",30,30);
    if (Msg !=null)
     g.drawString("HIT OR MISS: "
         + Msg,5,80);
  }
}
```

Java 1.0 provides for two keyboard events, these are:

- `keyUp(Event evt, int key)`. Called when a key has been released
- `keyDown(Event evt, int key)`. Called when a key has been pressed

The parameters passed into these methods are `event` (which defines the keyboard state) and an integer `Keypressed` which describes the key pressed.

📖   Java applet 7.6 (chap7_06.java)

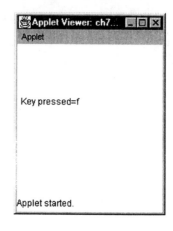

```java
import java.awt.*;
import java.applet.*;

public class chap7_06 extends Applet
{
String  Msg=null;

 public boolean keyUp(Event event,
  int KeyPress)
 {
   Msg="Key pressed="+(char)KeyPress;
   repaint();    // call paint()
   return(true);
  }
 public void paint(Graphics g)
  {
   if (Msg !=null)
        g.drawString(Msg,5,80);
  }
}
```

📖   HTML script 7.4 (chap7_06.html)
```html
<HTML><TITLE>Applet</TITLE>
<APPLET CODE=chap7_06.class WIDTH=200
HEIGHT=200></APPLET></HTML>
```

The event contains an identification as to the type of event it is. When one of the function keys is pressed then the variable `event.id` is set to the macro `Event.KEY_ACTION` (as shown in Java applet 7.7). Other keys, such as the Ctrl, Alt and Shift keys, set bits in the `event.modifier` variable. The test for the Ctrl key is:

```java
if ((event.modifiers & Event.CTRL_MASK) !=0)
    Msg="CONTROL KEY "+KeyPress;
```

This tests the `CTRL_MASK` bit; if it is a 1 then the CTRL key has been pressed. Java applet 7.7 shows its uses.

Java applet 7.7 (chap7_07.java)

```java
import java.awt.*;
import java.applet.*;

public class chap7_07 extends Applet
{
String  Msg=null;

 public boolean keyDown(Event event,
                        int KeyPress)
 {
 if (event.id == Event.KEY_ACTION)
   Msg="FUNCTION KEY "+KeyPress;
 else if ((event.modifiers & Event.SHIFT_MASK)!=0)
   Msg="SHIFT KEY "+KeyPress;
 else if ((event.modifiers & Event.CTRL_MASK)!=0)
   Msg="CONTROL KEY "+KeyPress;
 else if ((event.modifiers & Event.ALT_MASK)!=0)
   Msg="ALT KEY "+KeyPress;
 else Msg=""+(char)KeyPress;
 repaint();    // call paint()
 return(true);
 }
 public void paint(Graphics g)
 {
  if (Msg!=null)
     g.drawString(Msg,5,80);
 }
}
```

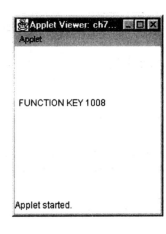

HTML script 7.5 (chap7_05.html)

```html
<HTML>
<TITLE>Applet</TITLE>
<APPLET CODE= chap7_07.class WIDTH=200 HEIGHT=200>
</APPLET></HTML>
```

For function keys the KeyPress variable has the following values:

Key	Value	Key	Value	Key	Value	Key	Value	Key	Value
F1	1008	F2	1009	F3	1010	F4	1011	F5	1012
F7	1014	F8	1015	F9	1016	F10	1017	F11	1018

Thus, to test for the function keys the following routine can be used:

```java
if (event.id == Event.KEY_ACTION)
      if (KeyPress==1008) Msg="F1";
      else if (KeyPress==1009) Msg="F2";
      else if (KeyPress==1010) Msg="F3";
      else if (KeyPress==1011) Msg="F4";
      else if (KeyPress==1012) Msg="F5";
      else if (KeyPress==1013) Msg="F6";
      else if (KeyPress==1014) Msg="F7";
      else if (KeyPress==1015) Msg="F8";
      else if (KeyPress==1016) Msg="F9";
      else if (KeyPress==1017) Msg="F10";
```

The function keys have constant definitions for each of the keys. These are

F1, F2, F3, and so. Thus the following is equivalent to the previous example:

```
if (event.id == Event.KEY_ACTION)
        if (KeyPress==F1) Msg="F1";
        else if (KeyPress==F2) Msg="F2";
        else if (KeyPress==F3) Msg="F3";
        else if (KeyPress==F4) Msg="F4";
        else if (KeyPress==F5) Msg="F5";
        else if (KeyPress==F6) Msg="F6";
        else if (KeyPress==F7) Msg="F7";
        else if (KeyPress==F8) Msg="F8";
        else if (KeyPress==F9) Msg="F9";
        else if (KeyPress==F10) Msg="F10";
```

For control keys the KeyPress variable has the following values:

Key	Value	Key	Value	Key	Value	Key	Value
Cntrl-A	1	Cntrl-B	2	Cntrl-C	3	Cntrl-D	4
Cntrl-E	5	Cntrl-F	6	Cntrl-G	7	Cntrl-H	8

Thus, to test for the control keys the following routine can be used:

```
if ((event.modifiers & Event.CTRL_MASK)!=0)
    if (KeyPress==1) Msg="Cntrl-A";
    else if (KeyPress==2) Msg="Cntrl-B";
    else if (KeyPress==3) Msg="Cntrl-C";
    else if (KeyPress==4) Msg="Cntrl-D";
```

The complete list of the keys defined by the KeyPress variable are:

Key	Value	Key	Value	Key	Value	Key	Value	Key	Value
HOME	1000	END	1001	PGUP	1002	PGDN	1003	UP	1004
DOWN	1005	LEFT	1006	RIGHT	1007	F1	1008	F2	1009
F3	1010	F4	1011	F5	1012	F7	1014	F8	1015
F9	1016	F10	1017	F11	1018	F12	1019		

7.8   Keyboard events in Java 1.1

Java 1.1 has changed the event handling. In its place is the concept of listeners. Each listener receivers notification about the types of events that it is interested in. For keyboard handling the two listeners are:

- KeyListener. This has the associated methods of:
    - keyPressed() which is equivalent to keyDown() in Java 1.0
    - keyReleased() which is equivalent to keyUp() in Java 1.0
    - keyTyped()

7.8.1 Key methods

The arguments passed to the methods have also changed. Their syntax is as follows:

```
public void keyPressed(KeyEvent event) {}
public void keyReleased(KeyEvent event) {}
public void keyTyped(KeyEvent event) {}
```

7.8.2 Event class

Another change to the Java program is to add the `java.awt.event` package, with:

```
import java.awt.event.*;
```

7.8.3 Class declaration

The class declaration is changed so that the appropriate listener is defined. If the key listener is required then the class declaration is as follows:

```
public class class_name extends Applet implements KeyListener
```

7.8.4 Defining components that generate events

The components which generate events must be defined. In the case of a key event these are added as:

```
compname.addKeyListener(this);
```

7.8.5 Updated Java program

Java applet 7.8 gives the updated Java program with Java 1.1 updates. In this case a `TextField` component is added to the applet (`text`). The `TextField` component will be discussed in Chapter 10. When a key is pressed on this component then the `keyPressed` event listener is called, when one is released the `keyReleased` is called.

The `getKeyCode()` method is used to determine the key that has been activated. In the event method the `KeyEvent` defines a number of `VK_` constants, such as:

VK_F1	Function Key F1	VK_A Character 'A'	VK_ALT	Alt key
VK_CONTROL	Control Key	VK_0 Character '0'	VK_SHIFT	Shift key

A full list of the `VK_` keys is given in Appendix D (Section D.4.11).

Java applet 7.8 (chap7_08.java)

```
import java.awt.*;
import java.applet.*;
import java.awt.event.*;

public class chap7_08 extends Applet implements KeyListener
{
String  Msg=null;
TextField text;

    public void init()
    {
        text=new TextField(20);

        add(text);
        text.addKeyListener(this);
    }

    public void keyPressed(KeyEvent event)
    {
    int KeyPress;

        KeyPress=event.getKeyCode();

        if (KeyPress == KeyEvent.VK_ALT)  Msg="ALT KEY";
        else if (KeyPress == KeyEvent.VK_CONTROL)  Msg="CNTRL KEY ";
        else if (KeyPress == KeyEvent.VK_SHIFT) Msg="SHIFT KEY ";
        else if (KeyPress == KeyEvent.VK_RIGHT) Msg="RIGHT KEY ";
        else if (KeyPress == KeyEvent.VK_LEFT) Msg="LEFT KEY ";
        else if (KeyPress == KeyEvent.VK_F1)   Msg="Function key F1";
        else Msg="Key:"+(char)KeyPress;

        text.setText(Msg);
    }
    public void keyReleased(KeyEvent event) { }
    public void keyTyped(KeyEvent event)  { }

}
```

Figure 7.2 Sample run

7.9.1   Explain how the six mouse events occur in Java 1.0 and how they have been modified in Java 1.1.

7.9.2   Write a Java applet which displays all the mouse and keyboard events. Display the parameters passed to them (such as the x, y co-ordinate for the mouse and the key pressed for the keyboard events).

7.9.3   Write a Java applet which displays the message "Mouse moving" and the x, y co-ordinate of the cursor when the mouse is moving.

7.9.4   Write a Java applet that contains a target which has areas with different point values. These point values are 50, 100 and 150. The program should accumulate the score so far. A sample screen is given in Figure 7.3 (refer to Java applet 7.4 for the outline of the program).

7.9.5   Modify the program in 7.9.4 so that a RESET area is displayed. When selected the points value should be reset to zero.

7.9.6   Write a Java applet which displays which function key or control key (Cntrl) has been pressed. The program should run continuously until the Cntrl-Z keystroke is pressed.

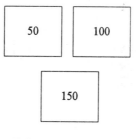

Points: 400

Figure 7.3

7.10 Project

Java applet 7.9 displays a small square, which can be moved around the screen with the arrowkeys. Sample run 7.4 shows a sample run. Modify the program for the following:

(i)   The program should quit when the user presses the ESC key (VK_ESCAPE).

(ii)   The program should stop the square going of the ends of the screen. For example to stop it going off the left hand side of the screen then the following can be used:

```
if (KeyPress == KeyEvent.VK_LEFT)   x--;
else if (KeyPress == KeyEvent.VK_RIGHT) x++;
else if (KeyPress == KeyEvent.VK_UP) y--;
else if (KeyPress == KeyEvent.VK_DOWN) y++;
if (x<0) x=0; // stops square from going of the screen
```

(iii)   If the user presses the backspace (VK_BACK_SPACE) then the square is returned to its starting position.

(iv)   The colour of the square is changed by pressing one of the function keys. For example F1 – red, F2 – green, F3 – blue, and so on. This could be achieved with the following:

```
public class chap7_09 extends Applet implements KeyListener
{
int x=0,y=0,oldx=0, oldy=0;
TextField text;
col=color.black;

    etc
}

public void keyPressed(KeyEvent event)
{
int KeyPress;

    KeyPress=event.getKeyCode();

    if (KeyPress == KeyEvent.VK_LEFT)   x--;
    else if (KeyPress == KeyEvent.VK_RIGHT) x++;
    else if (KeyPress == KeyEvent.VK_UP) y--;
    else if (KeyPress == KeyEvent.VK_DOWN) y++;
    else if (KeyPress == VK_F1) col=color.red;

    etc
    repaint();
}


public void paint(Graphics g)
{
    g.setColor(Color.white);   // draw in the background color
    g.fillRect(oldx,oldy,20,20);  // x,y,width,height
    g.setColor(col);
    g.fillRect(x,y,20,20);
    oldx=x;oldy=y;
}
```

(v)   The PgUp (VK_PAGE_UP) and PgDn (VK_PAGE_DOWN) keys are used to increment or decrement the step size. The increment should double or halve depending on whether PgUp or PgDn are pressed, respectively. An outline is shown next:

```
        if (KeyPress == KeyEvent.VK_LEFT)   x=x-increment;
        else if (KeyPress == KeyEvent.VK_RIGHT) x=x+increment;
        else if (KeyPress == KeyEvent.VK_UP) y=y-increment;
        else if (KeyPress == KeyEvent.VK_DOWN) y=y+increment;
        else if (KeyPress == KeyEvent.VK_PAGE_DOWN) increment=increment*2;
```

Java applet 7.9 (chap7_09.java)

```java
import java.awt.*;
import java.applet.*;
import java.awt.event.*;

public class chap7_09 extends Applet implements KeyListener
{
int          x=0,y=0,oldx=0, oldy=0;
TextField    text;

    public void init()
    {
    text=new TextField(3);
        add(text);
        text.addKeyListener(this);
    }

    public void keyPressed(KeyEvent event)
    {
    int KeyPress;

        KeyPress=event.getKeyCode();
        if (KeyPress == KeyEvent.VK_LEFT)   x--;
        else if (KeyPress == KeyEvent.VK_RIGHT) x++;
        else if (KeyPress == KeyEvent.VK_UP) y--;
        else if (KeyPress == KeyEvent.VK_DOWN) y++;
        repaint();
    }

    public void paint(Graphics g)
    {
        g.setColor(Color.white);   // draw in the background color
        g.fillRect(oldx,oldy,20,20);   // x,y,width,height
        g.setColor(Color.black);
        g.fillRect(x,y,20,20);
        oldx=x;oldy=y;
    }
  public void keyReleased(KeyEvent event) { }
  public void keyTyped(KeyEvent event)   { }
}
```

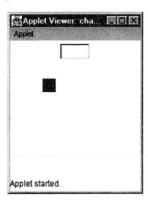

Figure 7.4 Sample run

8 Java Graphics and Sound

8.1 Introduction

Java has excellent support for images and sound. For graphics files it supports GIF (.gif) and JPEG (.jpg) files, each of which is in a compressed form. The image object is declared with:

```
Image mypic;
```

Next the graphics image is associated with the image object with the getImage() method:

```
mypic=getImage(getCodeBase(),"myson.gif");
```

where the getCodeBase() method returns the applet's URL (such as www.eece.napier.ac.uk) and the second argument is the name of the graphics file (in this case, myson.gif). After this the image can be displayed with:

```
g.drawImage(mypic,x,y,this);
```

where mypic is the name of the image object, and the x and y values are the co-ordinates of the upper-left hand corner of the image. The this keyword associates the current object (in this case it is the graphics image) and the current applet. Java applet 8.1 gives an applet which displays an image.

📖 Java applet 8.1

```
import java.awt.*;
import java.applet.*;

public class chap8_01 extends Applet
{
Image   mypic;
  public void init()
  {
   mypic = getImage(getCodeBase(),
             "myson.gif");
  }
  public void paint(Graphics g)
  {
    g.drawImage(mypic,0,0,this);
```

```
<HTML><TITLE>Applet</TITLE>
<APPLET CODE=chap8_01.class WIDTH=200
HEIGHT=200></APPLET></HTML>
```

8.2　Graphics

The `java.awt.Graphics` class contains a great deal of graphics-based methods; these are stated in Table 8.1.

Table 8.1 Java graphics methods

Graphics method	Description
`public abstract void translate( int x,int y)`	Translates the specified parameters into the origin of the graphics context. All subsequent operations on this graphics context will be relative to this origin. Parameters: x - the x co-ordinate y - the y co-ordinate.
`public abstract Color getColor()`	Gets the current colour.
`public abstract void setColor( Color c)`	Set current drawing colour.
`public abstract Font getFont()`	Gets the current font.
`public abstract void setFont( Font font)`	Set the current font.
`public FontMetrics getFontMetrics()`	Gets the current font metrics.
`public abstract FontMetrics getFontMetrics(Font f)`	Gets the current font metrics for the specified font.
`public abstract void copyArea( int x, int y, int width, int height, int dx,int dy)`	Copies an area of the screen where (x,y) is the co-ordinate of the top left-hand corner, width and height, and dx is the horizontal distance and dy the vertical distance.
`public abstract void drawLine( int x1,int y1,int x2, int y2)`	Draws a line between the (x1,y1) and (x2,y2).
`public abstract void fillRect( int x, int y, int width, int height)`	Fills the specified rectangle with the current colour.
`public void drawRect(int x,int y, int width, int height)`	Draws the outline of the specified rectangle using the current colour.
`public abstract void clearRect( int x, int y, int width, int height)`	Clears the specified rectangle by filling it with the current background colour of the current drawing surface.

Table 8.1 Java graphics methods (cont.)

Graphics method	Description

`public void draw3DRect(`
`  int x, int y, int width,`
`  int height,boolean raised)`
	Draws a highlighted 3-D rectangle where `raised` is a boolean value that defines whether the rectangle is raised or not.

`public void fill3DRect(int x,`
`  int y,int width,`
`  int height,boolean raised)`
	Paints a highlighted 3-D rectangle using the current colour.

`public abstract void drawOval(`
`  int x,int y, int width,`
`  int height)`
	Draws an oval inside the specified rectangle using the current colour.

`public abstract void fillOval(`
`  int x,int y, int width,`
`  int height)`
	Fills an oval inside the specified rectangle using the current colour.

`public abstract void drawArc(`
`  int x, int y, int width,`
`  int height, int startAngle,`
`  int arcAngle)`
	Draws an arc bounded by the specified rectangle starting. Zero degrees for `startAngle` is at the 3-o'clock position and `arcAngle` specifies the extent of the arc. A positive value for `arcAngle` indicates a counter-clockwise rotation while a negative value indicates a clockwise rotation. The parameter (x,y) specifies the centre point, and width and height specifies the width and height of a rectangle

`public abstract void fillArc(`
`  int x, int y, int width,`
`  int height, int startAngle,`
`  int arcAngle)`
	Fills a pie-shaped arc using the current colour.

`public abstract void drawPolygon(`
`  int xPoints[],int yPoints[],`
`  int nPoints)`
	Draws a polygon using an array of x and y points (`xPoints[]` and `yPoints[]`). The number of points within the array is specified by `nPoints`.

`public abstract void fillPolygon(`
`  int xPoints[],`
`  int yPoints[],int nPoints)`
	Fills a polygon with the current colour.

`public abstract void drawString(` `  String str, int x, int y)`	Draws the specified `String` using the current font and colour.
`public abstract boolean drawImage(` `  Image img,int x, int y)`	Draws the specified image at the specified coordinate (x, y).
`public abstract void dispose()`	Disposes of this graphics context.

8.2.1 Setting the colour

The current drawing colour is set using the `setColor()` method. It is used as follows:

```
g.setColor(Color.yellow);
```

Colours are defined in the `java.awt.Color` class and valid colours are:

```
Color.black    Color.blue     Color.cyan       Color.darkGray
Color.gray     Color.green    Color.lightGray  Color.magenta
Color.orange   Color.pink     Color.red        Color.white
Color.yellow
```

Any other 24-bit colour can be generated with the method `Color` which has the format:

```
public Color(int r, int g, int b);
```

where `r`, `g` and `b` are values of strength from 0 to 255. For example:

`Color(255,0,0)`   gives red;   `Color(255,255,255)` gives white;
`Color(0,128,128)` gives blue/green;   `Color(0,0,0)` gives black.

8.2.2 Drawing lines and circles

Normally to draw a graphics object the user must plan its layout for the dimension within the object. Figure 8.1 shows an example graphic with the required dimensions. The `drawOval()` method uses the top level hand point for the x and y parameters in the method and the width and height define the width and height of the oval shape. Thus the `drawOval()` method can be used to draw circles (if the width is equal to the height) or ovals (if the width is not equal to the height). Java applet 8.2 shows the Java code to draw the object. This applet uses the `setColor()` method to make the circle red and the other shapes blue.

📖 Java applet 8.2

```
import java.awt.*;
import java.applet.*;
public class chap8_02 extends Applet
{
  public void paint(Graphics g)
  {
    g.setColor(Color.red);
    g.fillOval(50,30,50,50);
    g.setColor(Color.blue);
    g.fillOval(30,80,90,100);
    g.fillRect(15,130,15,10);
    g.fillRect(120,130,15,10);
  }
}
```

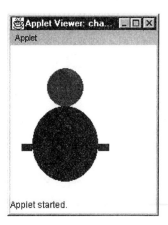

📖 HTML script 8.2

```
<HTML>
<TITLE>Applet</TITLE>
<APPLET CODE= chap8_02.class WIDTH=200
HEIGHT=200>
</APPLET>
</HTML>
```

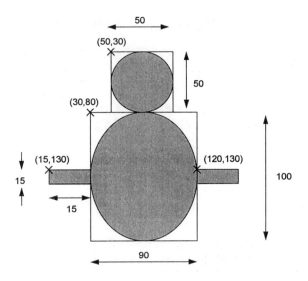

Figure 8.1 Dimensions for graphic

8.2.3 Drawing polygons

The drawPolygon() method can be used to draw complex objects where the object is defined as a group of (x,y) co-ordinates. Java applet 8.3 draws a basic picture of a car and the xpoints array holds the x co-ordinates and ypoints hold the y co-ordinates. Figure 8.2 illustrates the object.

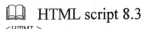 Java applet 8.3

```
import java.awt.*;
import java.applet.*;
public class chap8_03 extends Applet
{
int    xpoints[]={10,30,30,90,100,140,
      140,110,110,90,90,40,40,20,20,10,10},
      ypoints[]={50,50,30,30,50,50,70,
      70,60,60, 70, 70,60,60,70,70,50};
  public void paint(Graphics g)
  {
    g.drawPolygon(xpoints,ypoints,17);
  }
}
```

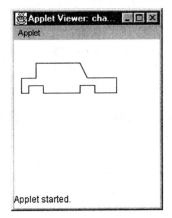

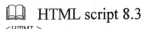 HTML script 8.3

```
<HTML>
<TITLE>Applet</TITLE>
<APPLET CODE= chap8_03.class WIDTH=200
HEIGHT=200>
</APPLET></HTML>
```

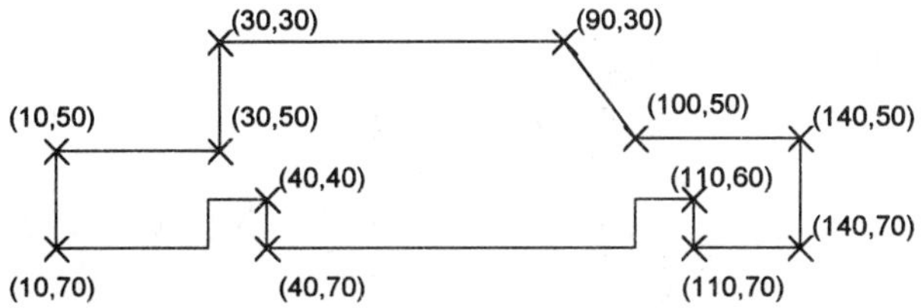

xpoints[]={10,30,30,90,100,140,140,110,110,90,
90,40,40,20,20,10,10},

ypoints[]={50,50,30,30,50,50,70,70,60,60,70,
70,60,60,70,70,50};

Figure 8.2 Co-ordinates of graphic

8.3 Moving objects with the arrowkeys

A graphic object can appear to move if it is drawn in a colour which is not the same as the background colour. The image can then be erased by re-drawing the image with the background colour. Next the image can be made to appear to move by changing the co-ordinates of the image and then re-drawing it with a colour which is not the same as the background colour. The movements can be controlled easily in Java with the arrowkeys.

The arrowkeys (UP, DOWN, LEFT and RIGHT) have defined values of 1004 (UP), 1005 (DOWN), 1006 (LEFT) and 1007 (RIGHT). These can be used to move graphics objects around the screen. The code is:

```
g.fillOval(x,y,10,10);
g.fillOval(x+30,y,10,10);
g.fillOval(x,y+30,40,20);
g.drawLine(x+5,y+10,x+5,y+35);
g.drawLine(x+35,y+10,x+35,y+35);
```

which draws an object at a position referenced to x and y. This can be made to move with the following:

```
public boolean keyDown(Event evt, int key)
{
        if (key==1006) { x-=5; repaint(); } // LEFT key
        else if (key==1007) { x+=5; repaint(); } // RIGHT key
        else if (key==1004) { y-=5; repaint(); } // UP key
        else if (key==1005) { y+=5; repaint(); } // DOWN key
        return true;
}
```

which when the RIGHT button is pressed it increments the x co-ordinate by 5, if the LEFT button is pressed then the x co-ordinate is decremented by 5. When the UP key is pressed the y co-ordinate is decremented by 5, if the DOWN key is pressed then the y co-ordinate is incremented by 5. Within each of these key presses, `paint()` is called.

Applet 8.4 shows a sample code which displays an object (`alien()`) which starts at the co-ordinates (100, 100) and is then moved with arrowkeys.

📖 Java applet 8.4 (⚡Java 1.0)

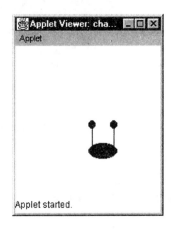

```java
import java.awt.*;
import java.applet.*;

public class chap8_04 extends Applet
{
int x=100,y=100;

 public void paint(Graphics g)
 {

    g.setColor(getBackground());
    alien(g);

    if ( x>100) x=200;
    if ( y>200) y=200;
    if ( x<0 )  x=0;
    if ( y<0 )  y=0;

    g.setColor(Color.black);
    alien(g);

 }

 public void alien(Graphics g)
 {
    g.fillOval(x,y,10,10);
    g.fillOval(x+30,y,10,10);
    g.fillOval(x,y+30,40,20);
    g.drawLine(x+5,y+10,x+5,y+35);
    g.drawLine(x+35,y+10,x+35,y+35);
 }

 public boolean keyDown(Event evt, int key)
 {
   if (key==1006) { x-=5; repaint(); }
   else if (key==1007) { x+=5; repaint(); }
   else if (key==1004) { y-=5; repaint(); }
   else if (key==1005) { y+=5; repaint(); }
   return true;
 }
}
```

📖 HTML script 8.4

```html
<HTML><TITLE>Applet</TITLE>
<APPLET CODE= chap8_04.class WIDTH=200
HEIGHT=200>
</APPLET></HTML>
```

8.3.1 Modified Java 1.1 program

📖 Java applet 8.5 (⚡Java 1.1)

```java
import java.awt.*;
import java.awt.event.*;
import java.applet.*;

public class chap8_05 extends Applet implements KeyListener
```

```
{
int x=100,y=100;
    public void init()
    {
    TextField text;
        text = new TextField(1);
        add(text);
        text.addKeyListener(this);
    }

    public void paint(Graphics g)
    {
        g.setColor(getBackground());
        alien(g);

        if ( x>100) x=200;
        if ( y>200) y=200;
        if ( x<0 )  x=0;
        if ( y<0 )  y=0;

     g.setColor(Color.black);
     alien(g);
    }

    public void alien(Graphics g)
    {
        g.fillOval(x,y,10,10);
        g.fillOval(x+30,y,10,10);
        g.fillOval(x,y+30,40,20);
        g.drawLine(x+5,y+10,x+5,y+35);
        g.drawLine(x+35,y+10,x+35,y+35);
    }

    public void keyPressed(KeyEvent evt)
    {
    int key;

        key=evt.getKeyCode();
        if (key==KeyEvent.VK_RIGHT) { x-=5; repaint(); }
        else if (key==KeyEvent.VK_LEFT) { x+=5; repaint(); }
        else if (key==KeyEvent.VK_DOWN) { y-=5; repaint(); }
        else if (key==KeyEvent.VK_UP) { y+=5; repaint(); }
    }

    public void keyReleased(KeyEvent evt) {  }
    public void keyTyped(KeyEvent evt) {  }
}
```

8.4 Sound

The playing of sound files is similar to displaying graphics files. Java applet
8.6 shows a sample applet which plays an audio file (in this case, test.au).
Unfortunately the current version of the Java compiler only supports the AU
format, thus WAV files need to be converted into AU format.

The initialisation process uses the getAudioClip() method and the audio
file is played with the loop() method. This method is contained in the
java.applet.AudioClip class, these methods are:

```
public abstract void play()      Plays the audio file and finishes at the end
public abstract void loop()      Starts playing the clip in a loop
public abstract void stop()      Stops playing the clip
```

📖 Java applet 8.6

```
import java.awt.*;
import java.applet.*;

public class chap8_06 extends Applet
{
AudioClip      audClip;
  public void paint(Graphics g)
  {
    audClip=getAudioClip(getCodeBase(),"hello.au");
    audClip.loop();
  }
}
```

📖 HTML script 8.5

```
<HTML><TITLE>Applet</TITLE>
<APPLET CODE=chap8_06.class WIDTH=200 HEIGHT=200>
</APPLET></HTML>
```

8.5   Exercises

8.5.1   Write separate Java applets, using simple rectangles and circles, to display the following graphics:

    (a)   a television (a sample graphic is shown in Figure 8.3)
    (b)   a face
    (c)   a house
    (d)   a robot

Figure 8.3

8.5.2   Modify the applets in Exercise 8.5.1 so that the user can move them around the screen with the arrowkeys.

8.5.3   Write an applet which displays two faces. One of the faces is moved with the arrowkeys, and the other is moved by the 'A' (LEFT), 'W' (UP), 'X' (DOWN) and 'D' (RIGHT).

8.5.4 Locate three GIF or JPEG files, then write a Java applet which allows the user to choose which one should be displayed. The function key F1 selects the first image, F2 the second, and F3 the third. The function key F4 should exit the applet.

8.5.5 Using an applet which displays the text TEST TEXT, determine the approximate colour of the following colour settings:

    (a)   `color(100, 50, 10)`
    (b)   `color(200,200,0)`
    (c)   `color(10,100,100)`
    (d)   `color(200,200,200)`
    (e)   `color(10,10,100)`

8.5.6 Write an applet using a polygon for the following shapes:

    (a)   a ship (a sample is shown in Figure 8.4)
    (b)   a tank
    (c)   a plane

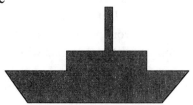

Figure 8.4

8.5.7 Locate a sound file and write an application which uses it.

8.6   Project

Write an applet which displays two faces. One of the faces is moved with the arrowkeys, and the other is moved by the 'A' (LEFT), 'W" (UP), 'X' (DOWN) and 'D' (RIGHT). The PgUp and PgDn keys should be used to double or halve the movement, respectively. See the project from the previous chapter for help.

9 Java Buttons and Menus

9.1 Introduction

One of the features of Java is that it supports many different types of menus items, these are:

- Buttons. Simple buttons which are pressed to select an item.
- Pop-up menus (or pull-down menus). Used to select from a number of items. The selected item is displayed in the pop-up menu window.
- List boxes.
- Dialog boxes. Used to either load or save files.
- Checkboxes. Used to select/deselect an item.
- Radio buttons. Used to select from one or several items.
- Menu bars. Used to display horizontal menus with pull-down menus.

These are used with event handlers to produce event-driven options.

9.2 Buttons and events

Java applet 9.1 creates three `Button` objects. These are created with the `add()` method which displays the button in the applet window.

📖 Java applet 9.1

```
import java.awt.*;
import java.applet.*;

public class chap9_01 extends Applet
{
  public void init()
  {
    add(new Button("Help"));
    add(new Button("Show"));
    add(new Button("Exit"));
  }
}
```

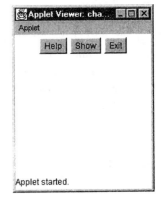

102

An alternative approach to creating buttons is to declare them using the `But-ton` type. For example the following applet is equivalent to Java applet 8.1. The names of the button objects, in this case, are `button1`, `button2` and `but-ton3`.

```
import java.applet.*;
import java.awt.*;

public class chap9_01 extends Applet
{
Button button1, button2, button3;

    public void init()
    {
        button1= new Button("Help");
        button2= new Button("Show");
        button3= new Button("Exit");
        add(button1);
        add(button2);
        add(button3);
    }
}
```

9.3   Action with Java 1.0

In Java 1.0, the `action` method is called when an event occurs, such as a key-press, button press, and so on. The information on the event is stored in the `Event` parameter. Its format is:

```
public boolean action(Event evt, Object obj)
```

where `evt` is made with the specified target component, time stamp, event type, x and y coordinates, keyboard key, state of the modifier keys and argu-ment. These are:

- `evt.target` is the target component
- `evt.when` is the time stamp
- `evt.id` is the event type
- `evt.x` is the x coordinate
- `evt.y` is the y coordinate
- `evt.key` is the key pressed in a keyboard event
- `evt.modifiers` is the state of the modifier keys
- `evt.arg` is the specified argument

Java applet 9.2 contains an example of the `action` method. It has two buttons (named `New1` and `New2`). When any of the buttons is pressed the `action` method is called. Figure 9.1 shows the display when either of the buttons are pressed. In the left hand side of Figure 9.1 the New1 button is pressed and the right-hand side shows the display after the New2 button is pressed. It can be seen that differences are in the target, arg parameter and the x, y co-ordinate parameters.

📖 Java applet 9.2 (⚡Java 1.0)

```
import java.applet.*;
import java.awt.*;

public class chap9_02 extends Applet
{
String Msg1=null, Msg2, Msg3, Msg4;
Button new1,new2;

    public void init()
    {
        new1=new Button("New 1");
        new2=new Button("New 2");
        add (new1); add(new2);
    }

    public boolean action(Event evt, Object obj)
    {
        Msg1= "Target= "+evt.target;
        Msg2= "When= " + evt.when + " id=" + evt.id +
            " x= "+ evt.x + " y= " + evt.y;
        Msg3= "Arg= " + evt.arg + " Key= " + evt.key;
        Msg4= "Click= " + evt.clickCount;
        repaint();
        return true;
    }

    public void paint(Graphics g)
    {
        if (Msg1!=null)
        {
            g.drawString(Msg1,30,80);
            g.drawString(Msg2,30,100);
            g.drawString(Msg3,30,120);
            g.drawString(Msg4,30,140);
        }
    }
}
```

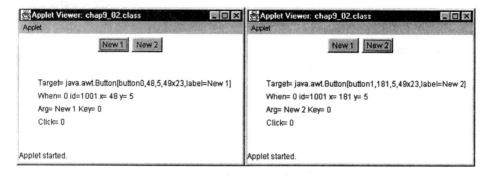

Figure 9.1 Sample runs

Thus to determine the button that has been pressed the evt.arg string can be tested. Java applet 9.3 shows an example where the evt.arg parameter is tested for its string content.

📖 Java applet 9.3 (⚡Java 1.0)

```java
import java.applet.*;
import java.awt.*;

public class chap9_03 extends Applet
{
String  Msg=null;
Button  new1, new2;
   public void init()
   {
      new1=new Button("New 1");    new2=new Button("New 2");
      add (new1); add(new2);
   }

   public boolean action(Event evt, Object obj)
   {
      if (evt.arg=="New 1") Msg= "New 1 pressed";
      else if (evt.arg=="New 2") Msg= "New 2 pressed";
      repaint();
      return true;
   }

   public void paint(Graphics g)
   {
      if (Msg!=null)
         g.drawString(Msg,30,80);
   }
}
```

Java applet 9.4 uses the action method which is called when an event occurs. Within this method the event variable is tested to see if one of the buttons caused the event. This is achieved with:

```java
if (event.target instanceof Button)
```

If this test is true then the Msg string takes on the value of the object, which holds the name of the button that caused the event.

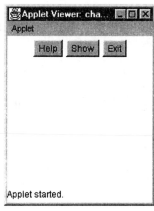

📖 Java applet 9.4 (⚡Java 1.0)

```java
import java.awt.*;
import java.applet.*;

public class chap9_04 extends Applet
{
String  Msg=null;

  public void init()
  {
   add(new Button("Help"));
   add(new Button("Show"));
   add(new Button("Exit"));
  }

  public boolean action(Event event,
```

```
  Object object)
{
 if (event.target instanceof Button)
 {
   Msg = (String) object;
   repaint();
 }
 return(true);
}

public void paint(Graphics g)
{
 if (Msg!=null)
 g.drawString("Button:" + Msg,30,80);
}
}
```

9.4   Action Listener in Java 1.1

As with mouse events, buttons, menus and textfields are associated with an action listener (named `ActionListener`). When an event associated with these occurs then the `actionPerformed` method is called. Its format is:

```
public void actionPerformed(ActionEvent evt)
```

where `evt` defines the event. The associated methods are:

- `getActionCommand()` is the action command
- `evt.getModifiers()` is the state of the modifier keys
- `evt.paramString()` is the parameter string

Java applet 9.5 contains an example of the `action` method. It has two buttons (named `New1` and `New2`). When any of the buttons is pressed the action method is called. Each of the buttons has an associated listener which is initiated with:

```
button1.addActionListener(this);
button2.addActionListener(this);
```

Figure 9.2 shows the display when either of the buttons are pressed. In the left-hand side of Figure 9.2 the `New1` button is pressed and the right-hand side shows the display after the `New2` button is pressed.

📖   Java applet 9.5 (⚡Java 1.1)
```
import java.applet.*;
import java.awt.*;
import java.awt.event.*;

public class chap9_05 extends Applet implements ActionListener
```

```
{
Button    button1, button2;
String    Msg1=null, Msg2, Msg3;

   public void init()
   {

      button1 = new Button("New 1");
      button2 = new Button("New 2");
      add(button1); add(button2);
      button1.addActionListener(this);
      button2.addActionListener(this);
   }

   public void actionPerformed(ActionEvent evt)
   {
      Msg1= "Command= "+evt.getActionCommand();
      Msg2= "Modifiers= " + evt.getModifiers();
      Msg3= "String= " + evt.paramString();
      repaint();
   }

   public void paint(Graphics g)
   {
      if (Msg1!=null)
      {
         g.drawString(Msg1,30,80);
         g.drawString(Msg2,30,100);
         g.drawString(Msg3,30,120);
      }
   }
}
```

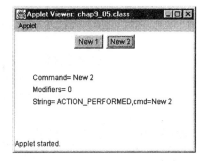

Figure 9.2 Sample run

Thus to determine the button that has been pressed the getActionCommand()
method is used. Java applet 9.6 shows an example where the getActionCom-
mand() method is tested for its string content. Figure 9.3 shows a sample run.

📖 Java applet 9.6 (⚡Java 1.1)

```
import java.applet.*;
import java.awt.*;
import java.awt.event.*;

public class chap9_06 extends Applet implements ActionListener
{

Button button1, button2;
```

```
String Msg=null;

    public void init()
    {

        button1 = new Button("New 1");
        button2 = new Button("New 2");
        add(button1); add(button2);
        button1.addActionListener(this);
        button2.addActionListener(this);
    }

    public void actionPerformed(ActionEvent evt)
    {
    String command;

        command=evt.getActionCommand();

        if (command.equals("New 1")) Msg="New 1 pressed";
        if (command.equals("New 2")) Msg="New 2 pressed";

        repaint();
    }

    public void paint(Graphics g)
    {
        if (Msg!=null)
        {
                g.drawString(Msg,30,80);
        }
    }
}
```

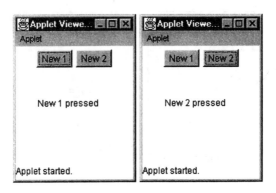

Figure 9.3 Sample run

9.5   Checkboxes

Typically checkboxes are used to select from a number of options. Java applet
9.7 shows how an applet can use checkboxes. As before, the `action` method is
called when a checkbox changes its state and within the method the
`event.target` parameter is tested for the checkbox with:

```
if (event.target instanceof Checkbox)
```

If this is true, then the method `DetermineCheckState()` is called which tests `event.target` for the checkbox value and its state (true or false).

📖 **Java applet 9.7 (⚡Java 1.0)**

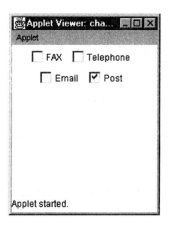

```
import java.awt.*;
import java.applet.*;
public class chap9_07 extends Applet
{
String  Msg=null;
Checkbox fax, telephone, email, post;

 public void init()
 {
  fax=new Checkbox("FAX");
  telephone=new Checkbox("Telephone");
  email=new Checkbox("Email");
  post=new Checkbox("Post",null,true);
  add(fax); add(telephone);
  add(email); add(post);
 }

 public void DetermineCheckState(
     Checkbox Cbox)
 {
  Msg=Cbox.getLabel()+" "+ Cbox.getState();
  repaint();
 }

 public boolean action(Event event,
     Object object)
 {
  if (event.target instanceof Checkbox)
    DetermineCheckState(
      (Checkbox)event.target);
  return(true);
 }
 public void paint(Graphics g)
 {
  if (Msg!=null)
   g.drawString("Check box:" + Msg,30,80);
 }
}
```

As with mouse events, checkboxes and lists are associated with an item listener (named `ItemListener`). When an event associated with these occur then the `itemStateChanged` method is called. Its format is:

```
public void itemStateChanged(ItemEvent event)
```

where `event` defines the event. The associated methods are:

- `getItem()` is the item selected
- `getStateChange()` is the state of the checkbox
- `paramString()` is the parameter string

Java applet 9.8 contains an example of checkboxes and Figure 9.4 shows a sample run. Each of the checkboxes has an associated listener which is initiated in the form:

> *chbox*.`addItemListener(this);`

📖 Java applet 9.8 (⚡Java 1.1)

```java
import java.awt.*;
import java.applet.*;
import java.awt.event.*;

public class chap9_08 extends Applet implements ItemListener
{
String      Msg1=null,Msg2,Msg3;
Checkbox    fax, telephone, email,post;

   public void init()
   {
     fax=new Checkbox("FAX");
     telephone=new Checkbox("Telephone");
     email=new Checkbox("Email");
     post=new Checkbox("Post",null,true);
     add(fax);
     add(telephone);
     add(email);
     add(post);

     fax.addItemListener(this);
     email.addItemListener(this);
     telephone.addItemListener(this);
     post.addItemListener(this);
   }

   public void itemStateChanged(ItemEvent event)
   {
     Msg1=""+event.getItem();
     Msg2=""+event.getStateChange();
     Msg3=event.paramString();
     repaint();
   }

   public void paint(Graphics g)
   {
     if (Msg1!=null)
     {
        g.drawString(Msg1,30,80);
        g.drawString(Msg2,30,110);
        g.drawString(Msg3,30,150);
     }
   }
}
```

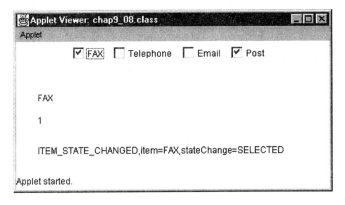

Figure 9.4 Sample run

The standard checkboxes allow any number of options to be selected. A radio button allows only one option to be selected at a time. The program is changed by:

- Adding checkbox names (such as fax, tele, email and post).
- Initialising the checkbox with CheckboxGroup() to a checkbox group identifier.
- Add the identifier of the checkbox group to the Checkbox() method.
- Testing the target property of the event to see if it equals a checkbox name.

Java applet 9.9 shows how this is achieved.

📖 Java applet 9.9 (⚡Java 1.0)

```
import java.awt.*;
import java.applet.*;

public class chap9_09 extends Applet
{
String     Msg=null;
Checkbox   fax, tele, email, post;

  public void init()
  {

  CheckboxGroup RadioGroup = new CheckboxGroup();

     add(fax=new Checkbox("FAX",RadioGroup,false));
     add(tele=new Checkbox("Telephone",RadioGroup,false));
     add (email=new Checkbox("Email",RadioGroup,false));
     add (post=new Checkbox("Post",RadioGroup,true));
```

```
    }

    public boolean action(Event event, Object object)
    {
        if (event.target.equals(fax)) Msg="FAX";
        else if (event.target.equals(tele)) Msg="Telephone";
        else if (event.target.equals(email)) Msg="Email";
        else if (event.target.equals(fax)) Msg="FAX";
        repaint();
        return(true);
    }

    public void paint(Graphics g)
    {

        if (Msg!=null) g.drawString("Check box:" + Msg,30,80);
    }
}
```

Java applet 9.10 show the Java 1.1 equivalent.

📖 Java applet 9.10 (⚡Java 1.1)

```
import java.awt.*;
import java.awt.event.*;
import java.applet.*;

public class chap9_10 extends Applet implements ItemListener
{
String  Msg=null;
Checkbox fax, tele, email, post;

 public void init()
   {

   CheckboxGroup RadioGroup = new CheckboxGroup();

       add(fax=new Checkbox("FAX",RadioGroup,true));
       add(tele=new Checkbox("Telephone",RadioGroup,false));
       add (email=new Checkbox("Email",RadioGroup,false));
       add (post=new Checkbox("Post",RadioGroup,false));
       fax.addItemListener(this);
       tele.addItemListener(this);
       email.addItemListener(this);
       post.addItemListener(this);
   }

   public void itemStateChanged(ItemEvent event)
   {
   Object obj;
       obj=event.getItem();

       if (obj.equals("FAX")) Msg="FAX";
       else if (obj.equals("Telephone")) Msg="Telephone";
       else if (obj.equals("Email")) Msg="Email";
       else if (obj.equals("Post")) Msg="Post";
       repaint();
   }

   public void paint(Graphics g)
   {
       if (Msg!=null)    g.drawString("Check box:" + Msg,30,80);
   }
}
```

This sets the checkbox type to `RadioGroup` and it can be seen that only one of the checkboxes is initially set (that is, 'FAX'). Figure 9.5 shows a sample run. It should be noted that grouped checkboxes use a round circle with a dot (⊙), whereas ungrouped checkboxes use a square box with a check mark (☑).

Figure 9.5 Sample run

9.8   Pop-up menu choices

To create a pop-up menu the `Choice` object is initially created with:

```
Choice mymenu = new Choice();
```

After this the menu options are defined using the `addItem` method. Java applet 9.11 shows an example usage of a pop-up menu.

📖 Java applet 9.11 (⚡Java 1.0)

```
import java.awt.*;
import java.applet.*;

public class chap9_11 extends Applet
{
String  Msg=null;
Choice  mymenu= new Choice();

  public void init()
  {
    mymenu.addItem("FAX");
    mymenu.addItem("Telephone");
    mymenu.addItem("Email");
    mymenu.addItem("Post");
    add(mymenu);
  }
  public void DetermineCheckState(
    Choice mymenu)
```

```
    {
      Msg=mymenu.getItem(
          mymenu.getSelectedIndex());
      repaint();
    }
    public boolean action(Event event,
        Object object)
    {
      if (event.target instanceof Choice)
      DetermineCheckState(
          (Choice)event.target);
      return(true);
    }

    public void paint(Graphics g)
    {
    if (Msg!=null)
      g.drawString("Menu select:"+Msg,30,120);
    }
  }
```

As before the arg property of the event can also be tested as shown in Java applet 9.12. Java applet 9.13 gives the Java 1.1 equivalent.

📖 Java applet 9.12 (⚡Java 1.0)

```
import java.awt.*;
import java.applet.*;

public class chap9_12 extends Applet
{
String  Msg=null;
Choice  mymenu= new Choice();

  public void init()
  {
    mymenu.addItem("FAX");
    mymenu.addItem("Telephone");
    mymenu.addItem("Email");
    mymenu.addItem("Post");
    add(mymenu);
  }
  public boolean action(Event event, Object object)
  {

    if (event.arg=="FAX") Msg="FAX";
    else if (event.arg=="Telephone") Msg="Telephone";
    else if (event.arg=="Email") Msg="Email";
    else if (event.arg == "Post") Msg="Post";
    repaint();
    return(true);
  }
  public void paint(Graphics g)
  {
    if (Msg!=null)
      g.drawString("Menu select:" + Msg,30,120);
  }
}
```

📖 Java applet 9.13 (⚡Java 1.1)

```
import java.awt.*;
```

```
import java.awt.event.*;
import java.applet.*;

public class chap9_13 extends Applet implements ItemListener
{
String  Msg=null;
Choice  mymenu= new Choice();

  public void init()
  {
    mymenu.addItem("FAX");
    mymenu.addItem("Telephone");
    mymenu.addItem("Email");
    mymenu.addItem("Post");
    add(mymenu);
    mymenu.addItemListener(this);
  }
  public void itemStateChanged(ItemEvent event)
  {
  Object obj;

    obj=event.getItem();

    if (obj.equals("FAX")) Msg="FAX";
    else if (obj.equals("Telephone")) Msg="Telephone";
    else if (obj.equals("Email")) Msg="Email";
    else if (obj.equals("Post")) Msg="Post";
    repaint();
  }
  public void paint(Graphics g)
  {
    if (Msg!=null)
      g.drawString("Menu select:" + Msg,30,120);
  }
}
```

9.9   Other pop-up menu options

The `java.awt.Choice` class allows for a pop-up menu. It includes the following methods:

`public void addItem(String item);`   Adds a menu item to the end.

`public void addNotify();`   Allows the modification of a list's appearance without changing its functionality.

`public int countItems();`   Returns the number of items in the menu.

`public String getItem(int index);`   Returns the string of the menu item at that index value.

`public int getSelectedIndex();`   Returns the index value of the selected item.

```
public String getSelectedItem();      Returns the string of the selected item.

protected String paramString();       Returns the parameter String of the list.

public void select(int pos);          Select the menu item at a given index.

public void select(String str);       Select the menu item with a given string
                                      name.
```

The `countItems` method is used to determine the number of items in a pop-up menu, for example:

```
Msg= "Number of items is " + mymenu.countItems()
```

The `getItem(int index)` returns the string associated with the menu item, where the first item has a value of zero. For example:

```
Msg= "Menu item number 2 is " + mymenu.getItem(2);
```

Java applet 9.14 uses the `select` method to display the second menu option as the default and the `getItem` method to display the name of the option.

📖 **Java applet 9.14 (⚡Java 1.1)**

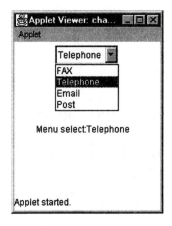

```
import java.awt.*;
import java.awt.event.*;
import java.applet.*;

public class chap9_14 extends Applet
     implements ItemListener
{
String  Msg=null;
Choice  mymenu= new Choice();

 public void init()
  {
    mymenu.addItem("FAX");
    mymenu.addItem("Telephone");
    mymenu.addItem("Email");
    mymenu.addItem("Post");
    add(mymenu);
    mymenu.addItemListener(this);
    mymenu.select(1);
        // Select item 1 (Telephone)
}

public void itemStateChanged(ItemEvent evt)
 {
Object obj;

 obj=evt.getItem();

 if (obj.equals("FAX"))
     Msg=mymenu.getItem(0);
 else if (obj.equals("Telephone"))
     Msg=mymenu.getItem(1);
```

```
    else if (obj.equals("Email"))
        Msg=mymenu.getItem(2);
    else if (obj.equals("Post"))
        Msg=mymenu.getItem(3);
    repaint();
}
public void paint(Graphics g)
{
  if (Msg!=null)
    g.drawString("Menu select:"+Msg,30,120);
  }
}
```

9.10 Multiple menus

Multiple menus can be created in a Java applet and the `action` event can be used to differentiate between the menus. Java applet 9.15 has two pull-down menus and two buttons (`age`, `gender`, `print` and `close`). The event method `getItem` is then used to determine which of the menus was selected. In this case the `print` button is used to display the options of the two pull-down menus and `close` is used to exit from the applet.

📖   Java applet 9.15 (⚡Java 1.1)

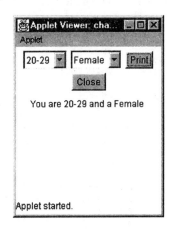

```
import java.applet.*;
import java.awt.*;
import java.awt.event.*;

public class chap9_15 extends Applet
    implements ItemListener, ActionListener
{
Choice age = new Choice();
Choice gender = new Choice();
Button print= new Button("Print");
Button close= new Button("Close");
String gendertype=null, agetype=null;

String Msg, Options[];

  public void init()
  {
      age.addItem("10-19");
      age.addItem("20-29");
      age.addItem("30-39");
      age.addItem("40-49");
      age.addItem("Other");
      add(age);

      gender.addItem("Male");
      gender.addItem("Female");
      add(gender);
      add(print);
      add(close);

      age.addItemListener(this);
      gender.addItemListener(this);
      print.addActionListener(this);
```

```
        close.addActionListener(this);
    }

    public void itemStateChanged(ItemEvent evt)
    {
      int i;
      Object obj;

        obj=evt.getItem();

      if (obj.equals("10-19")) agetype="10-19";
      else if (obj.equals("20-29"))
        agetype="20-29";
      else if (obj.equals("30-39"))
        agetype="30-39";
      else if (obj.equals("40-49"))
        agetype="40-49";
      else if (obj.equals("Other"))
        agetype="Other";
      else if (obj.equals("Male"))
        gendertype="Male";
      else if (obj.equals("Female"))
        gendertype="Female";
    }

    public void actionPerformed(ActionEvent evt)
    {
    String str;

      str=evt.getActionCommand();
      if (str.equals("Print"))  repaint();
      else if (str.equals("Close"))
        System.exit(0);
    }

    public void paint(Graphics g)
    {
      if ((agetype!=null) && (gendertype!=null))
       Msg="Your are " + agetype + " and a "
                     + gendertype;
      else Msg="Please select age and gender";

      if (Msg!=null) g.drawString(Msg,20,80);
    }
   }
```

9.11 Menu bar

Menu bars are now familiar in most GUIs (such as Microsoft Windows and Motif). They consist of a horizontal menu bar with pull-down submenus.

The java.awt.MenuBar class contains a constructor for a menu bar. Its format is:

```
    public MenuBar();
```

and the methods which can be applied to it are:

`public Menu add(Menu m);`	Adds the specified menu to the menu bar.
`public void addNotify();`	Allows a change of appearance of the menu bar without changing any of the menu bar's functionality.
`public int countMenus();`	Counts the number of menus on the menu bar.
`public Menu getHelpMenu();`	Gets the help menu on the menu bar.
`public Menu getMenu(int i);`	Gets the specified menu.
`public void remove(int index);`	Removes the menu located at the specified index from the menu bar.
`public void remove(` `     MenuComponent m);`	Removes the specified menu from the menu bar.
`public void removeNotify();`	Removes notify.
`public void setHelpMenu(` `   Menu m);`	Sets the help menu to the specified menu on the menu bar.

Java program 9.16 gives an example of using a menu bar. Initially the menu bar is created with the `MenuBar()` constructor, and submenus with the `Menu` constructors (in this case, `mfile`, `medit` and `mhelp`). Items are added to the submenus with the `MenuItem` constructor (such as `New`, `Open`, and so on). A `handleEvent()` method has been added to catch a close window operation. The `addSeparator()` method has been added to add a line between menu items. Note that this program is not an applet so that it can be run directly with the Java interpreter (such as `java.exe`).

📖 Java standalone program 9.16 (⚡Java 1.0)

```
import java.awt.*;

public class gomenu extends Frame
{
MenuBar mainmenu = new MenuBar();
Menu mfile = new Menu("File");
Menu medit = new Menu("Edit");
Menu mhelp = new Menu("Help");

    public gomenu()
    {
        mfile.add(new MenuItem("New"));
        mfile.add(new MenuItem("Open"));
        mfile.add(new MenuItem("Save"));
        mfile.add(new MenuItem("Save As"));
```

```
        mfile.add(new MenuItem("Close"));
        mfile.addSeparator();
        mfile.add(new MenuItem("Print"));
        mfile.addSeparator();
        mfile.add(new MenuItem("Exit"));

        mainmenu.add(mfile);

        medit.add(new MenuItem("Cut"));
        medit.add(new MenuItem("Copy"));
        medit.add(new MenuItem("Paste"));
        mainmenu.add(medit);

        mhelp.add(new MenuItem("Commands"));
        mhelp.add(new MenuItem("About"));
        mainmenu.add(mhelp);

        setMenuBar(mainmenu);
    }

    public boolean action(Event evt, Object obj)
    {
        if (evt.target instanceof MenuItem)
        {
            if (evt.arg=="Exit") System.exit(0);
        }
        return true;
    }

    public boolean handleEvent(Event evt)
    {
        if (evt.id == Event.WINDOW_DESTROY)
                System.exit(0);
        return true;
    }

    public static void main(String args[])
    {
        Frame f = new gomenu();
        f.resize(400,400);
        f.show();
    }
}
```

9.12 List box

A List component creates a scrolling list of options (where in a pull-down menu only one option can be viewed at a time). The java.awt.List class contains the List constructor which can be used to display a list component., which is in the form:

```
public List();
public List(int rows, boolean multipleSelections);
```

where row defines the number of rows in a list and multipleSelections is true when the user can select a number of selections, else it is false.

The methods that can be applied are:

`public void addItem(String item);`	Adds a menu item at the end.
`public void addItem(String item,` `   int index);`	Add a menu item at the end.
`public void addNotify();`	Allows the modification of a list's appearance without changing its functionality.
`public boolean` `   allowsMultipleSelections();`	Allows the selection of multiple selections.
`public void clear();`	Clears the list.
`public int countItems();`	Returns the number of items in the list.
`public void delItem(int position);`	Deletes an item from the list.
`public void delItems(int start,` `   int end);`	Deletes items from the list.
`Public void deselect(int index);`	Deselects the item at the specified index.
`Public String getItem(int index);`	Gets the item associated with the specified index.
`public int getRows();`	Returns the number of visible lines in this list.
`public int getSelectedIndex();`	Gets the selected item on the list.
`public int[] getSelectedIndexes();`	Gets selected items on the list.
`public String getSelectedItem();`	Returns the selected item on the list as a string.
`public String[] getSelectedItems();`	Returns the selected items on the list as an array of strings.
`public int getVisibleIndex();`	Gets the index of the item that was last made visible by the method `makeVisible`.
`public boolean isSelected(` `   int index);`	Returns true if the item at the specified index has been selected.
`public void makeVisible(int index);`	Makes a menu item visible.

`public Dimension minimumSize();`	Returns the minimum dimensions needed for the list.
`public Dimension minimumSize(int rows);`	Returns the minimum dimensions needed for the amount of rows in the list.
`protected String paramString();`	Returns the parameter String of the list.
`public Dimension preferredSize();`	Returns the preferred size of the list.
`public Dimension preferredSize(int rows);`	Returns the preferred size of the list.
`public void removeNotify();`	Removes notify.
`public void replaceItem( String newValue, int index);`	Replaces the item at the given index.
`Public void select(int index);`	Selects the item at the specified index.
`public void setMultipleSelections(boolean v);`	Allows multiple selections.

Java program 9.17 shows an example of a program with a list component. Intially the list is created with the `List` constructor. The `addItem` method is then used to add the four items ("Pop", "Rock", "Classical" and "Jazz"). Within `actionPerformed` the program uses the `Options` array of strings to build up a message string (`Msg`). The `Options.length` parameter is used to determine the number of items in the array.

📖 Java program 9.17 (⚡Java 1.1)

```
import java.awt.*;
import java.awt.event.*;
import java.applet.*;

public class chap9_17 extends Applet
                    implements ActionListener
{
List lmenu = new List(4,true);
String Msg, Options[];

    public void init()
    {
        lmenu.addItem("Pop");
        lmenu.addItem("Rock");
        lmenu.addItem("Classical");
        lmenu.addItem("Jazz");
        add(lmenu);
        lmenu.addActionListener(this);
```

```
        }
    public void actionPerformed(
                            ActionEvent evt)
    {
        int i;
        String str;

        str=evt.getActionCommand();
        Options=lmenu.getSelectedItems();
        Msg="";
        for (i=0;i<Options.length;i++)
                Msg=Msg+Options[i] + " ";
        repaint();
    }

    public void paint(Graphics g)
    {

        if (Msg!=null) g.drawString(Msg,20,80);
    }
}
```

<h2>9.13 File dialog</h2>

The `java.awt.Filedialog` class contains the `FileDialog` constructor which can be used to display a dialog window. To create a dialog window the following can be used:

```
public FileDialog(Frame parent, String title);
public FileDialog(Frame parent, String title, int mode);
```

where the `parent` is the owner of the dialog, `title` is the title of the dialog window and the `mode` is defined as whether the file is to be loaded or save. Two fields are defined for the mode, these are:

```
public final static int LOAD;
public final static int SAVE;
```

The methods that can be applied are:

`public void addNotify();`	Allows applications to change the look of a file dialog window without changing its functionality.
`public String getDirectory();`	Gets the initial directory.
`public String getFile();`	Gets the file that the user specified.
`public FilenameFilter getFilenameFilter();`	Sets the default file filter.

```
public int getMode();
```
Indicates whether the file dialog box is for file loading from or file saving.

```
protected String paramString();
```
Returns the parameter string representing the state of the file dialog window.

```
public void
   setDirectory(String dir);
```
Gets the initial directory.

```
public void
   setFile(String file);
```
Sets the selected file for this file dialog window to be the specified file.

```
public void
   setFilenameFilter(
   FilenameFilter filter);
```
Sets the filename filter for the file dialog window to the specified filter.

9.14 Exercises

9.14.1   Modify Applet 9.14 so that the following are added:

  (i)   a `countItems()` method which displays the number of items in the menu.
  (ii)   a `getSelectIndex()` method which displays the item value of the item selected.
  (iii) the `select()` method so that that email item is shown as the default. Note that it can be selected either with a string or the position.

9.14.2   Implement the two Java applets in Figure 9.6. The `Show` button should display all the selected options.

9.14.3   Add a `Reset` button to the applets developed in Exercise 9.14.2. This button should set the selected items back to their initial values.

9.14.4   Implement a Java applet which displays the button on a basic calculator. An example is shown in Figure 9.7.

9.14.5   Implement a Java applet, with checkboxes, which prompts a user for their personal information such as height, weight, and so on.

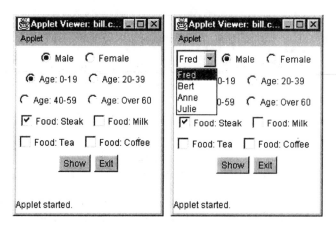

Figure 9.6 Sample runs

Figure 9.7 Sample runs

10.1.1 Single-line text input

Single-line text can be entered into a Java applet using the `TextField` action, which is contained in the `java.awt.TextField` class. Its format can be one of the following:

```
public TextField();
public TextField(int cols);
public TextField(String text);
public TextField(String text, int cols);
```

with the following methods:

```
public void addActionListener(ActionListener l)   // Java 1.1
public void addNotify();
public boolean echoCharIsSet();
public int getColumns();
public char getEchoChar();
public char getMinimumSize(int cols);             // Java 1.1
public char getMinimumSize ();                    // Java 1.1
public char getPreferredSize(int cols);           // Java 1.1
public char getPreferredSize();                   // Java 1.1
public Dimension minimumSize();                   // Java 1.0
public Dimension minimumSize(int cols);           // Java 1.0
protected String paramString();
public Dimension preferredSize();                 // Java 1.0
public Dimension preferredSize(int cols);         // Java 1.0
public void setEchoCharacter(char c);             // Java 1.0
public void setEchoChar(char c);                  // Java 1.1
```

Where the methods with the Java 1.0 comment are deprecated. The `java.awt.TextComponent` class contains a number of methods that can be used to get the entered text. The following methods can be applied:

```
public void addTextListener(Listener l);          // Java 1.1
public int getCaretPosition();                    // Java 1.1
public String getSelectedText();
public int getSelectionEnd();
public int getSelectionStart();
```

```
public String getText();
public boolean isEditable();
protected String paramString();
public void removeNotify();
public void removeTextListener();
public void select(int selStart, int selEnd);
public void selectAll();
public int setCaretPosition();                    // Java 1.1
public void setEditable(boolean t);
public void setSelectionEnd(int selEnd);          // Java 1.1
public void setSelectionStart(int selStart);      // Java 1.1
public void setText(String t);
```

In Java applet 10.1 the TextField(20) defines a 20-character input field. The getText() method is used within action() to get the entered text string. Java applet 10.2 shows the Java 1.1 equivalent.

📖 Java applet 10.1 (⚡Java 1.0)

```
import java.awt.*;
import java.applet.*;

public class chap10_01 extends Applet
{
String     Msg=null;
TextField  tfield = new TextField(20);

 public void init()
 {
   add(new Label("Enter your name"));
   add(tfield);
 }

 public boolean action(Event event,
    Object object)
 {
   if (event.target.equals(tfield))
       Msg=tfield.getText();
   repaint();
   return(true);
 }

  public void paint(Graphics g)
  {
    if (Msg!=null)
     g.drawString("Your name is:"+
                        Msg,30,120);
  }
}
```

📖 Java applet 10.2 (⚡Java 1.1)

```
import java.awt.*;
import java.applet.*;
import java.awt.event.*;

public class chap10_02 extends Applet implements ActionListener
{
String     Msg=null;
TextField  tfield = new TextField(20);
```

```
    public void init()
    {
        add(new Label("Enter your name"));
        add(tfield);
        tfield.addActionListener(this);
    }
    public void actionPerformed(ActionEvent event)
    {
        Msg=tfield.getText();
        repaint();
    }
    public void paint(Graphics g)
    {
        if (Msg!=null)
        g.drawString("Your name is:" + Msg,30,120);
    }
}
```

10.1.2 Setting text

In Java applet 10.3 the `TextField(20)` defines a 20-character input field. The `getText()` method is used within `actionPerformed()` to get the entered text string and the `setText()` method to put the text to a text field (`tfield2`).

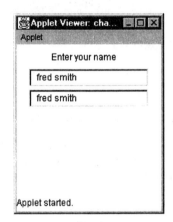

📖 Java applet 10.3 (⚡Java 1.1)

```
import java.awt.*;
import java.awt.event.*;
import java.applet.*;

public class chap10_03 extends Applet
        implements ActionListener
{
String    Msg=null;
TextField tfield1 = new TextField(20);
TextField tfield2 = new TextField(20);
 public void init()
   {
     add(new Label("Enter your name"));
     add(tfield1);
     add(tfield2);
     tfield1.addActionListener(this);
     tfield2.addActionListener(this);
   }

 public void actionPerformed(
                     ActionEvent event)
   {
     Msg=tfield1.getText();
     tfield2.setText(Msg);
   }
 }
```

10.1.3 Password entry

Many programs require the user to enter a password before they can execute a certain part of the program. Normally this password should be displayed in a manner in which no other user can view. Thus Java has the `setEchoChar()` method (in Java 1.0 this is `setEchoCharacter()`) to define which character is displayed in the given text field. Java applet 10.4 is an example applet where the user enters their name and it is displayed with the '*' character. When the user presses the Enter key the entered name is displayed in the second text field.

📖 Java applet 10.4 (⚡Java 1.1)

```
import java.awt.*;
import java.awt.event.*;
import java.applet.*;

public class chap10_04 extends Applet
                implements ActionListener
{
String     Msg=null;
TextField  tfield1 = new TextField(20);
TextField  tfield2 = new TextField(20);

  public void init()
  {
    add(new Label("Enter your name"));
    add(tfield1);
    tfield1.setEchoChar('*');
     // this is setEchoCharacter() in Java 1.0
    add(tfield2);
    tfield1.addActionListener(this);
    tfield2.addActionListener(this);
  }

public void actionPerformed(ActionEvent event
{
    Msg=tfield1.getText();
    tfield2.setText(Msg);
}
}
```

10.1.4 Multiple-line text input

Multiple-line text can be entered into a Java applet using the `TextArea` action, which is contained in the `java.awt.TextArea` class. Its format can be one of the following:

```
public TextArea();
public TextArea(int rows, int cols);
public TextArea(String text);
public TextArea(String text, int rows, int cols)·
```

with the following methods:

```
public void addNotify();
public void append(String str);                    // Java 1.1
public void appendText(String str);                // Java 1.0
public int getColumns();
public char getMinimumSize(int cols);              // Java 1.1
public char getMinimumSize ();                     // Java 1.1
public char getPreferredSize(int cols);            // Java 1.1
public char getPreferredSize();                    // Java 1.1
public int getRows();
public void insertText(String str, int pos);
public Dimension minimumSize();                    // Java 1.0
public Dimension minimumSize(int rows, int cols);  // Java 1.0
```

```
protected String paramString();                      // Java 1.0
public Dimension preferredSize();                    // Java 1.0
public Dimension preferredSize(int rows, int cols);  // Java 1.0
public void replaceText(String str, int start, int end);
                                                     // Java 1.0
public int setColumns(int cols);                     // Java 1.1
public int setRows(int rows);                        // Java 1.1
```

10.2 Fonts

Java is well supported with different fonts. The class library `java.awt.Font` defines the Font class and the general format for defining the font is:

Font *font* = new **Font** (*font_type*, *font_attrib*, *font_size*)

and the methods are:

```
public Font decode(String str);
public boolean equals(Object obj);
public String getFamily();
public static Font getFont(String nm);
public static Font getFont(String nm, Font font);
public String getName();
public FontPeer getPeer();                           // Java 1.1
public int getSize();
public int getStyle();
public int hashCode();
public boolean isBold();
public boolean isItalic();
public boolean isPlain();
public String toString();
```

The font class has various fields, these are:

```
protected String name;
protected int size;
protected int style;
```

and the defined bit masks are:

```
public final static int BOLD;
public final static int ITALIC;
public final static int PLAIN;
```

The `java.awt.Graphics` class also contains a number of methods related to fonts, these include:

```
public abstract Font getFont();
public FontMetrics getFontMetrics();
```

```
public abstract FontMetrics getFontMetrics(Font f);
public abstract void setColor(Color c);
public abstract void setFont(Font font);
```

In Java 1.0, the main font types are:

```
"TimesRoman"    "Helvetica"    "Courier"    "Symbol"
```

In Java 1.1 the font names "Serif", "SanSerif" and "Monospaced" should be used instead of the ones given above. This book is written in Times Roman. Helvetica looks good as a header, such as **Header 1**. Courier produces a mono-space font where all of the characters have the same width. The Java applets in this chapter use the Courier font. Symbol is normally used when special symbols are required. The *font_attrib* can either be BOLD (Value of 1), ITALIC (Value of 2) or NORMAL (Value of 0) and the font_size is an integer value which is supported by the compiler. The font size of this text is 11 and most normal text varies between 8 and 12.

Java applet 10.5 shows an example applet using different fonts.

📖 Java applet 10.5

```
import java.awt.*;
import java.applet.*;

public class chap10_05 extends Applet
{
Font   TimesRoman= new
            Font("TimesRoman",Font.BOLD,24);
Font   Courier= new Font("Courier",Font.BOLD,24)
Font   Helvetica= new
            Font("Helvetica",Font.BOLD,24);
Font   Symbol= new Font("Symbol",Font.BOLD,24);

  public void paint(Graphics g)
  {
    g.setFont(TimesRoman);
    g.drawString("Sample text",10,40);
    g.setFont(Courier);
    g.drawString("Sample text",10,60);
    g.setFont(Helvetica);
    g.drawString("Sample text",10,80);
    g.setFont(Symbol);
    g.drawString("Sample text",10,100);
  }
}
```

Java applet 10.6 shows an example applet using a pull-down menu to select from a number of different fonts.

Java applet 10.6 (⚡Java 1.1)

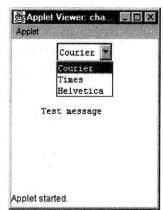

```
import java.applet.*;
import java.awt.event.*;
import java.awt.*;
public class chap10_06 extends Applet
                        implements ItemListener
{
Choice font= new Choice();

 public void init()
 {
   font.addItem("Courier");
   font.addItem("Times");
   font.addItem("Helvetica");
   add(font);
   font.addItemListener(this);
 }
 public void itemStateChanged(ItemEvent evt)
 {
Object obj;

 obj=evt.getItem();
 if (obj.equals("Courier"))
  setFont(new Font("Courier",Font.PLAIN,12));
 else if (obj.equals("Times"))
  setFont(new Font("Times",Font.PLAIN,12));
 else if (obj.equals("Helvetica"))
  setFont(new Font("Helvetica",Font.PLAIN,12))
 repaint();
 }
 public void paint(Graphics g)
 {
   g.drawString("Test message",40,100);
 }
}
```

10.3 Date

Java has a wide range of date constructors and methods. They are defined in
the `java.util.Date` class. The constructors for a date are:

```
public Date();
public Date(int year, int month, int date);          //Java 1.0
public Date(int year, int month, int date, int hrs, int min);
                                                     //Java 1.0
public Date(int year, int month, int date, int hrs, int min,
            int sec);                                //Java 1.0
public Date(long date);
public Date(String s);                               // Java 1.0
```

and the methods are as follows:

```
public boolean after(Date  when);
public boolean before(Date  when);
public boolean equals(Object  obj);
```

```
public int getDate();                              // Java 1.0
public int getDay();                               // Java 1.0
public int getHours();                             // Java 1.0
public int getMinutes();                           // Java 1.0
public int getMonth();                             // Java 1.0
public int getSeconds();                           // Java 1.0
public long getTime();
public int getTimezoneOffset();                    // Java 1.0
public int getYear();                              // Java 1.0
public int hashCode();
public static long parse(String  s);
public void setDate(int  date);                    // Java 1.0
public void setHours(int  hours);                  // Java 1.0
public void setMinutes(int  minutes);              // Java 1.0
public void setMonth(int  month);                  // Java 1.0
public void setSeconds(int  seconds);              // Java 1.0
public void setTime(long  time);
public void setYear(int  year);                    // Java 1.0
public String toGMTString();                       // Java 1.0
public String toLocaleString();                    // Java 1.0
public String toString();
public static long UTC(int  year, int  month, int  date, int  hrs,
                       int  min, int  sec);
```

In Java 1.1, many of the date methods have been deprecated. The Calendar class has thus been favoured. Java applet 10.7 shows an applet which displays the date in two different formats. The first ("Date 1") displays it using the toString() method and the second ("Date 2") displays it by building up a string using the getMinutes(), getHours(), getDay(), getMonth() and getYear() methods.

📖 Java applet 10.7 (⚡Java 1.0)

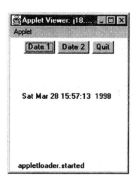

```
import java.applet.*;
import java.awt.*;
import java.util.Date;

public class chap10_07 extends Applet
{
String Msg;
Button dbutton1 = new Button("Date 1");
Button dbutton2 = new Button("Date 2");
Button quit = new Button("Quit");
Date newDate= new Date();

    public void init()
    {
        add(dbutton1);
        add(dbutton2);
        add(quit);
    }

    public boolean action(Event evt, Object obj)
    {
        if (evt.arg=="Date 1")
                Msg=newDate.toString();
        else if (evt.arg=="Date 2")
                Msg=newDate.getHours() + ":" +
                    newDate.getMinutes() + " " +
```

```
                    newDate.getDay() + "/" +
                    newDate.getMonth() + "/" +
                    newDate.getYear();
      else if (evt.arg=="Quit") System.exit(0);
      repaint();
      return true;
    }
    public void paint(Graphics g)
    {
        if (Msg!=null)
                g.drawString(Msg,20,100);
    }
}
```

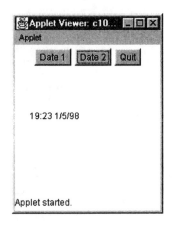

The date format is specified with the following:

- Year. The year value of the date is the year minus 1990. Thus the year 1998 is specified with the year value of 98, and the year 2000 by 100.
- Day. The day value of the date is the day number, from 1 to 31.
- Month. The month value of the date is the month number minus 1. Thus January is represented by 0, February by 1, and so on.
- Hour. The hour value of the date is the hour number, from 0 to 23.
- Minute. The minute value of the date is the minute number, from 0 to 59.
- Second. The second value of the date is the second number, from 0 to 59.

Java applet 10.8 shows an applet which displays the day of the week for a certain entered date (note that the day array is incomplete as it only ranges from day 1 to day 12). Three arrays of strings are setup for the day ("1", "2", and so on), month ("Jan", "Feb", and so on) and year (such as "1998", "1999" and "2000"). These arrays are named Days[], Months[] and Years[], and are used to set the text on the pull-down menu.

It can be seen from the sample run that the 3 May 1998 is on a Sunday.

📖 Java applet 10.8 (⚡Java 1.0)

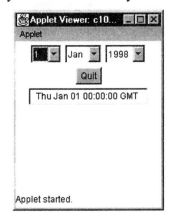

```
import java.applet.*;
import java.awt.*;
import java.util.Date;

public class cap10_08 extends Applet
{
String Msg;
Choice day = new Choice();
Choice year = new Choice();
Choice month = new Choice();
Button quit = new Button("Quit");
Date   newDate= new Date(98,0,1);
                // 1 Jan 1998
String Days[]={"1", "2", "3", "4","5","6",
       "7","8","9","10","11","12"}; // TBC
```

```
String Month[]={"Jan","Feb","Mar","Apr","May",
    "Jun","Jul","Aug","Sep","Oct","Nov","Dec"};
String Years[]={"1998", "1999", "2000"};
int i,inday=1,inmonth=0,inyear=98;
TextField tfield = new TextField(20);

  public void init()
  {
    for (i=0;i<12;i++) day.addItem(Days[i]);
    add(day);

    for (i=0;i<12;i++) month.addItem(Month[i]);
    add(month);

    for (i=0;i<3;i++) year.addItem(Years[i]);
    add(year);

    add(quit);
    add(tfield);

    Msg=newDate.toString();
    tfield.setText(Msg);
  }

  public boolean action(Event evt, Object obj)
  {
    if (evt.target.equals(day))
      inday=day.getSelectedIndex()+1;
    if (evt.target.equals(month))
      inmonth=month.getSelectedIndex();
    if (evt.target.equals(year))
      inyear=year.getSelectedIndex()+98;
    if (evt.target.equals(quit))
      System.exit(0);
    newDate= new Date(inyear,inmonth,inday);
    Msg=newDate.toString();
    tfield.setText(Msg);
    return true;
  }
}
```

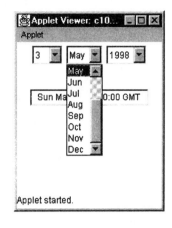

10.3.1 Java time

Java keeps time by incrementing a long value every 1ms. Java applet 10.9 shows an applet which determines the amount of time that a program has been running. It uses the `getTime()` method to initially get a value for the current time and puts it into `oldtime`. Then when the user presses the "Show Time" button the number of seconds is calculated by subtracting the new time (`newtime`) from `oldtime`, and dividing by 1000 (so that it can be displayed in seconds).

📖   Java applet 10.9 (⚡Java 1.0)

```
import java.applet.*;
import java.awt.*;
import java.util.Date;

public class chap10_09 extends Applet
{
String Msg;
Button dbutton1 = new Button("Show Time");
```

```
Button quit = new Button("Quit");
long   newtime,oldtime;
TextField tfield = new TextField(20);

  public void init()
  {
      add(dbutton1);
      add(quit);
      add(tfield);
      Date newDate= new Date();
      oldtime=newDate.getTime();
      tfield.setText("Press Show Time");
  }

  public boolean action(Event evt, Object obj)
  {

      if (evt.arg=="Show Time")
      {
        Date newDate= new Date();
        newtime=newDate.getTime();
        Msg=" " + (newtime-oldtime)/1000 +
                " seconds";
      }
      else if (evt.arg=="Quit") System.exit(0);
      tfield.setText(Msg);
      return true;

  }
}
```

10.3.2 UTC format

UTC (Co-ordinated Universal Time) is a machine-independent method of representing time. It assumes that there are 86 400 seconds each day ($24 \times 60 \times 60$) and once every year or two an extra second is added (a "leap" second). This is normally added on 31 December or 30 June.

Most computer systems define time with GMT (Greenwich Mean Time) which is UT (Universal Time). UTC is based on an atomic clock whereas GMT is based on astronomical observations. Unfortunately, because the earth rotation is not uniform, it is not as accurate as UTC.

10.4 Exercises

10.4.1   Write a Java applet which displays the following:

Sample Applet

Please press the x key to exit

Note that Sample Applet is bold Arial text with a size of 20 and the other text is Courier of size of 14.

10.4.2 Write a Java applet in which the user enters some text. If the user enters EXIT then the program will exit.

10.4.3 Modify Java applet 10.1 so that the default name of Fred Smith is set in the text field. The user can either accept this or re-type a new name. The entered name should be displayed in another text field.

10.4.4 Modify Java applet 10.2/3 so that the user enters a password. If entered password is "Anonymous" then the text "Success" should be displayed in a text field, else the program should display "Failure". If the user fails three times then the program should exit.

10.4.5 Modify Java applet 10.6 so that the user can change the size of the font which is displayed. Java applet 10.10 shows an outline. Remember the font should not change when the size is changed, and vice versa. A possible method is to store the font type and size as a variable. Also convert it to Java 1.1.

Java applet 10.10 (⚡Java 1.0)

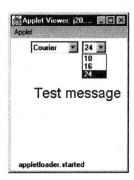

```java
import java.applet.*;
import java.awt.*;

public class chap10_10 extends Applet
{
Choice font= new Choice();
Choice size= new Choice();

    public void init()
    {
        font.addItem("Courier");
        font.addItem("Times");
        font.addItem("Helvetica");
        add(font);

        size.addItem("10");
        size.addItem("16");
        size.addItem("24");
        add(size);
    }

    public boolean action(Event evt, Object obj)
    {
        if (evt.target.equals(font))
        {
            // TBC
        }
        if (evt.target.equals(size))
        {
```

```
        // TBC
    }

    return true;
    }

  public void paint(Graphics g)
  {
      g.drawString("Test message",40,100);
  }
}
```

10.4.6 Modify the Java applet in Exercise 10.4.5 so that the user selects whether the font style is PLAIN, BOLD or ITALIC.

10.4.7 Modify the Java applet in Exercise 10.4.6 so that the user can enter some text in a text field and the program displays it with the selected font, size and style.

10.4.8 Modify the Java applet in Exercise 10.4.6 so that the font size and style are selected with a checkbox rather than a pull-down menu.

10.4.9 Write a Java applet which shows the current GMT time and date, and local time and date. The program should determine the difference in hours between the two.

10.4.10 Complete Java applet 10.8 so that it contains a complete range of days of the month (assume each month has 31 days in it). Also add the years up to 2010.

10.4.11 Write a Java applet in which the user enters two dates and the Java program determines which one occurs first (note, use the `after()` or `before()` methods).

10.4.12 Write a Java applet which stores the current date and then allows the user to change the current date. When the program is complete the applet should be able to set the date and time back to the original date and time.

10.4.13 Modify Java applet 10.9 so that it displays the run time with two decimal places. Also make the program quit when the user presses any button after 60 seconds.

10.4.14 Using the `getTime()` method, determine the date at which Java time is referenced to. Refer to Java applet 10.9 and display the value of `oldtime`.

10.5 Project 1

Java applet 10.11 implements a basic calculator in which the user enters values in two text fields and the result appears in another text field. The applet has four basic arithmetic operators, these are: add, subtract, multiply and divide. Figure 10.1 shows two sample runs with a '+' and a '/' operation. Modify the applet with the following:

(i)   Display a divide-by-zero message when the user enters a value of zero in the second value box with a divide operation.
(ii) Add an x to the power of y button (x^y).
(iii) Add a button that takes displays the exponential value of the first text field (e^y).

📖 Java applet 10.11 (⚡Java 1.1)

```
import java.applet.*;
import java.awt.event.*;
import java.awt.*;

public class chap10_11 extends Applet implements ActionListener
{
Button addop,subop,multiop,divop, quit;
TextField text1,text2,result;

   public void init()
   {
      text1=new TextField(20);
      text2=new TextField(20);
      result=new TextField(20);

      addop=new Button("+");
      subop=new Button("-");
      multiop=new Button("*");
      divop=new Button("/");
      quit=new Button("Quit");

      add(text1); add(text2);
      add(result);add(quit);
      add(addop); add(subop);
      add(multiop); add(divop);

      addop.addActionListener(this);
      subop.addActionListener(this);
      multiop.addActionListener(this);
      divop.addActionListener(this);
   }

   public void actionPerformed(ActionEvent evt)
   {
   String str,str1;
```

```
double val1,val2,res=0;

    str=evt.getActionCommand();
    str1=text1.getText();
    val1=Double.valueOf(str1).doubleValue();
    str1=text2.getText();
    val2=Double.valueOf(str1).doubleValue();

    if (str.equals("+")) res=val1+val2;
    else if (str.equals("-")) res=val1-val2;
    else if (str.equals("/")) res=val1/val2;
    else if (str.equals("*")) res=val1*val2;
    else if (str.equals("Quit")) System.exit(0);

    str=Double.toString(res);
    result.setText(str);
  }
}
```

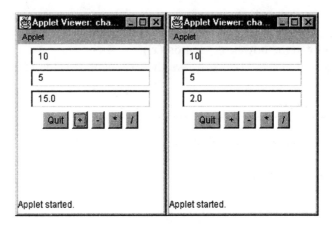

Figure 10.1 Sample run

Project 1 operates on double values. Develop an applet in which the user enters two integer values. The operators will then be integer operators, such as:

- AND (&).
- OR (|).
- XOR (~).
- SHIFT LEFT (>>).
- SHIFT RIGHT (<<).
- MODULUS (%).

Figure 10.2 show two sample runs for:

- 10 AND 12 (1010 AND 1100 = 1000) which gives the result of 8.
- 10 XOR 12 (1010 XOR 1100 = 0110) which gives the result of 6.

An outline of the code is given in applet 10.12.

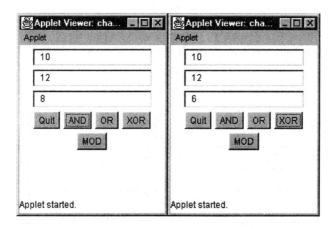

Figure 10.2 Sample run for AND and XOR operations

📖 Java applet 10.12 (⚡Java 1.1)

```
import java.applet.*;
import java.awt.event.*;
import java.awt.*;
import java.lang.*;

public class chap10_12 extends Applet implements ActionListener
{
Button      andop,orop,xorop,modop, quit;
TextField   text1,text2,result;
   public void init()
   {
       text1=new TextField(20);
       text2=new TextField(20);
       result=new TextField(20);
       andop=new Button("AND");
       orop=new Button("OR");
          etc
   }

   public void actionPerformed(ActionEvent evt)
   {
   String str,str1;
   int val1,val2,res=0;
       str=evt.getActionCommand();
       str1=text1.getText();
       val1=Integer.valueOf(str1).intValue();
       str1=text2.getText();
       val2=Integer.valueOf(str1).intValue();

       if (str.equals("AND")) res=val1&val2;
          etc
```

```
        str=Integer.toString(res);
        result.setText(str);
    }
}
```

10.7 Project 3

Develop an applet in which the user enters two Boolean values (true or false) and the program will operate on them with the following logical operations:

- AND (&&).
- OR (||).
- EQUALS (==).
- NOT EQUALS (!=).
- GREATER THAN (>).
- LESS THAN (<).
- GREATER THAN OR EQUAL TO(>=).
- LESS THAN OR EQUAL TO (<=).

10.8 Project 4

Modify the applet developed in Exercise 9.14.5 so that it operates as a calculator. A text box should show the result of any calculation.

11 Strings

11.1 Introduction

C has strong support for strings, Java greatly enhances the use of strings and makes it easy to initialise and copy strings. A string is declared with:

```
String Msg;
```

There is no need to declare the size of the string as it is automatically allocated. The methods that can be used with strings are:

```
public char charAt(int index);
public int compareTo(String anotherString);
public String concat(String str);
public static String copyValueOf(char data[]);
public static String copyValueOf(char data[], int offset,
     int count);
public boolean endsWith(String suffix);
public boolean equals(Object anObject);
public boolean equalsIgnoreCase(String anotherString);
public void getBytes(int srcBegin, int srcEnd,
     byte dst[], int dstBegin);                     // Java 1.0
public void getBytes();                             // Java 1.1
public void getChars(int srcBegin, int srcEnd,
     char dst[], int dstBegin);
public int hashCode();
public int indexOf(int ch);
public int indexOf(int ch, int fromIndex);
public int indexOf(String str);
public int indexOf(String str, int fromIndex);
public String intern();
public int lastIndexOf(int ch);
public int lastIndexOf(int ch, int fromIndex);
public int lastIndexOf(String str);
public int lastIndexOf(String str, int fromIndex);
public int length();
public boolean regionMatches(boolean ignoreCase,
        int toffset, String other, int ooffset, int len);
public boolean regionMatches(int toffset, String other,
        int ooffset, int len);
public String replace(char oldChar,  char newChar);
public boolean startsWith(String prefix);
public boolean startsWith(String prefix, int toffset);
```

143

```
public String substring(int beginIndex);
public String substring(int beginIndex, int endIndex);
public char[] toCharArray();
public String toLowerCase();
public String toLowerCase(Local locale);              // Java 1.1
public String toString();
public String toUpperCase();
public String toUpperCase(Local locale);              // Java 1.1
public String trim();
public static String valueOf(boolean b);
public static String valueOf(char c);
public static String valueOf(char data[]);
public static String valueOf(char data[], int offset, int count);
public static String valueOf(double d);
public static String valueOf(float f);
public static String valueOf(int i);
public static String valueOf(long l);
public static String valueOf(Object obj);
```

Java applet 11.1 compares two entered strings and uses the `equal()` method
to compare them. A compare button (`comp`) is used to initiate the comparison.

📖 Java applet 11.1 (⚡Java 1.0)

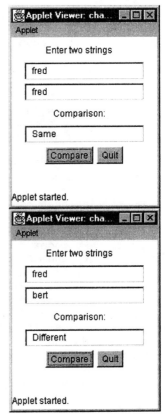

```
import java.applet.*;
import java.awt.*;
import java.lang.String;

public class chap11_01 extends Applet
{
String str1,str2;
TextField tfield1 = new TextField(20);
TextField tfield2 = new TextField(20);
TextField tfield3 = new TextField(20);
Button comp = new Button("Compare");
Button quit = new Button("Quit");

 public void init()
 {
   add(new Label("Enter two strings"));
   add(tfield1); add(tfield2);
   add(new Label("Comparison:"));
   add(tfield3);
   add(comp); add(quit);
 }
 public boolean action(Event evt, Object obj)
 {
   if (evt.target.equals(comp))
   {
      str1=tfield1.getText();
      str2=tfield2.getText();
      if (str1.equals(str2))
         tfield3.setText("Same");
      else tfield3.setText("Different");
   }
   else if (evt.target.equals(quit))
         System.exit(0);
   return true;
 }
}
```

Java applet 11.2 shows the Java 1.1 equivalent.

📖 **Java applet 11.2 (⚡ Java 1.1)**

```java
import java.applet.*;
import java.awt.*;
import java.awt.event.*;
import java.lang.String;

public class chap11_02 extends Applet implements ActionListener
{
TextField    tfield1 = new TextField(20);
TextField    tfield2 = new TextField(20);
TextField    tfield3 = new TextField(20);
Button       comp = new Button("Compare");
Button       quit = new Button("Quit");

    public void init()
    {
        add(new Label("Enter two strings"));
        add(tfield1); add(tfield2);
        add(new Label("Comparison:"));
        add(tfield3);
        add(comp); add(quit);
        comp.addActionListener(this);
        quit.addActionListener(this);
    }
    public void actionPerformed(ActionEvent evt)
    {
    String str, str1, str2;

        str=evt.getActionCommand();
        if (str.equals("Compare"))
        {
            str1=tfield1.getText();
            str2=tfield2.getText();
            if (str1.equals(str2)) tfield3.setText("Same");
            else tfield3.setText("Different");
        }
        else if (str.equals("quit")) System.exit(0);
    }
}
```

Applet 11.1 compares the characters in two strings and will display that the strings differ when the letters are the same but their case differs. Java applet 11.3 uses a checkbox (ccase) to define whether the case of the entered strings should be ignored, or not. If the checkbox is checked then the entered strings are converted into lowercase with the toLowerCase() method.

📖 **Java applet 11.3 (⚡ Java 1.1)**

```java
import java.applet.*;
import java.awt.*;
import java.awt.event.*;
import java.lang.String;

public class chap11_03 extends Applet implements
                                ActionListener, ItemListener
{
String       str1,str2;
TextField    tfield1 = new TextField(20);
```

```
TextField   tfield2 = new TextField(20);
TextField   tfield3 = new TextField(20);
Button      comp = new Button("Compare");
Button      quit = new Button("Quit");
Checkbox    ccase = new Checkbox("Case");
boolean     case_show=false;

    public void init()
    {
        add(new Label("Enter two strings"));
        add(tfield1); add(tfield2);
        add(new Label("Comparison:"));
        add(tfield3);
        add(comp); add(quit);
        add(ccase);
        comp.addActionListener(this);
        quit.addActionListener(this);
        ccase.addItemListener(this);
    }

    public void actionPerformed(ActionEvent evt)
    {
    String str;
        str=evt.getActionCommand();
        if (str.equals("Compare"))
        {
            str1=tfield1.getText();
            str2=tfield2.getText();
            if (case_show)
            {
                str1=str1.toLowerCase();
                str2=str2.toLowerCase();
            }
            if (str1.equals(str2)) tfield3.setText("Same");
            else tfield3.setText("Different");
        }
        else if (str.equals("Quit")) System.exit(0);
    }
    public void itemStateChanged(ItemEvent evt)
    {
    Object obj;
        obj=evt.getItem();
        if (obj.equals("Case")) case_show=ccase.getState();
    }
}
```

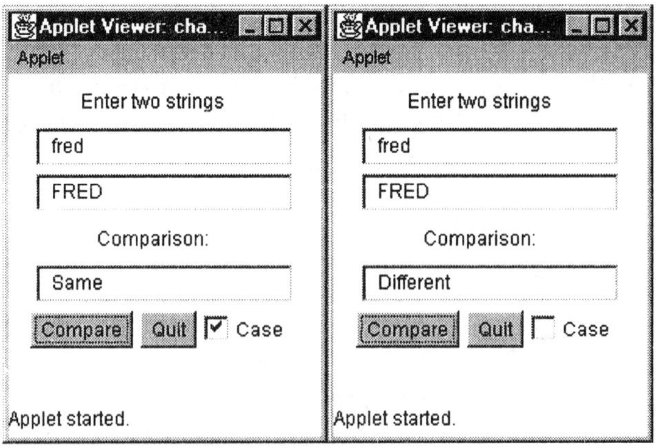

Figure 11.1 Sample runs

Note that the `equalsIgnoreCase()` method could have also been used. For example the lines:

```
if (case_show)
{
        str1=str1.toLowerCase();
        str2=str2.toLowerCase();
}
if (str1.equals(str2))
        tfield3.setText("Same");
else    tfield3.setText("Different");
```

could be replaced with:

```
if (case_show)
{
    if (str1.equalsIgnoreCase(str2)) tfield3.setText("Same");
    else tfield3.setText("Different");
}
else
{
    if (str1.equals(str2)) tfield3.setText("Same");
    else tfield3.setText("Different");
}
```

Applet 11.4 uses the `indexOf()` method to find a given character in an entered string. It can be seen in the sample runs, in Figure 11.2, that a run value of –1 identifies that the character has not been found in the string. As with C, the first indexed value of a string is a 0, the second at 1, and so on.

📖 Java applet 11.4 (⚡Java 1.1)

```java
import java.applet.*;
import java.awt.*;
import java.awt.event.*;
import java.lang.String;

public class chap11_04 extends Applet implements ActionListener
{
String     str1,str2;
TextField tfield1 = new TextField(20);
TextField tfield2 = new TextField(2);
TextField tfield3 = new TextField(20);
Button    find = new Button("Find");
Button    quit = new Button("Quit");

    public void init()
    {
        add(new Label("Enter a string"));
        add(tfield1);
        add(new Label("Character to find:"));
        add(tfield2);
        add(new Label("Dialog"));
        add(tfield3);
        add(find); add(quit);
        find.addActionListener(this);
        quit.addActionListener(this);
    }

    public void actionPerformed(ActionEvent evt)
    {
```

```
    int index;
    String Msg,str;
        str=evt.getActionCommand();
        if (str.equals("Find"))
        {
                str1=tfield1.getText();
                str2=tfield2.getText();
                index=str1.indexOf(str2);
                Msg="Found at " + index;
                tfield3.setText(Msg);
        }
        else if (str.equals("Quit"))  System.exit(0);
    }
}
```

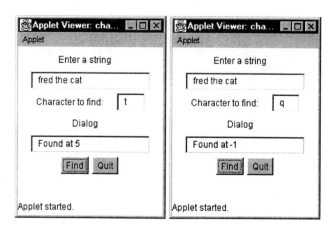

Figure 11.2 Sample run

Applet 11.4 only displays the first occurrence of a character in a string. Applet 11.5 adds an index term to the indexOf() method to find multiple occurrences of a character in the string. A loop is set up to test the value of index and will quit from the loop when the index term is –1.

📖 Java applet 11.5 (⚡Java 1.1)

```
import java.applet.*;
import java.awt.*;
import java.awt.event.*;
import java.lang.String;

public class chap11_05 extends Applet
        implements ActionListener
{
TextField  tfield1 = new TextField(20);
TextField  tfield2 = new TextField(2);
TextArea   tarea = new TextArea(4,20);
Button     find = new Button("Find");
Button     quit = new Button("Quit");

  public void init()
  {
    add(new Label("Enter a string"));
    add(tfield1);
```

```
        add(new Label("Character to find:"));
        add(tfield2);
        add(new Label("Dialog"));
        add(tarea);
        add(find); add(quit);
        find.addActionListener(this);
        quit.addActionListener(this);
    }

    public void actionPerformed(ActionEvent evt)
    {
    int index,curr;
        String Msg=null, str1, str2, str;
        str=evt.getActionCommand();

        if (str.equals("Find"))
        {
          str1=tfield1.getText();
          str2=tfield2.getText();
          curr=0;
          do
          {
            index=str1.indexOf(str2,curr);
            curr=index+1;
            if (Msg!=null)
                Msg=Msg+"Found at "+index + "\n";
            else Msg="Found at "+index + "\n";

            if (index!=-1) tarea.setText(Msg);
          } while (index!=-1);
        }
        else if (str.equals("Quit"))
                    System.exit(0);
    }
}
```

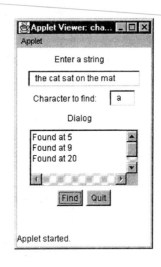

Java applet 11.6 allows a user to enter a string and then replace a given character with another given character. The `replace()` method is used to replace
the characters in the string, while the `charAt(0)` is used to determine the first
character in the entered character replacement strings (`str2` and `str3`).

📖 Java applet 11.6 (⚡Java 1.1)

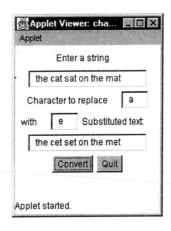

```
import java.applet.*;
import java.awt.*;
import java.awt.event.*;
import java.lang.String;

public class chap11_06 extends Applet
        implements ActionListener
{
TextField tfield1 = new TextField(20);
TextField tfield2 = new TextField(2);
TextField tfield3 = new TextField(2);
TextField tfield4 = new TextField(20);
Button convert = new Button("Convert");
Button quit = new Button("Quit");

    public void init()
    {
      add(new Label("Enter a string"));
```

```
        add(tfield1);
        add(new Label("Character to replace"));
        add(tfield2);
        add(new Label("with"));
        add(tfield3);
        add(new Label("Substituted text:"));
        add(tfield4);

        add(convert); add(quit);
        convert.addActionListener(this);
        quit.addActionListener(this);
    }

 public void actionPerformed(ActionEvent
evt)
 {
 int index,curr;
 String str1,str2,str3,str4,str;

    str=evt.getActionCommand();

    if (str.equals("Convert"))
    {
       str1=tfield1.getText();
       str2=tfield2.getText();
       str3=tfield3.getText();
       str4=str1.replace(str2.charAt(0),
                str3.charAt(0));
       tfield4.setText(str4);
    }
    else if (str.equals("Quit"))
            System.exit(0);
 }
}
```

Java applet 11.7 converts an entered string (str) into a character array (c). It
uses the length() method to determine the number of characters in the string.

📖 **Java applet 11.7 (↯Java 1.1)**

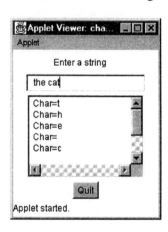

```
import java.applet.*;
import java.awt.*;
import java.awt.event.*;
import java.lang.String;

public class chap11_07 extends Applet
    implements ActionListener
{
TextField  tfield1 = new TextField(20);
TextArea   tarea = new TextArea(6,20);
Button     quit = new Button("Quit");

 public void init()
 {
    add(new Label("Enter a string"));
    add(tfield1);
    tfield1.addActionListener(this);
    add(tarea);
    add(quit);  quit.addActionListener(this);
 }

public void actionPerformed(ActionEvent evt)
{
char c[];
```

```
String Msg=null,str;
    int i=0;

    str=evt.getActionCommand();
    if (str.equals("Quit")) System.exit(0);
    else
    {
      str=tfield1.getText();
      c=str.toCharArray();
      for (i=0;i<str.length();i++)
      {
         if (Msg!=null) Msg=Msg + " Char=" +
                       c[i] + "\n";
         else Msg= " Char=" + c[i] + "\n";
      }
      tarea.setText(Msg);
    }
  }
}
```

11.2 Exercises

11.2.1 Write a Java applet in which the user enters a line of text and the applet displays the string in uppercase. Figure 11.3 shows a sample run.

11.2.2 Write a Java applet in which the user enters a line of text and the applet displays the string in either uppercase or lowercase. A checkbox should be used define whether the conversion is uppercase or lowercase. Figure 11.4 shows a sample run.

11.2.3 Modify the applet in Exercise in 11.2.2 so that it has a radio button to differentiate between uppercase and lowercase.

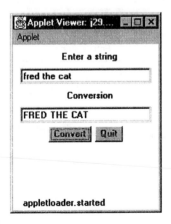

Figure 11.3 Sample run

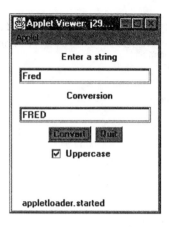

Figure 11.4 Sample run

11.2.4 Write a Java applet in which the user enters a string and the applet displays the number of characters in the entered string. (Hint: use the length() method.)

11.2.5 Modify Java applet 11.7 so that it displays the entered string without whitespaces. Figure 11.5 shows a sample run.

11.2.6 Write a Java applet in which the user enters two strings and the applet identifies that one of the strings is contained at the start of the other. (Hint: use the startsWith() method.)

11.2.7 Write a Java applet in which the user enters two strings and the applet identifies that one of the strings is contained at the end of the other. (Hint: use the endWith() method.)

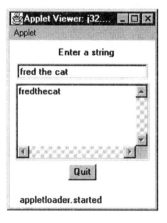

Figure 11.5 Sample run

11.2.8   Write a Java applet in which the user enters two strings and the applet identifies that one of the strings is contained within the other (at any place).

11.2.9   Write a Java applet which uses the `valueOf()` method with differing data types. State the result of each of the data types.

<hr>

11.3 Project

Develop a string manipulation applet which contains two text entry fields and a results field. The user can then select from the following options:

(i)   A checkbox which converts the two entered strings into lowercase.
(ii)   A checkbox which converts the two entered strings into uppercase.
(iii)   A button which concatenates the two entered strings together.
(iv)   A button which determines the total length of the two entered strings.
(v)   A button which determines if the two entered strings are equal (the case is either ignored or not, depending on an ignore case checkbox).
(vi)   A checkbox which identifies whether the string compare should ignore the case of the characters, or not.

Java applet 11.8 shows a very rough outline of the project, but does not have the full functionality. Figure 11.6 shows a sample run. Note that the `equalsIgnoreCase(Str)` can be used to ignore the case of two strings.

📖 Java applet 11.8 (⚡Java 1.1)

```
import java.applet.*;
import java.awt.event.*;
import java.awt.*;

public class chap11_08 extends Applet implements ActionListener,
                                                 ItemListener
{
Checkbox    upperop,lowerop;
Button      catop,lenop, eqop, quit;
TextField   text1,text2,result;

   public void init()
   {
      text1=new TextField(20);
      text2=new TextField(20);
      result=new TextField(20);
      upperop=new Checkbox("Upper");
      lowerop=new Checkbox("Lower");
      catop=new Button("Cat");
      lenop=new Button("Length");
      eqop=new Button("Equals");
      quit=new Button("Quit");
```

```
      add(text1); add(text2);
      add(result);add(quit);
      add(upperop); add(lowerop);
      add(catop); add(lenop);
      add(eqop);
      upperop.addItemListener(this);
      lowerop.addItemListener(this);
      catop.addActionListener(this);
      lenop.addActionListener(this);
      eqop.addActionListener(this);
   }
public void itemStateChanged(ItemEvent evt)
{
Object str;
String str1="",str2="";

      str=evt.getItem();
      if (str.equals("Lower"))
      {
         str1=text1.getText().toLowerCase();
         str2=text2.getText().toLowerCase();
      }
      else
      {
         str1=text1.getText().toUpperCase();
         str2=text2.getText().toUpperCase();
      }
      text1.setText(str1);
      text2.setText(str2);
   }

   public void actionPerformed(ActionEvent evt)
   {
     String str,str1, str2, Msg="";
     int val1,val2,res=0;
       str=evt.getActionCommand();
       str1=text1.getText();
       str2=text2.getText();
       if (str.equals("Cat")) Msg=str1+str2;
       else if (str.equals("Quit")) System.exit(0);
       result.setText(Msg);
   }
}
```

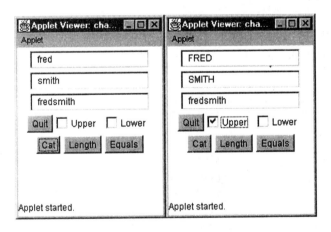

Figure 11.6 Sample run

Develop a Java applet which converts from one number format to another. The input and output formats are binary (base-2), octal (base-8), hexadecimal (base-16) and decimal. Java applet 11.9 shows an outline of the applet and Figure 11.7 shows two sample runs. Modify the program so that the output displays a hexadecimal value with a following h, an octal value with an o and a binary value with a b.

📖 Java applet 11.9 (⚡Java 1.1)

```
import java.applet.*;
import java.awt.event.*;
import java.awt.*;

public class chap10_09 extends Applet implements ActionListener,
              ItemListener
{
Checkbox    oct,dec,hex;
Button      toOct,toHex, toDec, quit;
TextField   text1, result;
static int  HEXREAD=0, OCTREAD=1, DECREAD=2;
int         read=DECREAD;

    public void init()
    {
    CheckboxGroup RadioGroup = new CheckboxGroup();

        text1=new TextField(20);

        hex=new Checkbox("Hex",RadioGroup,false);
        oct=new Checkbox("Oct",RadioGroup,false);
        dec=new Checkbox("Dec",RadioGroup,true);

        result=new TextField(20);

        toOct=new Button("ToOct");
        toHex=new Button("ToHex");
        toDec=new Button("ToDec");
        quit=new Button("Quit");

        add(text1);    add(result);

        add(hex); add(oct);
        add(dec);

        add(toOct); add(toHex);
        add(toDec); add(quit);

        hex.addItemListener(this);
        oct.addItemListener(this);
        dec.addItemListener(this);
        toOct.addActionListener(this);
        toHex.addActionListener(this);
        toDec.addActionListener(this);
        quit.addActionListener(this);

    }
    public void itemStateChanged(ItemEvent evt)
    {
    Object str;
```

```
        str=evt.getItem();

        if (str.equals("Hex")) read=HEXREAD;
        else if (str.equals("Oct")) read=OCTREAD;
        else if (str.equals("Dec")) read=DECREAD;
}

public void actionPerformed(ActionEvent evt)
{
String str,str1, Msg="";
int    val1=0;

        str=evt.getActionCommand();

        if (str.equals("Quit")) System.exit(0);

        str1=text1.getText();

        if (read==HEXREAD)  val1=Integer.parseInt(str1,16);
        else if (read==OCTREAD) val1=Integer.parseInt(str1,8);
        else if (read==DECREAD) val1=Integer.parseInt(str1,10);

        // other way is->        else if (read==DECREAD)
        //                       val1=Integer.valueOf(str1).intValue();

        if (str.equals("ToOct"))
        {
                Msg=Integer.toOctalString(val1);
                result.setText(Msg);
        }
        else if (str.equals("ToHex"))
        {
                Msg=Integer.toHexString(val1);
                result.setText(Msg);
        }
        else if (str.equals("ToDec"))
        {
                Msg=Integer.toString(val1);
                result.setText(Msg);
        }
    }
}
```

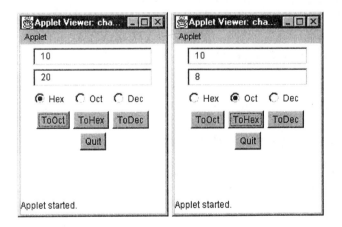

Figure 11.7 Sample run

12 Exceptions

12.1 Exception handling

Many errors can occur in a program. In most programming languages they can cause a program to crash or act unpredictably. For example C and Pascal can cause a run-time error when the program accesses an array element which does not correspond with the number of elements which have been declared. In Java an error causes an exception, which can be tested and handled in the required mode. The format is:

```
try
{
    // statements to catch if an exception occurs
}
catch
{
   // the catch is called when an exception occurs
}
```

When an exception occurs the rest of the statements are not executed and the program goes to the catch statements. After completing the exception the program does not return to the try statement. Multiple catch statements can also be inserted after a try statement, such as:

```
try
{
   // statements which might cause an exception
}
catch NumberFormatException()
{
    // exception caused when a numeric value conversion has an
    // invalid format
}
catch NegativeArraySizeException()
{
   // exception caused when there is a negative array size
}
```

The constructors are:

```
public Exception()
```
     Constructs an exception with no specified detail message.

```
public Exception(String s)
```
     Constructs a exception with the specified detail message (s).

Java applet 12.1 shows an example of an exception in a program which accesses an array element which has not been declared. It can be seen in Test run 12.1 that the exception message is:

```
java.lang.ArrayIndexOutOfBoundsException: 4.
```

📖 Java applet 12.1

```
import java.net.*;
import java.awt.*;
import java.applet.*;
public class chap12_01 extends Applet
{
    public void paint(Graphics g)
    {
    float arr[]=new float[4];
    int i;
        arr[0]=1; arr[1]=2; arr[2]=3; arr[3]=4;
        try
        {
            for (i=0;i<100;i++)
                System.out.println(" " + arr[i]);
        }
        catch (Exception e)
        {
            System.out.println("Error :" + e);
        }
    }
}
```

💻 Test run 12.1

```
C:\java\temp>appletviewer chap12_01.html
 1
 2
 3
 4
Error :java.lang.ArrayIndexOutOfBoundsException: 4
```

12.2 Typical exceptions

The `java.lang` package contains a number of exceptions, these include:

```
public ArithmeticException()
```
     Thrown when an exceptional arithmetic condition has occurred, such as a division-by-zero or a square root of a negative number.

```
public ArrayIndexOutOfBoundsException()
```
Thrown when an illegal index term in an array has been accessed.

```
public ArrayStoreException()
```
Thrown when the wrong type of object is stored in an array of objects.

```
public ClassCastException()
```
Exception that is thrown when an object is casted to a subclass which it is not an instance.

```
public Exception()
```
Exception that indicates conditions that a reasonable application might want to catch.

```
public IllegalArgumentException()
```
Thrown when a method has been passed an illegal or inappropriate argument.

```
public IllegalThreadStateException()
```
Thrown to indicate that a thread is not in an appropriate state for the requested operation.

```
public IndexOutOfBoundsException()
```
Thrown to indicate that an index term is out of range.

```
public InterruptedException()
```
Thrown when a thread is waiting, sleeping, or otherwise paused for a long time and another thread interrupts it using the interrupt method in class Thread.

```
public NegativeArraySizeException()
```
Thrown when an array is created with a negative size.

```
public NullPointerException()
```
Thrown when an application attempts to use a null pointer.

```
public NumberFormatException()
```
Thrown when an application attempts to convert a string to one of the numeric types, but that the string does not have the appropriate format.

```
public StringIndexOutOfBoundsException()
```
Thrown when a string is indexed with a negative value or a value which is greater than or equal to the size of the string.

Other exceptions will be discussed in the following chapters.

Java applet 12.2 shows a simple applet which determines the value of a division between two integer numbers. It uses the `ArithmeticException` exception which will be thrown when there is a divide-by-zero error (or any other exceptional arithmetic condition). The second sample run shows a divide-by-zero error.

The statement:

```
val1=Integer.valueOf(str);
```

converts a string (`str`) in an `Integer`. To convert it to an `int` type (in order to perform a calculation) the following is used:

```
val1.intValue();
```

📖 Java applet 12.2 (⚡Java 1.1)

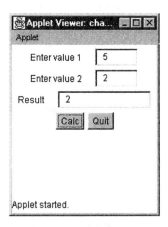

```java
import java.applet.*;
import java.awt.*;
import java.awt.event.*;

public class chap12_02 extends Applet
       implements ActionListener
{
TextField tfield1 = new TextField(5);
TextField tfield2 = new TextField(5);
TextField tfield3 = new TextField(15);
Button calc = new Button("Calc");
Button quit = new Button("Quit");

  public void init()
  {
    add(new Label("Enter value 1"));
    add(tfield1);
    add(new Label("Enter value 2"));
    add(tfield2);
    add(new Label("Result"));
    add(tfield3);
    add(calc); calc.addActionListener(this);
    add(quit); quit.addActionListener(this);
  }

public void actionPerformed(ActionEvent evt)
{
String    str,str1;
Integer   val1,val2;
int       val3;

  str=evt.getActionCommand();
  if (str.equals("Calc"))
  {
    str1=tfield1.getText();
    val1=Integer.valueOf(str1);
    str1=tfield2.getText();
    val2=Integer.valueOf(str1);
    try
    {
```

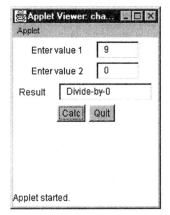

```
      val3=val1.intValue()/val2.intValue();
      tfield3.setText(""+val3);
    }
    catch (ArithmeticException err)
    {
      tfield3.setText("Divide-by-0");
    }
  }
  else if (str.equals("Quit"))
              System.exit(0);
  }
}
```

Note that `val3` could also have been calculated directly with the following line:

```
val3=Integer.valueOf(str).intValue();
```

Java applet 12.3 calculates the square root of an entered floating point value. If the entered value is a negative then an exception is thrown when the applet tries to determine the square root of the negative value.

📖   Java applet 12.3 (⚡Java 1.1)

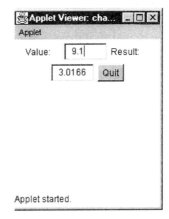

```
import java.applet.*;
import java.awt.*;
import java.awt.event.*;

public class chap12_03 extends Applet
    implements ActionListener
{
TextField tfield1 = new TextField(5);
TextField tfield2 = new TextField(5);
Button    quit = new Button("Quit");

  public void init()
  {
      add(new Label("Value:"));
      add(tfield1);
      add(new Label("Result:"));
      add(tfield2);
      add(quit);
      quit.addActionListener(this);
      tfield1.addActionListener(this);
  }

  public void actionPerformed(
                    ActionEvent evt)
  {
String str=null;
Double val1;
double val,res;

str=evt.getActionCommand();

if (str.equals("Quit"))
    System.exit(0);
else
{
  val1=Double.valueOf(tfield1.getText());
  try
```

```
      {
        val=val1.floatValue();
        res=Math.sqrt(val);
        tfield2.setText(""+res);
      }
      catch (ArithmeticException err)
      {
        tfield2.setText("Exception");
      }
    }
  }
}
```

Note that val1 could also have been calculated directly with the following line:

```
val1= Double.valueOf(tfield1.getText()).doubleValue();
```

Java applet 12.4 calculates the square root of an entered floating point value. It uses the NumberFormatException exception to determine if the entered value is not in the correct format.

Java applet 12.4 (✝Java 1.1)

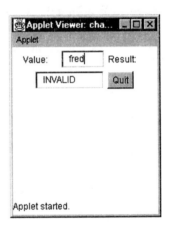

```
import java.applet.*;
import java.awt.*;
import java.awt.event.*;
import java.lang.*;

public class chap12_04 extends Applet
        implements ActionListener
{
TextField tfield1 = new TextField(5);
TextField tfield2 = new TextField(10);
Button    quit = new Button("Quit");

    public void init()
    {
        add(new Label("Value:"));
        add(tfield1);
        add(new Label("Result:"));
        add(tfield2);       add(quit);
        quit.addActionListener(this);
        tfield1.addActionListener(this);
    }

    public void actionPerformed(
                        ActionEvent evt)
    {
    String str=null;
    Double val1;
    double val,res;

        str=evt.getActionCommand();

        if (str.equals("Quit"))
            System.exit(0);
        else
        {
            try
```

```
        {
            val1=Double.valueOf(
               tfield1.getText());
            val=val1.floatValue();
            res=Math.sqrt(val);
            tfield2.setText(""+res);
        }
        catch (NumberFormatException err)
        {
            tfield2.setText("INVALID");
        }
    }
  }
}
```

12.4 Exercises

12.4.1 Modify Java applet 12.4 so that it detects both a square root of a negative number and an invalid number format.

12.4.2 Write a Java applet which throws the `StringIndexOutOfBoundsException()` exception.

12.4.3 Write a Java applet which throws some of the other exceptions.

13 Java Networking

13.1 Introduction

Networking technologies, such as Ethernet only provide a data link layer function; that is, they allow a reliable connection between one node and another on the same network. They do not provide internetworking where data can be transferred from one network to another or from one network segment to another. For data to be transmitted across the network, it requires an addressing structure which is read by a bridge, gateway and router. The interconnection of networks is known as internetworking (or internet). Each part of an internet is a subnetwork (or subnet). TCP/IP are a pair of protocols which allow one subnet to communicate with another. A protocol is a set of rules which allow the orderly exchange of information. The IP part corresponds to the network layer of the OSI model and the TCP part to the transport layer. Their operation is transparent to the physical and data link layers and can thus be used on Ethernet, FDDI or Token Ring networks. This is illustrated in Figure 13.1. The address of the data link layer corresponds to the physical address of the node, such as the MAC address (in Ethernet and Token Ring) or the telephone number (for a modem connection). The IP address is assigned to each node on the internet. It is used to identify the location of the network and any subnets.

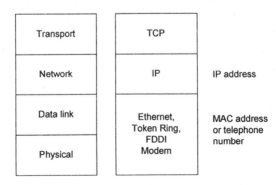

Figure 13.1 TCP/IP and the OSI model

164

TCP/IP was originally developed by the US Defense Advanced Research Projects Agency (DARPA). Their objective was to connect a number of universities and other research establishments to DARPA. The resultant internet is now known as the Internet. It has since outgrown this application and many commercial organisations now connect to the Internet. The Internet uses TCP/IP to transfer data. Each node on the Internet is assigned a unique network address, called an IP address. Note that any organisation can have its own internets, but if it is to connect to the Internet then the addresses must conform to the Internet addressing format.

The International Standards Organization has adopted TCP/IP as the basis for the standards relating to the network and transport layers of the OSI model. This standard is known as ISO-IP. Most currently available systems conform to the IP addressing standard.

13.2 TCP/IP gateways and hosts

TCP/IP hosts are nodes which communicate over interconnected networks using TCP/IP communications. A TCP/IP gateway node connects one type of network to another. It contains hardware to provide the physical link between the different networks, and the hardware and software to convert frames from one network to the other. Typically, it converts a Token Ring MAC layer to an equivalent Ethernet MAC layer, and vice versa.

A router connects two networks of the same kind through a point-to-point link. The main operational difference between a gateway, a router and a bridge is that, for a Token Ring and Ethernet network, the bridge uses the 48-bit MAC address to route frames, whereas the gateway and router use an IP network address. In the public telephone system, the MAC address would be equivalent to a randomly assigned telephone number, whereas the IP address would give logical information about where the telephone was located, such as the country code, the area code, and so on.

Figure 13.2 shows how a gateway routes information. The gateway reads the frame from the computer on network A. It then reads the IP address contained in the frame and makes a decision whether it is routed out of network A to network B. If it does, then it relays the frame to network B.

13.3 Functions of the IP protocol

The main functions of the IP protocol are to:

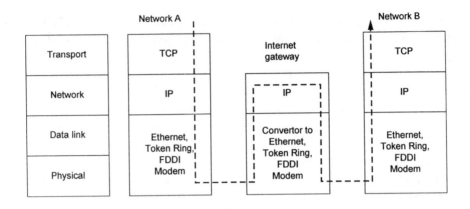

Figure 13.2 Internet gateway layers

- Route IP data frames – which are called internet datagrams – around an internet. The IP protocol program running on each node knows the location of the gateway on the network. The gateway must then be able to locate the interconnected network. Data then passes from node to gateway through the internet.
- Fragment the data into smaller units if it is greater than 64 kB.
- Report errors when a datagram is being routed or reassembled. If this happens, then the node that detects the error reports back to the source node. Datagrams are deleted from the network if they travel through the network for more than a set time. Again, an error message is returned to the source node to inform it that the internet routing could not find a route for the datagram or that the destination node, or network, does not exist.

13.4 Internet datagram

The IP protocol is an implementation of the network layer of the OSI model. It adds a data header onto the information passed from the transport layer; the resultant data packet is known as an internet datagram. The header contains information such as the destination and source IP addresses, the version number of the IP protocol, and so on. Its format is given in Figure 13.3.

The datagram contains up to 65 536 bytes (64 kB) of data. If the data to be transmitted is less than or equal to 64 kB, then it is sent as one datagram. If it is greater, then the source splits the data into fragments and sends multiple datagrams. When transmitted from the source, each datagram is routed separately through the internet and the received fragments are finally reassembled at the destination.

The TCP/IP `version number` helps gateways and nodes interpret the data unit correctly. Differing versions may have a different format or the IP protocol may interpret the header differently.

The `type of service` bit field is an 8-bit bit pattern in the form PPPDTRXX. PPP which defines the priority of the datagram (from 0 to 7), D sets a low-delay service, T sets high throughput, R sets high reliability and XX are currently not used.

The `header length` defines the size of the data unit in multiplies of 4 bytes (32 bits). The minimum length is 5 bytes and the maximum is 65 536 bytes. Padding bytes fill any unused spaces.

A gateway may route a datagram and split it into smaller fragments. The D bit informs the gateway that it should not fragment the data and thus signifies that a receiving node should receive the data as a single unit or not at all. The M bit is the more fragments bit and is used when data is split into fragments. The fragment offset contains the fragment number.

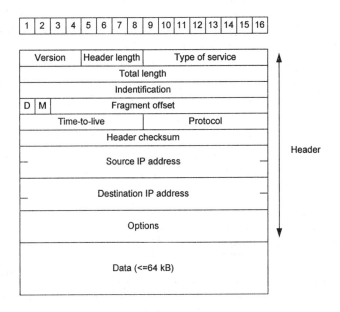

Figure 13.3 Internet datagram format and contents

A datagram could be delayed in the internet indefinitely. To prevent this the 8-bit `time-to-live` value is set to the maximum transit time in seconds. It is set initially by the source IP. Each gateway then decrements this value by a defined amount. When it becomes zero the datagram is discarded. It also defines the maximum amount of time that a destination IP node should wait for the next datagram fragment.

Different IP protocols can be used on the datagram. The 8-bit `protocol` field defines which type is to be used.

The `header checksum` contains a 16-bit pattern for error detection. The `source` and `destination IP addresses` are stored in the 32-bit source and destination IP address fields. The `options` field contains information such as debugging, error control and routing information.

13.5 TCP/IP internets

Figure 13.4 illustrates a sample TCP/IP implementation. A gateway MERCURY provides a link between a Token Ring network (NETWORK A) and the Ethernet network (ETHER C). Another gateway PLUTO connects NETWORK B to ETHER C. The TCP/IP protocol allows a host on NETWORK A to communicate with VAX01.

13.5.1 Selecting internet addresses

Each node using TCP/IP communications requires an IP address which is then matched to its Token Ring or Ethernet MAC address. The MAC address allows nodes on the same segment to communicate with each other. In order for nodes on a different network to communicate, each must be configured with an IP address.

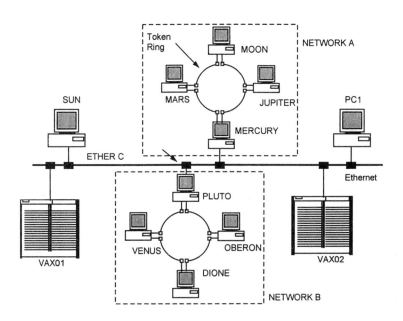

Figure 13.4 Example internet

Nodes on a TCP/IP network are either hosts or gateways. Any nodes that run application software or function as terminals are hosts. Any node which routes TCP/IP packets between networks is called a TCP/IP gateway node. This node must have the necessary network controller boards to physically interface with other networks it connects to.

13.5.2 Format of the IP address

A typical IP address consists of two fields: the left field (or the network number) which identifies the network, and the right number (or the host number) which identifies the particular host within that network. Figure 13.5 illustrates this.

The IP address is 32 bits long and can address over 4 million physical networks (2^{32} or 4 294 967 296 hosts). There are three different address formats, these are shown in Figure 13.6. Each of these types is applicable to certain types of networks. Class A allows up to 128 (2^7) different networks and up to 16 777 216 (2^{24}) hosts on each network. Class B allows up to 16 384 networks and up to 65 536 hosts on each network. Class C allows up to 2 097 152 networks each with up to 256 hosts.

The class A address is thus useful where there are a small number of networks with a large number of hosts connected to them. Class C is useful where there are many networks with a relatively small number of hosts connected to each network. Class B addressing gives a good compromise of networks and connected hosts.

When selecting internet addresses for the network, the address can be specified simply with decimal numbers within a specific range. The standard DARPA IP addressing format is of the form:

```
X.Y.Z.W
```

where W, X, Y and Z represent 1 byte of the IP address. As decimal numbers they range from 0 to 255. The 4 bytes together represent both the network and host address.

The valid range of the different IP addresses is given in Figure 13.6 and Table 13.1 defines the valid IP addresses. Thus for a class A type address there can be 127 networks and 16 711 680 (256×256×255) hosts. Class B can have 16 320 (64×255) networks and class C can have 2 088 960 (32×256×255) networks and 255 hosts.

Addresses above 223.255.254 are reserved, as are addresses with groups of zeros.

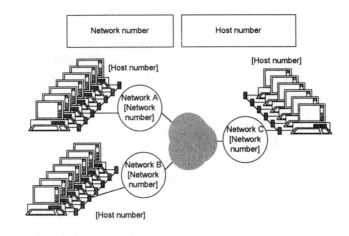

Figure 13.5 IP addressing over networks

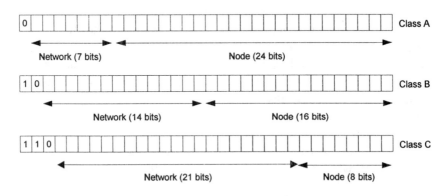

Figure 13.6 Type A, B and C IP address classes

Table 13.1 Ranges of addresses for type A, B and C internet address

Type	Network portion	Host portion
A	1 - 126	0.0.1 - 255.255.254
B	128.1 - 191.254	0.1 - 255.254
C	192.0.1 - 223.255.254	1 - 254

13.6 Domain name system

An IP address can be defined in the form xxx.yyy.zzz.www, where xxx, yyy, zzz and www are integer values in the range 0 to 255. On the Internet it is xxx.yyy.zzz that normally defines the subnet and www that defines the host.

Such names may be difficult to remember. A better method is to use symbolic names rather than IP addresses.

Users and application programs can then use symbolic names rather than IP addresses. The directory network services on the Internet determine the IP address of the named destination user or application program. This has the advantage that users and application programs can move around the Internet and are not fixed to an IP address.

An analogy relates to the public telephone service. A phone directory contains a list of subscribers and their associated telephone number. If someone looks for a telephone number, first the user name is looked up and their associated phone number found. The telephone directory listing maps a user name (symbolic name) to an actual telephone number (the actual address).

Table 13.2 lists some Internet domain assignments for World Wide Web (WWW) servers. Note that domain assignments are not fixed and can change their corresponding IP addresses, if required. The binding between the symbolic name and its address can thus change at any time.

Table 13.2 Internet domain assignments for WWW servers

Web server	Internet domain names	Internet IP address
NEC	web.nec.com	143.101.112.6
Sony	www.sony.com	198.83.178.11
Intel	www.intel.com	134.134.214.1
IEEE	www.ieee.com	140.98.1.1
University of Bath	www.bath.ac.uk	136.38.32.1
University of Edinburgh	www.ed.ac.uk	129.218.128.43
IEE	www.iee.org.uk	193.130.181.10
University of Manchester	www.man.ac.uk	130.88.203.16

13.7 Internet naming structure

The Internet naming structure uses labels separated by periods; an example is eece.napier.ac.uk. It uses a hierarchical structure where organisations are grouped into primary domain names. These are com (for commercial organisations), edu (for educational organisations), gov (for government organisations), mil (for military organisations), net (Internet network support centres) or org (other organisations). The primary domain name may also define the country in which the host is located, such as uk (United Kingdom), fr (France), and so on. All hosts on the Internet must be registered to one of these primary domain names.

The labels after the primary field describe the subnets within the network. For example in the address eece.napier.ac.uk, the ac label relates to an academic institution within the uk, napier to the name of the institution and eece the subnet with that organisation. An example structure is illustrated in Figure 13.7.

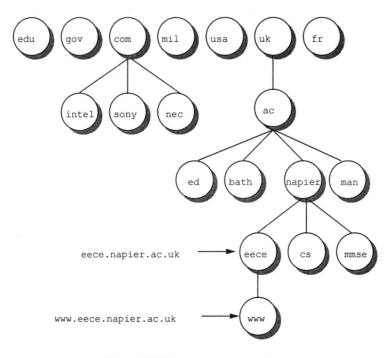

Figure 13.7 Example domain naming

13.8 HTTP protocol

The foundation protocol of the WWW is the Hypertext Transfer Protocol (HTTP) which can be used in any client/server application involving hypertext. It is used in the WWW for transmitting information using hypertext jumps and can support the transfer of plaintext, hypertext, audio, images, or any Internet-compatible information. The most recently defined standard is HTTP 1.1, which has been defined by the IETF standard.

HTTP is a stateless protocol where each transaction is independent of any previous transactions. The advantage of being stateless is that it allows the rapid access of WWW pages over several widely distributed servers. It uses the TCP protocol to establish a connection between a client and a server for each transaction then terminates the connection once the transaction completes.

HTTP also supports many different formats of data. Initially a client issues a request to a server which may include a prioritised list of formats that it can handle. This allows new formats to be added easily and also prevents the transmission of unnecessary information.

A client's WWW browser (the user agent) initially establishes a direct connection with the destination server which contains the required WWW page. To make this connection the client initiates a TCP connection between the client and the server. After this is established the client then issues an HTTP request, such as the specific command (the method), the URL, and possibly extra information such as request parameters or client information. When the server receives the request, it attempts to perform the requested action. It then returns an HTTP response which includes status information, a success/error code, and extra information itself. After this is received by the client, the TCP connection is closed.

13.8.1 Intermediate systems

The previous section discussed the direct connection of a client to a server. Many system organisations do not wish a direct connection to an internal network. Thus HTTP supports other connections which are formed through intermediate systems, such as:

- A proxy
- A gateway
- A tunnel

Each intermediate system is connected by a TCP and acts as a relay for the request to be sent out and returned to the client. Figure 13.8 shows the set up of the proxies and gateways.

Proxy

A proxy connects to a number of clients; it acts on behalf of other clients and sends requests from the clients to a server. It thus acts as a client when it communicates with a server, but as a server when communicating with a client. A proxy is typically used for security purposes where the client and server are separated by a firewall. The proxy connects to the client side of the firewall and the server to the other side of the firewall. Thus the server must authenticate itself to the firewall before a connection can be made with the proxy. Only after this has been authenticated will the proxy pass requests through the firewall.

Gateway

Gateways are servers that act as if they are the destination server. They are typically used when clients cannot get direct access to the server, and typically for one of the security reasons where the gateway acts as a firewall so that the gateway communicates with the Internet and the server only communicates with the Internet through the gateway. The client must then authenticate itself to the proxy, which can then pass the request on to the server.

They can also be used when the destination is a non-HTTP server. Web browsers have built into them the capability to contact servers for protocols other than HTTP, such as FTP and Gopher servers. This capability can also be provided by a gateway. The client makes an HTTP request to a gateway server. The gateway server than contacts the relevant FTP or Gopher server to obtain the desired result. This result is then converted into a form suitable for HTTP and transmitted back to the client.

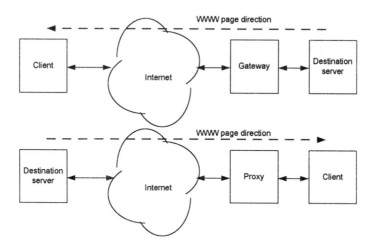

Figure 13.8 Usage of proxies and gateways

Tunnel

A tunnel does not perform any operation on the HTTP message; it passes messages onto the client or server unchanged. This differs from a proxy or a gateway, which modify the HTTP messages. Tunnels are typically used as firewalls, where the firewall authenticates the connection but simply relays the HTTP messages.

13.8.2 Cache

In a computer system a cache is an area of memory that stores information likely to be accessed in a fast access memory area. For example a cache controller takes a guess on which information the process is likely to access next. When the processor wishes to access the disk then, if it has guessed right it will load, the cache controller will load from the electronic memory rather than loading it from the disk. A WWW cache stores cacheable responses so that there is a reduction in network traffic and an improvement in access times.

Java directly supports TCP/IP communications and has the following classes:

- `java.net.ContentHandler`. Class which reads data from a URLConnection and also supports MIME (Multipurpose Internet Mail Extension).
- `java.net.DatagramPacket`. Class representing a datagram packet which contains packet data, packet length, Internet addresses and the port number.
- `java.net.DatagramSocket`. Class representing a datagram socket class.
- `java.net.InetAddress`. Class representing Internet addresses.
- `java.net.ServerSocket`. Class representing Socket server class.
- `java.net.Socket`. Class representing Socket client classes.
- `java.net.SocketImpl`. Socket implementation class.
- `java.net.URL`. Class URL representing a Uniform Reference Locator (URL) which is a reference to an object on the WWW.
- `java.net.URLConnection`. Class representing an active connection to an object represented by a URL.
- `java.net.URLEncoder`. Converts strings of text into URLEncoded format.
- `java.net.URLStreamHandler`. Class for opening URL streams.

When an error occurs in the connection or in the transmission and reception of data it causes an exception. The classes which handle these are:

- `java.io.IOException`. To handle general errors.
- `java.net.MalformedURLException`. Malformed URL.
- `java.net.ProtocolException`. Protocol error.
- `java.net.SocketException`. Socket error.
- `java.net.UnknownHostException`. Unknown host error.
- `java.net.UnknownServiceException`. Unknown service error.

13.9.1 Class j12_ava.net.InetAddress

This class represents Internet addresses. The methods are:

```
public static synchronized InetAddress[] getAllByName(String
host)
```
    This returns an array with all the corresponding `InetAddresses` for a given host name (`host`).

```
public static synchronized InetAddress getByName(String host)
```
    This returns the network address of an indicated host. A host name of null returns the default address for the local machine.

```
public String getHostAddress()
```
    This returns the IP address string (WW.XX.YY.ZZ) in a string format.

```
public byte[] getAddress()
```
    This returns the raw IP address in network byte order. The array position 0 (addr[0]) contains the highest order byte.

```
public String getHostName()
```
    Gets the hostname for this address. If the host is equal to null, then this address refers to any of the local machine's available network addresses.

```
public static InetAddress getLocalHost()
```
    Returns the local host.

```
public String toString()
```
    Converts the InetAddress to a String.

Java applet 13.1 uses the getAllByName method to determine all the IP addresses associated with an Internet host. In this case the host is named www.microsoft.com. It can be seen from the test run that there are 18 IP addresses associated with this domain name. It can be seen that the applet causes an exception error as the loop tries to display 30 such IP addresses. When the program reaches the 19th InetAddress, the exception error is displayed (ArrayIndexOutOfBoundsException).

📖 Java applet 13.1

```java
import java.net.*;
import java.awt.*;
import java.applet.*;

public class chap13_01 extends Applet
{
InetAddress[] address;
int          i;
   public void start()
   {
      System.out.println("Started");
      try
      {
         address=InetAddress.getAllByName("www.microsoft.com");

         for (i=0;i<30;i++)
         {
            System.out.println("Address " + address[i]);
         }
      }
      catch (Exception e)
      {
         System.out.println("Error :" + e);
      }
   }
}
```

```
C:\java\temp>appletviewer chap13_01.html
Started
Address www.microsoft.com/207.68.137.59
Address www.microsoft.com/207.68.143.192
Address www.microsoft.com/207.68.143.193
Address www.microsoft.com/207.68.143.194
Address www.microsoft.com/207.68.143.195
Address www.microsoft.com/207.68.156.49
Address www.microsoft.com/207.68.137.56
Address www.microsoft.com/207.68.156.51
Address www.microsoft.com/207.68.156.52
Address www.microsoft.com/207.68.137.62
Address www.microsoft.com/207.68.156.53
Address www.microsoft.com/207.68.156.54
Address www.microsoft.com/207.68.137.65
Address www.microsoft.com/207.68.156.73
Address www.microsoft.com/207.68.156.61
Address www.microsoft.com/207.68.156.16
Address www.microsoft.com/207.68.156.58
Address www.microsoft.com/207.68.137.53
Error :java.lang.ArrayIndexOutOfBoundsException: 18
```

Java applet 13.2 overcomes the problem of displaying the exception. In this case the exception is caught by inserting the address display within a `try {}` statement then having a `catch` statement which does nothing. Test run 13.2 shows a sample run.

📖 **Java applet 13.2**

```
import java.net.*;
import java.awt.*;
import java.applet.*;
public class chap13_02 extends Applet
{
InetAddress[]  address;
int            i;
   public void start()
   {
      System.out.println("Started");
      try
      {
         address=InetAddress.getAllByName("www.microsoft.com");

         try
         {
            for (i=0;i<30;i++)
            {
               System.out.println("Address " + address[i]);
            }
         }
         catch(Exception e)
         { /* Do nothing about the exception, as it is not really
              an error */}
      }
      catch (Exception e)
      {
         System.out.println("Error :" + e);
      }
   }
}
```

```
C:\java\temp>appletviewer chap13_02.html
Started
Address www.microsoft.com/207.68.137.59
Address www.microsoft.com/207.68.143.192
Address www.microsoft.com/207.68.143.193
Address www.microsoft.com/207.68.143.194
Address www.microsoft.com/207.68.143.195
Address www.microsoft.com/207.68.156.49
Address www.microsoft.com/207.68.137.56
Address www.microsoft.com/207.68.156.51
Address www.microsoft.com/207.68.156.52
Address www.microsoft.com/207.68.137.62
Address www.microsoft.com/207.68.156.53
Address www.microsoft.com/207.68.156.54
Address www.microsoft.com/207.68.137.65
Address www.microsoft.com/207.68.156.73
Address www.microsoft.com/207.68.156.61
Address www.microsoft.com/207.68.156.16
Address www.microsoft.com/207.68.156.58
Address www.microsoft.com/207.68.137.53
```

Java applet 13.3 shows an example of displaying the local host name (getLo-calHost), the host name (getHostName) and the host's IP address (getHostAddress). Test run 13.3 shows a sample run.

Java applet 13.3

```java
import java.net.*;
import java.awt.*;
import java.applet.*;

public class chap13_03 extends Applet
{
InetAddress host;
String str;
int i;
   public void start()
   {
      System.out.println("Started");

      try
      {
         host=InetAddress.getLocalHost();
         System.out.println("Local host " + host);

         str=host.getHostName();
         System.out.println("Host name: " + str);

         str=host.getHostAddress();
         System.out.println("Host address: " + str);
      }

      catch (Exception e)
      {
         System.out.println("Error :" + e);
      }
   }
}
```

```
C:\java\temp>appletviewer chap13_03.html
Started
Local host toshiba/195.232.26.125
Host name: toshiba
Host address: 195.232.26.125
```

The previous Java applets have all displayed their output to the output terminal (with System.out.println). Java applet 13.4 uses the drawString method to display the output text to the Applet window. Figure 13.9 shows a sample run.

📖 Java applet 13.4

```
import java.net.*;
import java.awt.*;
import java.applet.*;

public class chap13_04 extends Applet
{
InetAddress[] address;
int i;

    public void paint(Graphics g)
    {

        g.drawString("Addresses for WWW.MICROSOFT.COM",5,10);

        try
        {
            address=InetAddress.getAllByName("www.microsoft.com");

            for (i=0;i<30;i++)
            {
                g.drawString(" "+address[i].toString(),5,20+10*i);
            }
        }
        catch (Exception e)
        {
            System.out.println("Error :" + e);
        }
    }
}
```

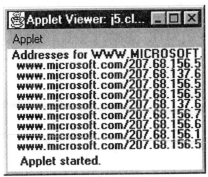

Figure 13.9 Sample run

13.9.2 class java.net.URL

The URL (Uniform Reference Locator) class is used to reference to an object on the World Wide Web. The main constructors are:

`public URL(String protocol, String host, int port, String file)`
> Creates an absolute URL from the specified protocol (`protocol`), host (`host`), port (`port`) and file (`file`).

`public URL(String protocol, String host, String file)`
> Creates an absolute URL from the specified protocol (`protocol`), host (`host`) and file (`file`).

`public URL(String spec)`
> Creates a URL from an unparsed absolute URL (`spec`).

`public URL(URL context, String spec)`
> Creates a URL from an unparsed absolute URL (`spec`) in the specified context.

The methods are:

`public int getPort()`
> Returns a port number. A return value of −1 indicates that the port is not set.

`public String getProtocol()`
> Returns the protocol name.

`public String getHost()`
> Returns the host name.

`public String getFile()`
> Returns the file name.

`public boolean equals(Object obj)`
> Compares two URLs, where `obj` is the URL to compare against.

`public String toString()`
> Converts to a string format.

`public String toExternalForm()`
> Reverses the URL parsing.

`public URLConnection openConnection()`
> Creates a URLConnection object that contains a connection to the remote object referred to by the URL.

```
public final InputStream openStream()
```
    Opens an input stream.

```
public final Object getContent()
```
    Gets the contents from this opened connection.

13.9.3 class java.net. URLConnection

Represents an active connection to an object represented by a URL. The main methods are:

```
public abstract void connect()
```
    URLConnection objects are initially created and then they are connected.

```
public URL getURL()
```
    Returns the URL for this connection.

```
public int getContentLength()
```
    Returns the content length, a -1 if not known.

```
public String getContentType()
```
    Returns the content type, a null if not known.

```
public String getContentEncoding()
```
    Returns the content encoding, a null if not known.

```
public long getExpiration()
```
    Returns the expiration date of the object, a 0 if not known.

```
public long getDate()
```
    Returns the sending date of the object, a 0 if not known.

```
public long getLastModified()
```
    Returns the last modified date of the object, a 0 if not known.

```
public String getHeaderField(String name)
```
    Returns a header field by name (name), a null if not known.

```
public Object getContent()
```
    Returns the object referred to by this URL.

```
public InputStream getInputStream()
```
    Used to read from objects.

```
public OutputStream getOutputStream()
```
    Used to write to objects.

```
public String toString()
```
   Returns the String URL representation.

13.9.4 class java.net.URLEncoder

This class converts text strings into x-www-form-urlencoded format.

```
public static String encode(String s)
```
   Translates a string (s) into x-www-form-urlencoded format.

13.9.5 class java.net.URLStreamHandler

Abstract class for URL stream openers. Subclasses of this class know how to create streams for particular protocol types.

```
protected abstract URLConnection openConnection(URL u)
```
   Opens an input stream to the object referenced by the URL (u).

```
protected void parseURL(URL u, String spec,
        int start, int limit)
```
   Parses the string (spec) into the URL (u), where start and limit refer to the range of characters in spec that should be parsed.

```
protected String toExternalForm(URL u)
```
   Reverses the parsing of the URL.

```
protected void setURL(URL u,  String protocol,String host,
        int port, String file, String ref)
```
   Calls the (protected) set method out of the URL given.

13.9.6 java.applet.AppletContext

The AppletContext can be used by an applet to obtain information from the applet's environment, which is usually the browser or the applet viewer. Related methods are:

```
public abstract void showDocument(URL url)
```
   Shows a new document.

```
public abstract void showDocument(URL url,  String target)
```
   Shows a new document in a target window or frame.

13.10 Connecting to a WWW site

Java applet 13.5 shows an example of an applet that connects to a WWW site. In this case it connects to the www.microsoft.com site.

Java applet 13.5 (⚡Java 1.1)

```java
import java.net.*;
import java.awt.*;
import java.awt.event.*;
import java.applet.*;

public class chap13_05 extends Applet implements ActionListener
{
URL     urlWWW;
Button  btn;

    public void init()
    {
        btn = (new Button("Connect to Microsoft WWW site"));
        add(btn);
        btn.addActionListener(this);
    }

    public void start()
    {
        //Check for valid URL
        try
        {
            urlWWW  = new URL("http://www.microsoft.com");
        }
        catch (MalformedURLException e)
        {
            System.out.println("URL Error: " + e);
        }
    }

    public void actionPerformed(ActionEvent evt)
    {

      if (evt.getActionCommand().equals(
              "Connect to Microsoft WWW site"))
      {
            getAppletContext().showDocument(urlWWW);
      }
    }
}
```

Figure 13.10 Sample run

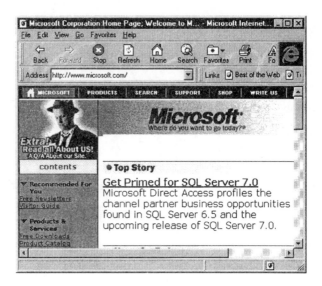

Figure 13.11 WWW connection

Java applet 13.6 extends the previous applet by allowing the user to enter a URL and it also shows a status window (status). Figures 13.12, 13.13 and 13.14 show sample runs. In Figure 13.12 the user has added an incorrect URL (www.sun.com). The status windows shows that this is an error. In Figure 13.13 the user enters a correct URL (http://www.sun.com) and Figure 13.14 show the result after the Connect button is pressed.

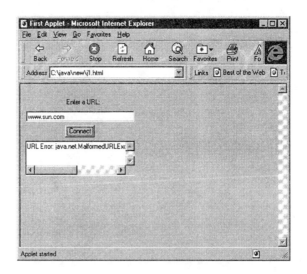

Figure 13.12 WWW connection

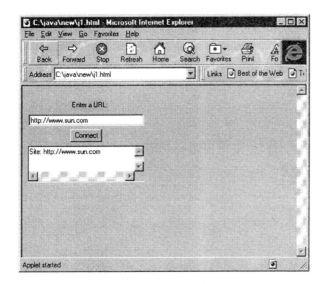

Figure 13.13 WWW connection

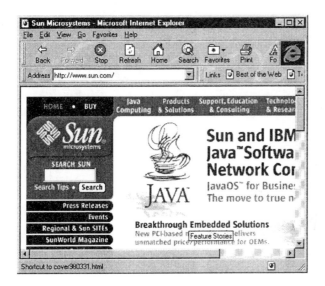

Figure 13.14 WWW connection

Java applet 13.6

```java
import java.net.*;
import java.awt.*;
import java.awt.event.*;
import java.applet.*;

public class chap13_06 extends Applet implements ActionListener
{
URL       urlWWW;
Button    btn;
Label     label = new Label("Enter a URL:");
TextField inURL = new TextField(30);
```

```
TextArea status = new TextArea(3,30);
   public void init()
   {
       add(label);
       add(inURL);
       btn = (new Button("Connect"));
       add(btn);
       add(status);
       btn.addActionListener(this);
   }
   public void getURL()//Check for valid URL
   {
       try
       {
       String str;
           str=inURL.getText();
           status.setText("Site: " + str);
           urlWWW  = new URL(str);
       }
       catch (MalformedURLException e)
       {
           status.setText("URL Error: " + e);
       }
   }

   public void actionPerformed(ActionEvent evt)
   {
   String str;
       str=evt.getActionCommand();

       if (str.equals("Connect"))
       {
           status.setText("Connecting...\n");
           getURL();
           getAppletContext().showDocument(urlWWW);
       }
   }
}
```

13.11 Exercises

13.11.1 Modify Java applet 13.4 so that it uses a text window instead of a graphic window.

13.11.2 Write a Java applet in which the user selects from one of the following pop-up menu URLs. Theses are:

www.microsoft.com   www.ibm.com
www.intel.com   www.sun.com

13.11.3 Modify the Java applet developed in Exercise 13.11.2 so that the user selects from a pull-down menu for one of the URLs. Figure 13.15 shows a sample run. Also, modify the applet so that the user enters the name of the HTML file in a text field.

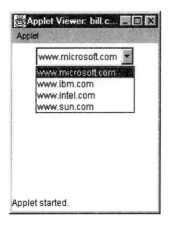

Figure 13.15 Sample run

14.1 Transmission control protocol

In the OSI model, TCP fits into the transport layer and IP fits into the network layer. TCP thus sits above IP, which means that the IP header is added onto the higher-level information (such as transport, session, presentation and application). The main functions of TCP are to provide a robust and reliable transport protocol. It is characterised as a reliable, connection-oriented, acknowledged and datastream-oriented server. IP, itself, does not support the connection of two nodes, whereas TCP does. With TCP, a connection is initially established and is then maintained for the length of the transmission.

The TCP information contains simple acknowledgement messages and a set of sequential numbers. It also supports multiple simultaneous connections using destination and source port numbers, and manages them for both transmission and reception. As with IP, it supports data fragmentation and reassembly and data multiplexing/demultiplexing.

The setup and operation of TCP is as follows:

1. When a host wishes to make a connection, TCP sends out a request message to the destination machine which contains a unique number, called a socket number and a port number. The port number has a value which is associated with the application (for example a TELNET connection has the port number 23 and an FTP connection has the port number 21). The message is then passed to the IP layer, which assembles a datagram for transmission to the destination.
2. When the destination host receives the connection request, it returns a message containing its own unique socket number and a port number. The socket number and port number thus identify the virtual connection between the two hosts.
3. After the connection has been made the data can flow between the two hosts (called a data stream).

After TCP receives the stream of data, it assembles the data into packets, called TCP segments. After the segment has been constructed, TCP adds a header (called the protocol data unit) to the front of the segment. This header contains information such as a checksum, port number, destination and source socket numbers, socket number of both machines and segment sequence numbers. The TCP layer then sends the packaged segment down to the IP layer, which encapsulates it and sends it over the network as a datagram.

14.1.1 Ports and sockets

As previously mentioned, TCP adds a port number and socket number for each host. The port number identifies the required service, whereas the socket number is a unique number for that connection. Thus a node can have several TELNET connections with the same port number but each connection will have a different socket number. A port number can be any value but there is a standard convention which most systems adopt. Table 14.1 defines some of the most common values; they are defined from 0 to 255. Port numbers above 255 can be used for unspecified applications.

Table 14.1 Typical TCP port numbers

Port	Process name	Notes
20	FTP-DATA	File Transfer Protocol - data
21	FTP	File Transfer Protocol - control
23	TELNET	Telnet
25	SMTP	Simple Mail Transfer Protocol
49	LOGIN	Login Protocol
53	DOMAIN	Domain Name Server
79	FINGER	Finger
161	SNMP	SNMP

14.1.2 TCP header format

The sender's TCP layer communicates with the receiver's TCP layer using the TCP protocol data unit. It defines parameters such as the source port, destination port, and so on, and is illustrated in Figure 14.1. The fields are:

- Source and destination port number – which are 16-bit values to identify the local port number (source number and destination port number or destination port).
- Sequence number – which identifies the current sequence number of the data segment. This allows the receiver to keep track of the data segments received. Any segments that are missing can be easily identified.
- Data offset – which is a 32-bit value and identifies the start of the data.
- Flags – the flag field is defined as UAPRSF, where U is the urgent flag, A the acknowledgement flag, P the push function, R the reset flag, S the sequence synchronise flag and F the end-of-transmission flag.
- Windows – which is a 16-bit value and gives the number of data blocks that the receiving host can accept at a time.

- Checksum – which is a 16-bit checksum for the data and header.
- UrgPtr – which is the urgent pointer and is used to identify an important area of data (most systems do not support this facility).

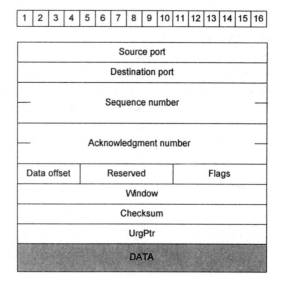

Figure 14.1 TCP header format

14.2 Socket programming

The main calls in standard socket programming are:

`socket()`   Creates a socket.
`accept()`   Accepts a connection on a socket.
`connect()`   Establishes a connection to a peer.
`bind()`   Associates a local address with a socket.
`listen()`   Establishes a socket to listen for incoming connection.
`getInputStream()`
             Gets an input data stream for a socket. This can be used to create a `receive()` method.
`getOutputStream()`
             Gets an output data stream for a socket. This can be used to create a `send()` method.
`close()`   Closes a socket.

Figure 14.2 shows the operation of a connection of a client to a server. The server is defined as the computer which waits for a connection, the client is the computer which initially makes contact with the server.

On the server the computer initially creates a socket with `socket()` method, this is bound to a name with the `bind()` method. After this the server listens for a connection with the `listen()` method. When the client calls the `connect()` method the server then accepts the connection with `accept()`. After this the server and client can send and receive data with the `send()` or `receive()` functions (these are created with the `getInputStream()` and `getOutputStream()` methods). When the data transfer is complete the `close()` method is used to close the socket.

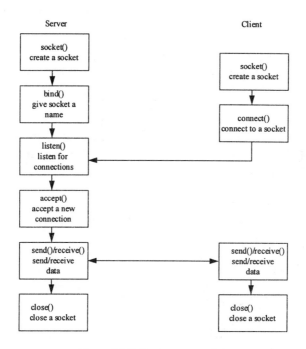

Figure 14.2 Socket connection

The implementation for `send()` and `receive()` is:

```
public static void send(Socket client,String str)
{
 try
 {
  DataOutputStream send=new DataOutputStream(client.getOutputStream());
  send.writeUTF(str);
 }
 catch (IOException e)
 {
   //something
 }
}

public static String receive(Socket client)
```

```
{
 String str="";
 try
 {
   DataInputStream receive=new DataInputStream(client.getInputStream());
   str=receive.readLine();
 }
 catch (IOException e)
 {
       //something
 }
 return str;
}
```

14.2.1 class java.net.Socket

The TCP protocol links two computers using sockets and ports. The constructors for `java.net.Socket` are:

public **Socket**(InetAddress address, int port)
> Creates a stream socket and connects it to the specified address (address) on the specified port (port).

public **Socket**(InetAddress address, int port, boolean stream)
> Creates a socket and connects it to the specified address (address) on the specified port (port). The boolean value stream indicates whether this is a stream or datagram socket.

public **Socket**(String host, int port)
> Creates a stream socket and connects it to the specified port (port) on the specified host (host).

public **Socket**(String host, int port, boolean stream)
> Creates a socket and connects it to the specified port (port) on the specified host (host). The boolean value stream indicates whether this is a stream or datagram socket.

The methods are:

public synchronized void **close**()
> Closes the socket.

public InetAddress **getInetAddress**()
> Returns the address to which the socket is connected.

public InputStream **getInputStream**()
> Returns the InputStream for this socket.

public int **getLocalPort**()
> Returns the local port to which the socket is connected.

```
public OutputStream getOutputStream()
```
Returns an OutputStream for this socket.

```
public int getPort()
```
Returns the remote port to which the socket is connected.

```
public String toString()
```
Converts the Socket to a String.

14.2.2 class java.net.SocketImpl

The SocketImpl class implements sockets. The methods are:

```
protected abstract void create(boolean stream)
```
Creates a socket where stream indicates whether the socket is a stream or a datagram.

```
protected abstract void connect(String host, int port)
```
Connects the socket to the specified port (port) on the specified host (host).

```
protected abstract void connect(InetAddress address, int port)
```
Connects the socket to the specified address (address) on the specified port (port).

```
protected abstract void bind(InetAddress host, int port)
```
Binds the socket to the specified port (port) on the specified host (host).

```
protected abstract void listen(int backlog)
```
This specifies the number of connection requests (backlog) the system will queue up while waiting to execute accept().

```
protected abstract void accept(SocketImpl s)
```
Accepts a connection (s).

```
protected abstract InputStream getInputStream()
```
Returns an InputStream for a socket.

```
protected abstract OutputStream getOutputStream()
```
Returns an OutputStream for a socket.

```
protected abstract int available()
```
Returns the number of bytes that can be read without blocking.

```
protected abstract void close()
```
Closes the socket.

```
protected InetAddress getInetAddress()

protected int getPort()

protected int getLocalPort()

public String toString()
```
Returns the address and port of this Socket as a String.

14.3   Creating a socket

Java applet 14.1 sets a constructs a socket for www.sun.com using port 4001
(`Socket remote = new Socket("www.sun.com",4001)`). After this the data
stream is created and assigned to `DataIn`. The `readln()` method is then used
to get the text from the stream.

📖   Java applet 14.1

```
import java.io.*;
import java.net.*;
import java.awt.*;
import jacva.applet.*;

public class chap14_01 extends Applet
{

 public void init()
 {

 String      Instr;
 InputStream  Instream;

     try
     {
         Socket remote = new Socket("www.sun.com",4001);
         Instream = remote.getInputStream();
         DataInputStream DataIn = new DataInputStream(Instream);

         do
         {

             Instr = DataIn.readLine();
             if (Instr!=null)  System.out.println(str);
         } while (Instr!=null);
     }
     catch (UnknownHostException err)
     {
         System.out.println("UNKNOWN HOST: "+err);
     }
     catch (IOException err)
     {
         System.out.println("Error" + err); }
     }
 }
}
```

Java program 14.2 contacts a server on a given port and returns the local and remote port. It uses command line arguments where the program is run in the form:

```
java chap14_01 host port
```

where java is the Java interpreter, chap14_01 is the name of the class file, *host* is the name of the host to contact and *port* is the port to use. The args.length parameter is used to determine the number of command line options, anything other than two will display the following message:

```
Usage : chap14_01 host port
```

📖 Java program 14.2

```java
import java.net.*;
import java.io.*;

public class chap14_02
{
 public static void main (String args[])
  {
   if (args.length !=2)
    System.out.println(" Usage : chap14_01 host port");

   else
   {
    String inp;
    try
    {
     Socket sock = new Socket(args[0], Integer.valueOf(args[1]).intValue());
     DataInputStream is = new DataInputStream(sock.getInputStream());

     System.out.println("address : " + sock.getInetAddress());
     System.out.println("port : " + sock.getPort());
     System.out.println("Local address : " + sock.getLocalAddress());
     System.out.println("Localport : " + sock.getLocalPort());

     while((inp = is.readLine()) != null)
     { System.out.println(inp);}
    }
    catch (UnknownHostException e)
    {
     System.out.println(" Known Host : " + e.getMessage());
    }
    catch (IOException e)
    {
     System.out.println("error I/O : " + e.getMessage());
    }
    finally
    {
     System.out.println("End of program");
    }
   }
  }
}
```

Test run 14.1 shows a test run which connects to port 13 on `www.eece.napier.ac.uk`. It can be seen that the connection to this port causes the server to return back the current date and time. Test run 14.2 connects into the same server, in this case on port 19. It can be seen that a connection to this port returns a sequence of characters.

🖳 **Test run 14.1**
```
>> java chap14_02 www.eece.napier.ac.uk 13
Host and IP address : www.eece.napier.ac.uk/146.176.151.139
port : 13
Local address :pc419.eece.napier.ac.uk
Localport : 1393
Fri May  8 13:19:59 1998
End of program
```

🖳 **Test run 14.2**
```
>> java chap14_02 www.eece.napier.ac.uk 19
Host and IP address : www.eece.napier.ac.uk/146.176.151.139
port : 19
Local IP address :pc419.eece.napier.ac.uk
Localport : 1403
 !"#$%&'()*+,-./0123456789:;<=>?@ABCDEFGHIJKLMNOPQRSTUVWXYZ[\]^_`abcdefg
!"#$%&'()*+,-./0123456789:;<=>?@ABCDEFGHIJKLMNOPQRSTUVWXYZ[\]^_`abcdefgh
"#$%&'()*+,-./0123456789:;<=>?@ABCDEFGHIJKLMNOPQRSTUVWXYZ[\]^_`abcdefghi
#$%&'()*+,-./0123456789:;<=>?@ABCDEFGHIJKLMNOPQRSTUVWXYZ[\]^_`abcdefghij
$%&'()*+,-./0123456789:;<=>?@ABCDEFGHIJKLMNOPQRSTUVWXYZ[\]^_`abcdefghijk
%&'()*+,-./0123456789:;<=>?@ABCDEFGHIJKLMNOPQRSTUVWXYZ[\]^_`abcdefghijkl
&'()*+,-./0123456789:;<=>?@ABCDEFGHIJKLMNOPQRSTUVWXYZ[\]^_`abcdefghijklm
'()*+,-./0123456789:;<=>?@ABCDEFGHIJKLMNOPQRSTUVWXYZ[\]^_`abcdefghijklmn
()*+,-./0123456789:;<=>?@ABCDEFGHIJKLMNOPQRSTUVWXYZ[\]^_`abcdefghijklmno
)*+,-./0123456789:;<=>?@ABCDEFGHIJKLMNOPQRSTUVWXYZ[\]^_`abcdefghijklmnop
*+,-./0123456789:;<=>?@ABCDEFGHIJKLMNOPQRSTUVWXYZ[\]^_`abcdefghijklmnopq
+,-./0123456789:;<=>?@ABCDEFGHIJKLMNOPQRSTUVWXYZ[\]^_`abcdefghijklmnopqr
,-./0123456789:;<=>?@ABCDEFGHIJKLMNOPQRSTUVWXYZ[\]^_`abcdefghijklmnopqrs
-./0123456789:;<=>?@ABCDEFGHIJKLMNOPQRSTUVWXYZ[\]^_`abcdefghijklmnopqrst
./0123456789:;<=>?@ABCDEFGHIJKLMNOPQRSTUVWXYZ[\]^_`abcdefghijklmnopqrstu
/0123456789:;<=>?@ABCDEFGHIJKLMNOPQRSTUVWXYZ[\]^_`abcdefghijklmnopqrstuv
0123456789:;<=>?@ABCDEFGHIJKLMNOPQRSTUVWXYZ[\]^_`abcdefghijklmnopqrstuvw
123456789:;<=>?@ABCDEFGHIJKLMNOPQRSTUVWXYZ[\]^_`abcdefghijklmnopqrstuvwx
```

14.4 Client/server program

A server is a computer which runs a special program which waits for another computer (a client) to connect to it. This server normally performs some sort of special operation, such as:

- File Transfer Protocol. Transferring files
- Telnet. Remote connection
- WWW service

Java program 14.3 acts as a server program and waits for a connection on port 1111. When a connection is received on this port it sends its current date and time back to the client. This program can be run with Java program 14.2 (which is running on a remote computer) with a connection to the server's IP address (or domain name) and using port 1111. When the client connects to the server, the server responds back to the client with its current date and time.

Test run 14.3 shows a sample run from the server (NOTE THE SERVER PROGRAM MUST BE RUN BEFORE THE CLIENT IS STARTED). It can be seen that it has received connection from the client with the IP address of 146.176.150.120 (Test run 14.4 shows the client connection).

Java program 14.3

```
import java.net.*;
import java.io.*;
import java.util.*;

class chap14_03
{
 public static void main( String arg[])
  {
   try
   {
    ServerSocket sock = new ServerSocket(1111);
    Socket sock1 = sock.accept();

    System.out.println(sock1.toString());
    System.out.println("address : " + sock1.getInetAddress());
    System.out.println("port    : " + sock1.getPort());

    DataOutputStream out = new DataOutputStream(sock1.getOutputStream());

    out.writeBytes("Welcome "+ sock1.getInetAddress().getHostName()+
         ". We are "+ new Date()+ "\n");

    sock1.close();
    sock.close();
   }
   catch(IOException err)
   {
    System.out.println(err.getMessage());
   }
   finally
   {
    System.out.println("End of the program");
   }
  }
}
```

Test run 14.3 (Server)
```
>> java chap14_03
address : pc419.eece.napier.ac.uk/146.176.151.130
port : 1111
End of program
```

```
>> java chap14_02 146.176.150.120 1111
Host and IP address : pc419.eece.napier.ac.uk/146.176.151.130
port : 1111
Local address :pc419.eece.napier.ac.uk
Localport : 1393
Fri May  8 13:19:59 1998
End of program
```

14.5 Exercises

14.5.1 Using Java program 14.2 connect to some WWW servers. Try different port values.

14.5.2 Find two computers which can be connected over TCP/IP. Determine their IP addresses (or DNS) and connect them over a network.

14.5.3 Connect two computers over a network and set up a chat connection. One of the computers should be the chat server and the other the chat client. Modify it so that the server accepts calls from one or many clients.

14.6 Project

Develop a Java program which has send and receive text windows. The program should allow the user to specify the IP address (or DNS) of the server. The send and receive windows will then show the text sent and received.

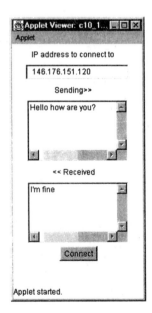

15 Multithreading

15.1 Introduction

Multitasking involves running several tasks at the same time. It normally involves each task running on a process for a given amount of time, before it is released and another process is given some time. There are two forms of multitasking, these are:

- Pre-emptive multitasking. This type involves the operating system controlling how long a process stays on the processor. This allows for smooth multitasking and is used in Windows NT/95 32-bit programs.
- Co-operative multitasking. This type of multitasking relies on a process giving up the processor. It is used with Windows 3.1 programs and suffers from processor hogging, where a process can stay on a processor and the operating system cannot kick it off.

The logical extension to multitasking programs is to split programs into a number a parts (threads) and running each of these on the multitasking system (multithreading). A program which is running more than one thread at a time is known as a multithreaded program. Multithreaded programs have many advantages over non-multithreaded programs, including:

- They make better use of the processor, where different threads can be run when one or more threads are waiting for data. For example a thread could be waiting for keyboard input, while another thread could be searching the Internet for information.
- They are easier to test, where each thread can be tested independently of other threads.
- They can use standard threads, which are optimised for a given hardware.

They also have disadvantages, including:

- The program has to be planned properly so that threads must know on which threads they depend on.
- A thread may wait indefinitely for another thread has which crashed.

The main difference between multiple processes and multiple threads is that each process has independent variables and data, while multiple threads share data from the main program.

15.2 Threads class

The `java.lang.Thread` class implements one or more threads. A thread is typically constructed with:

```
Thread proc=null;

    proc = new Thread(this);
```

where *proc* defines the name of the thread. The main methods that can be applied to the thread are:

```
public void destroy();
public void interrupt();
public static boolean interrupted();
public final boolean isAlive();
public final boolean isDaemon();
public boolean isInterrupted();
public final void resume();
public void run();
public final void setDaemon(boolean on);
public static void sleep(long millis);
public void start();
public final void stop();
public final void stop(Throwable obj);
public final void suspend();
public static void yield();
```

The `start()` method starts the thread and the `stop()` method stops it. The `sleep()` method suspends the thread for a number of milliseconds. For example to suspend a thread of 0.5 seconds and then stop it, the following can be used:

```
Thread proc = null;

    proc = new Thread(this);
    proc.start();
    proc.sleep(500);
    proc.stop();
```

Java applet 15.1 implements a basic time and date display. The thread is initially started with:

```
mytimer = new Thread(this);
    mytimer.start();
```

The timer routine is contained within run(), with:

```
try {   mytimer.sleep(1000); }
catch (InterruptedException e) {}
repaint();
```

The `sleep(1000)` method causes the thread to suspend for 1 second (1000 milliseconds). After this `paint()` is called, which implements:

```
g.setColor(getBackground());

if (lastdate!=null)
        g.drawString(lastdate, 5, 40);

g.setColor(Color.darkGray);
g.drawString(today, 5, 40);
lastdate = today;
```

This sets the drawing colour to the background colour (typically either white or grey). The previous time and date string is then erased from the screen. Next the text colour is changed to dark grey and the new date and time is then re-drawn.

📖 Java applet 15.1

```
import java.util.*;
import java.awt.*;
import java.applet.*;

public class chap15_01 extends Applet
                    implements Runnable
{
Thread mytimer = null;
String lastdate = null;

    public void paint(Graphics g)
    {
    String today;
    Date ddd = new Date();

    today = ddd.toLocaleString();

    g.setFont(new Font("TimesRoman",
            Font.BOLD, 22));

    // Erase and redraw time
    g.setColor(getBackground());

    if (lastdate!=null)
        g.drawString(lastdate, 5, 40);

    g.setColor(Color.darkGray);
    g.drawString(today, 5, 40);
    lastdate = today;
    }
```

```
public void start()
{
  if(mytimer == null)
  {
     mytimer = new Thread(this);
     mytimer.start();
  }
}

public void stop()
{
    mytimer = null;
}

public void run()
{
  while (mytimer != null)
  {
     try {mytimer.sleep(1000);}
     catch (InterruptedException e){}
     repaint();
  }
  mytimer = null;
  }
}
```

Java applet 15.2 uses the `suspend()`, `resume()` and `stop()` methods to suspend, resume (after a suspend) and stop a thread, respectively.

📖 Java applet 15.2

```
import java.util.*;
import java.awt.*;
import java.applet.*;

public class chap15_02 extends Applet
        implements Runnable
{
Thread mytimer = null;
String lastdate = null;
Button dstart= new Button("Start");
Button dsus=new Button("Suspend");
Button dend=new Button("Stop");
Button quit=new Button("Quit");

  public void init()
  {
     add(dstart);
     add(dsus);
     add(dend);
     add(quit);
  }

  public boolean action(Event evt,
      Object obj)
  {
     if (evt.target.equals(dstart))
          mytimer.resume();
     else if (evt.target.equals(dsus))
          mytimer.suspend();
     else if (evt.target.equals(dend))
```

```
                mytimer.stop();
        else if (evt.target.equals(quit))
        {
                    mytimer=null;
                    System.exit(0);
        }
        return true;
    }

    public void paint(Graphics g)
    {
     String today;
     Date ddd = new Date();

        today = ddd.toLocaleString();

        g.setFont(new Font("TimesRoman",
                Font.BOLD, 22));

         // Erase and redraw time
        g.setColor(getBackground());

        if (lastdate!=null)
          g.drawString(lastdate, 5, 40);

        g.setColor(Color.darkGray);
        g.drawString(today, 5, 80);
        lastdate = today;
    }

    public void start()
    {
      if(mytimer == null)
      {
        mytimer = new Thread(this);
        mytimer.start();
      }
    }

    public void stop()
    {
        mytimer = null;
    }

    public void run()
    {
        while (mytimer != null)
        {
          try {mytimer.sleep(1000);}
          catch (InterruptedException e){}
          repaint();
        }
        mytimer = null;
      }
}
```

Note that a general purpose delay method can be constructed as follows:

```
    public void delay(int ms)
    {
        try {mytimer.sleep(ms);}
        catch (InterruptedException e){}
    }
```

which will delay the thread by a number of milliseconds (ms). This could be used as follows:

```
public void run()
{
    while (mytimer != null)
    {
        delay(2000);   // Delay for 2 seconds (2000 ms)
        repaint();
    }
    mytimer = null;
}
```

15.3 Simple animation

The previous Java applet can be modified so that it can display an animated object. In Java applet 15.3 an oval graphic is randomly moved around the screen. Each update is 100 ms and the object will be constrained with a (0, 0) to (200, 200) window. The 100 ms delay is set up with:

```
delay(100);   // try {mytimer.sleep(100);}
```

and the graphic is constrained with:

```
if ( x>200) x=200;        if ( y>200) y=200;
if ( x<0 )  x=0;          if ( y<0 )  y=0;
```

As before (in applet 15.2) the graphic is erased from the window by drawing it with the background colour of the window, then redrawing it with a blue colour.

📖 Java applet 15.3
```
import java.util.*;
import java.awt.*;
import java.applet.*;

public class chap15_03 extends Applet
            implements Runnable
{
Thread timer = null;
int x=0,y=0;

  public void paint(Graphics g)
  {
     g.setColor(getBackground());
     g.fillOval(x,y,20,10);

     x+=(Math.random()*10)-5;
     y+=(Math.random()*10)-5;

     if ( x>200) x=200;
```

```
   if ( y>200) y=200;
   if ( x<0 )  x=0;
   if ( y<0 )  y=0;

   g.setColor(Color.blue);
   g.fillOval(x,y,20,10);
 }

 public void start()
 {
  if(timer == null)
  {
     timer = new Thread(this);
     timer.start();
  }
 }

 public void stop()
 {
    timer = null;
 }

 public void run()
 {
    while (timer != null)
    {
       delay(100); // wait 100 ms
       repaint();
    }
    timer = null;
 }

 public void delay(int ms)
 {
   try {timer.sleep(ms);}
   catch (InterruptedException e){}
 }
}
```

Java applet 15.4 is similar to the previous applet but the image now has three ovals and two lines. The oval and line drawing have also been put into `alien()`. This is called when the image is erased (with the background colour set) and then to draw it again in blue.

📖 **Java applet 15.4**

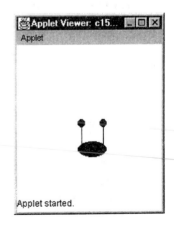

```
import java.util.*;
import java.awt.*;
import java.applet.*;

public class chap15_04 extends Applet
      implements Runnable
{
Thread  timer = null;
int     x=100,y=100;//put alien in middle of
                    //screen

  public void paint(Graphics g)
  {
    g.setColor(getBackground());
    alien(g);

    x+=(Math.random()*10)-5;
```

```
    y+=(Math.random()*10)-5;

    if ( x>200) x=200;    if ( y>200) y=200;
    if ( x<0 )  x=0;      if ( y<0 )  y=0;

    g.setColor(Color.blue);
    alien(g);
}

public void alien(Graphics g)
{
    g.fillOval(x,y,10,10);
    g.fillOval(x+30,y,10,10);
    g.fillOval(x,y+30,40,20);
    g.drawLine(x+5,y+10,x+5,y+35);
    g.drawLine(x+35,y+10,x+35,y+35);
}

public void start()
{
  if(timer == null)
  {
    timer = new Thread(this);
    timer.start();
  }
}

public void stop()
{
    timer = null;
}
public void run()
{
  while (timer != null)
  {
     delay(100); // wait 100 ms
     repaint();
  }
  timer = null;
}

public void delay(int ms)
{
  try {timer.sleep(ms);}
  catch (InterruptedException e){}
}
}
```

15.4 Exercises

15.4.1   Modify Java applet 15.2 so that it checks that the thread is suspended before it resumes it.

15.4.2   Modify Java applet 15.1 so that it displays the time as local time and as GMT. Also modify it so that it displays the date to a text field, rather than a graphics window.

15.4.3 Modify Java applet 15.1 so that it displays a 'TICK' message beside the date and time which blinks on for one second and then off for the next second, and so on.

A possible implement is to set up a flag (such as `tflag`) which is toggled in `paint()`, such as:

```
boolean tflag=true;

paint()
{
    . . .

    if (tflag==true) tflag=false; else tflag=true;

    if (tglag==true)
        lastdate+" TICK";

    . . .
}
```

15.4.4 Modify Java applet 15.3 so that it initially draws the graphic object in the centre of the window (Hint: modify the initialisation values of x and y).

15.4.5 Modify Java applet 15.3 so that the user can select the step increment of the movement. This increment is set to +/– 5 in applet 15.3, that is:

```
y+=(Math.random()*10)-5; x+=(Math.random()*10)-5;
```

The entered value should be set from a pop-up menu.

15.4.6 Write a Java applet which displays a small blue circle which randomly moves around the screen and leaves a red trail. (Hint: draw the circle in blue and then erase it with red.)

15.4.7 Modify Java applet 15.4 so that it draws the alien invader given below.

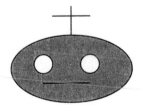

15.4.8 Modify the `delay` method in Java applet 15.3 so that it automatically initiates the `timer` thread (Hint: delete the `start` method and test `timer` to see if it is a `null`. If it is start the thread.)

15.5 Project

Develop a Java applet which displays nine GIF images with a given time delay between displays. The applet should have a play button and a stop button. The stop button should exit the applet and the play button should be used to start the display of the nine images. The graphics files should be named img001.gif, img002.gif ... img009.gif. An outline of the code is as follows:

```
Image    pic;
String   fname;

    // within event handler when play is pressed
    for (i=0;  i<10;i++)
    {
        fname="img00"+i+".gif";
        delay(1000);  // wait 1 second
        pic=getImage(getCodeBase(),fname);
        paint();
    }

  public void paint(Graphics g)
  {
     g.drawImage(pic,0,0,this);
  }
```

Modify the project so that the delay time is variable and can be increased or decreased with a faster and a slower button.

A Introduction to HTML

A.1 Introduction

HTML is a standard hypertext language for the WWW and has several different versions. Most WWW browsers support HTML 2 and most of the new versions of the browsers support HTML 3. WWW pages are created and edited with a text editor, a word processor or, as is becoming more common, within the WWW browser.

HTML tags contain special formatting commands and are contained within a less than (<) and a greater than (>) symbol (which are also known as angled brackets). Most tags have an opening and closing version; for example, to highlight bold text the bold opening tag is <B> and the closing tag is </B>. Table A.1 outlines a few examples.

Table A.1 Example HTML tags

Open tag	Closing tag	Description
<HTML>	</HTML>	Start and end of HTML
<HEAD>	</HEAD>	Defines the HTML header
<BODY>	</BODY>	Defines the main body of the HTML
<TITLE>	</TITLE>	Defines the title of the WWW page
<I>	</I>	Italic text
<B>	</B>	Bold text
<U>	</U>	Underlined text
<BLINK>	</BLINK>	Make text blink
<EM>	</EM>	Emphasise text
<FONT SIZE=+1>	</FONT>	Increase font size by one increment
<FONT SIZE=-1>	</FONT>	Reduce font size by one increment
<CENTER>	</CENTER>	Centre text
<H1>	</H1>	Section header, level 1
<H2>	</H2>	Section header, level 2
<H3>	</H3>	Section header, level 3
<P>		Create a new paragraph
 		Create a line break
<!-->	-->	Comments
<SUPER>	</SUPER>	Superscript
_		Subscript

HTML script 1 gives an example script and Figure A.1 shows the output from the WWW browser. The first line is always <HTML> and the last line is

</HTML>. After this line the HTML header is defined between <HEAD> and </HEAD>. The title of the window in this case is My first HTML page. The main HTML text is then defined between <BODY> and </BODY>.

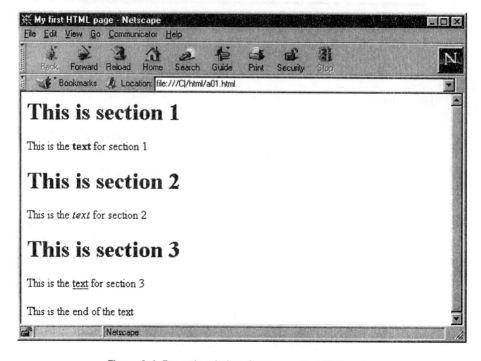

Figure A.1 Example window from example HTML script

📖 HTML script A.1

```
<HTML>
<HEAD>
<TITLE>My first HTML page</TITLE>
</HEAD>
<BODY>
<H1> This is section 1</H1>
This is the <b>text</b> for section 1
<H1> This is section 2</H1>
This is the <i>text</i> for section 2
<H1> This is section 3</H1>
This is the <u>text</u> for section 3
<p>
This is the end of the text
</BODY>
</HTML>
```

The WWW browser fits text into the window size and does not interpret line breaks in the HTML source. To force a new line the
 (line break) or a new paragraph (<P>) is used. The example also shows bold, italic and underlined text.

A.2 Links

The topology of the WWW is set-up using links where pages link to other related pages. A reference takes the form:

```
<A HREF="url"> Reference Name </A>
```

where *url* defines the URL for the file, *Reference Name* is the name of the reference and </A> defines the end of the reference name. HTML script A.2 shows an example of the uses of references and Figure A.2 shows a sample browser page. The background colour is set using the <BODY BGCOLOR="#FFFFFF"> which sets the background colour to white. In this case the default text colour is black and the link is coloured blue.

📖 HTML script A.2

```
<HTML>

<HEAD>
<TITLE>Fred's page</TITLE>
</HEAD>

<BODY BGCOLOR="#FFFFFF">

<H1>Fred's Home Page</H1>

If you want to access information on
this book <A HREF="softbook.html">click here</A>.

<P>

A reference to the <A REF="http:www.iee.com/">IEE</A>

</BODY>
</HTML>
```

A.2.1 Other links

Links can be set-up to send to e-mail addresses and newsgroups. For example:

```
<A HREF="news:sport.tennis"> Newsgroups for tennis</A>
```

to link to a tennis newsgroup and

```
<A HREF="mailto:f.bloggs@fredco.co.uk">Send a message to me</A>
```

to send a mail message to the e-mail address: f.bloggs@ fredco.co.uk.

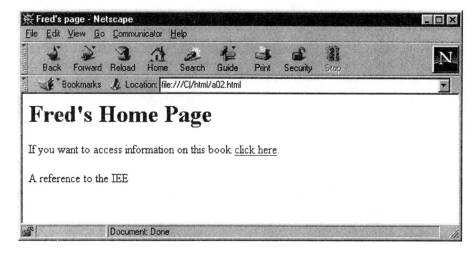

Figure A.2 Example window from example HTML script A.2

HTML allows ordered and unordered lists. Lists can be declared anywhere in the body of the HTML.

A.3.1 Ordered lists

The start of an ordered list is defined with <OL> and the end of the list by </OL>. Each part of the list is defined after the <LI> tag. Unordered lists are defined between the <UL> and </UL> tags. HTML script A.3 gives examples of an ordered and an unordered list. Figure A.3 shows the output from the browser.

📖 HTML script A.3

```
<HTML><HEAD><TITLE>Fred's page</TITLE></HEAD>
<BODY BGCOLOR="#FFFFFF">
<H1>List 1</H1>
<OL>
<LI>Part 1
<LI>Part 2
<LI>Part 3
</OL>
<H1>List 2</H1>
<UL>
<LI>Section 1
<LI>Section 2
<LI>Section 3
</UL>
</BODY></HTML>
```

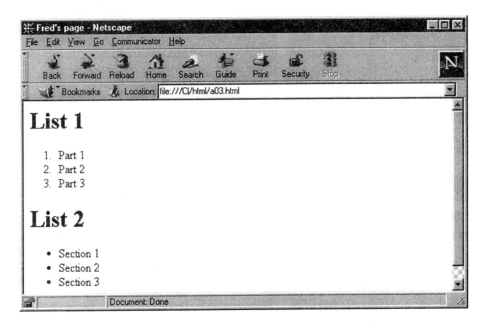

Figure A.3 WWW browser with an ordered and unordered lists

Some browsers allow the type of numbered list to be defined with the <OL TYPE=x>, where x can either be:

- A for capital letters (such as A, B, C, and so on).
- a for small letters (such as a, b, c, and so on).
- I for capital roman letters (such as I, II, III, and so on).
- i for small roman letters (such as i, ii, iii, and so on).
- I for numbers (which is the default).

```
<OL Type=I>
<LI> List 1
<LI> List 2
<LI> List 3
</OL>

<OL Type=A>
<LI> List 1
<LI> List 2
<LI> List 3
</OL>
```

would be displayed as:

I.   List 1
II.   List 2
III.   List 3

A.   List 1
B.   List 2
C.   List 3

The starting number of the list can be defined using the `<LI VALUE=n>` where *n* defines the initial value of the defined item list.

A.3.2 Unordered lists

Unordered lists are used to list a series of items in no particular order. They are defined between the `<UL>` and `</UL>` tags. Some browsers allow the type of bullet point to be defined with the `<LI TYPE=shape>`, where *shape* can either be:

- *disc* for round solid bullets (which is the default for first level lists).
- *round* for round hollow bullets (which is the default for second level lists).
- *square* for square bullets (which is the default for third).

HTML script A.4 gives an example of an unnumbered list and Figure A.4 shows the WWW page output for this script. It can be seen from this that the default bullets for level 1 lists are discs, for level 2 they are round and for level 3 they are square.

📖 HTML script A.4

```
<HTML><HEAD><TITLE>Example list</TITLE></HEAD>
<H1> Introduction </H1>
<UL>
<LI> OSI Model
<LI> Networks
  <UL>
  <LI> Ethernet
      <UL>
      <LI> MAC addresses
      </UL>
  <LI> Token Ring
  <LI> FDDI
  </UL>
<LI> Conclusion
</UL>
<H1> Wide Area Networks </H1>
<UL>
<LI> Standards
<LI> Examples
  <UL>
  <LI> EastMan
  </UL>
<LI> Conclusion
</UL>
</BODY>
</HTML>
```

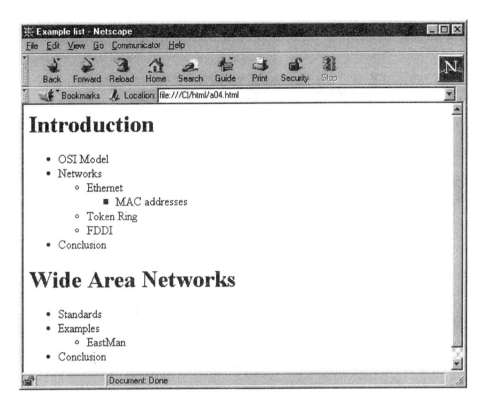

Figure A.4 WWW page with an unnumbered list

A.3.3 Definition lists

HTML uses the `<DL>` and `</DL>` tags for definition lists. These are normally used when building glossaries. Each entry in the definition is defined by the `<DT>` tag and the text associated with the item is defined after the `<DD>` tag. The end of the list is defined by `</DL>`. HTML script A.5 shows an example with a definition list and Figure A.5 gives a sample output. Note that it uses the `<EM>` tag to emphasise the definition subject.

📖 HTML script A.5

```
<HTML><HEAD><TITLE>Example list</TITLE></HEAD>
<H1> Glossary </H1>
<DL>
<DT> <EM> Address Resolution Protocol (ARP) </EM>
<DD> A TCP/IP process which maps an IP address to an Ethernet
address.
<DT> <EM> American National Standards Institute (ANSI) </EM>
<DD> ANSI is a non-profit organization which is made up of ex-
pert committees that publish standards for national industries.
<DT> <EM> American Standard Code for Information Interchange
(ASCII) </EM>
```

```
<DD> An ANSI-defined character alphabet which has since been
adopted as a standard international alphabet for the interchange
of characters.
</DL></BODY></HTML>
```

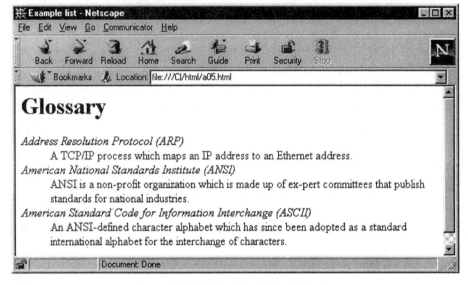

Figure A.5 WWW page with definition list

A.4 Colours

Colours in HTML are defined in the RGB (red/green/blue) strength. The format is `#rrggbb`, where `rr` is the hexadecimal equivalent for the red component, `gg` the hexadecimal equivalent for the green component and `bb` the hexadecimal equivalent for the blue component. Table A.2 lists some of the codes for certain colours.

Individual hexadecimal numbers use base 16 and range from `0` to `F` (in decimal this ranges from 0 to 15). A two-digit hexadecimal number ranges from `00` to `FF` (in decimal this ranges from 0 to 255). Table A.3 outlines hexadecimal equivalents.

Table A.2 Hexadecimal colours

Colour	Code	Colour	Code
White	#FFFFFF	Dark red	#C91F16
Light red	#DC640D	Orange	#F1A60A
Yellow	#FCE503	Light green	#BED20F
Dark green	#088343	Light blue	#009DBE
Dark blue	#0D3981	Purple	#3A0B59
Pink	#F3D7E3	Nearly black	#434343
Dark grey	#777777	Grey	#A7A7A7
Light grey	#D4D4D4	Black	#000000

Table A.3 Hexadecimal to decimal conversions

Hex.	Dec.	Hex.	Dec.	Hex.	Dec.	Hex.	Dec.
0	0	1	1	2	2	3	3
4	4	5	5	6	6	7	7
8	8	9	9	A	10	B	11
C	12	D	13	E	14	F	15

HTML uses percentage strengths for the colours. For example, FF represents full strength (100%) and 00 represent no strength (0%). Thus, white is made from FF (red), FF (green) and FF (blue) and black is made from 00 (red), 00 (green) and 00 (blue). Grey is made from equal weighting of each of the colours, such as 43, 43, 43 for dark grey (#434343) and D4, D4 and D4 for light grey (#D4D4D4). Thus, pure red with be #FF0000, pure green will be #00FF00 and pure blue with be #0000FF.

Each colour is represented by 8 bits, thus the colour is defined by 24 bits. This gives a total of 16 777 216 colours (2^{24} different colours). Note that some video displays will not have enough memory to display 16.777 million colours in a certain mode so that colours may differ depending on the WWW browser and the graphics adapter.

The colours of the background, text and the link can be defined with the BODY tag. An example with a background colour of white, a text colour of orange and a link colour of dark red is:

```
<BODY BGCOLOR="#FFFFFF" TEXT="#F1A60A"  LINK="#C91F16">
```

and for a background colour of red, a text colour of green and a link colour of blue:

```
<BODY BGCOLOR="#FF0000" TEXT="#00FF00"  LINK="#0000FF">
```

When a link has been visited its colour changes. This colour itself can be changed with the VLINK. For example, to set-up a visited link colour of yellow:

```
<BODY VLINK="#FCE503" "TEXT=#00FF00"  "LINK=#0000FF">
```

Note that the default link colours are:

Link: #0000FF   (Blue)
Visited link: #FF00FF   (Purple)

Images (such as GIF and JPEG) can be used as a background to a WWW page. For this purpose the option BACKGROUND='*src.gif*' is added to the <BODY> tag. An HTML script with a background of CLOUDS.GIF is given in HTML script A.6. A sample output from a browser is shown in Figure A.6.

📖 HTML script A.6

```
<HTML><HEAD><TITLE>Fred's page</TITLE></HEAD>
<BODY BACKGROUND="clouds.gif">
<H1>Fred's Home Page</H1>
If you want to access information on
this book <A HREF="gbook.html">click here</A>.<P>
A reference to the <A HREF="http://www.iee.com/">IEE</A>
</BODY></HTML>
```

Figure A.6 WWW page with CLOUDS.GIF as a background

A.6   Displaying images

WWW pages can support graphics images within a page. The most common sources of images are either JPEG or GIF files, as these types of images normally have a high degree of compression. GIF images, as was previously mentioned, support only 256 colours from a pallet of 16.7 million colours, whereas JPEG supports more than 256 colours.

A.6.1 Inserting an image

Images can be displayed within a page with the `<IMG SRC='src.gif'>` which inserts the graphic *src.gif*. HTML script A.7 contains three images: `mypic1.jpg`, `me.gif` and `mypic2.jpg`. These are aligned either to the left or the right using the `ALIGN` option within the `<IMG SRC>` tag. The first image (`mypic1.jpg`) is aligned to the right, while the second image (`mypic2.jpg`) is aligned to the left. Figure A.7 shows a sample output from this script. Note that images are left aligned by default.

📖 HTML script A.7

```
<HTML><HEAD>
<TITLE>My first home page</TITLE>
</HEAD>
<BODY BGCOLOR="#ffffff">
<IMG SRC ="mypic1.jpg" width=120 ALIGN=RIGHT>
<H1> Picture gallery </H1>
<P><P>
Here are a few pictures of me and my family. To the right
is a picture of my sons taken in the garden. Below to the
left is a picture of my two youngest sons under an
umbrella and to the right is a picture of me taken in my office.
<P>
<IMG SRC ="mypic2.jpg" ALIGN=LEFT width=200>
<IMG SRC ="me.gif" ALIGN=RIGHT width=300>
</BODY></HTML>
```

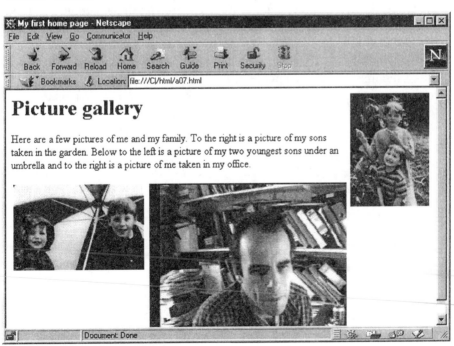

Figure A.7 WWW page with three images

A.6.2 Alternative text

Often users choose not to view images in a page and select an option on the viewer which stops the viewer from displaying any graphic images. If this is the case then the HTML page can contain substitute text which is shown instead of the image. For example:

```
<IMG SRC ="mypic1.jpg" ALT="In garden" ALIGN=RIGHT>
<IMG SRC ="mypic2.jpg" ALT="Under umbrella" ALIGN=LEFT>
<IMG SRC ="me.gif" ALT="Picture of me" ALIGN=RIGHT>
```

A.6.3 Other options

Other image options can be added, such as:

- HSPACE=x VSPACE=y defines the amount of space that should be left around images. The x value defines the number of pixels in the x-direction and the y value defines the number of pixels in the y-direction.
- WIDTH= x HEIGHT=y defines the scaling in the x- and y-direction, where x and y are the desired pixel width and height, respectively, of the image.
- ALIGN=*direction* defines the alignment of the image. This can be used to align an image with text. Valid options for aligning with text are *texttop*, *top*, *middle*, *absmiddle*, *bottom*, *baseline* or *absbottom*. HTML script A.8 shows an example of image alignment with the image a.gif (which is just the letter 'A' as a graphic) and Figure A.8 shows a sample output. It can be seen that *texttop* aligns the image with highest part of the text on the line, *top* aligns the image with the highest element in the line, *middle* aligns with the middle of the image with the baseline, *absmiddle* aligns the middle of the image with the middle of the largest item, *bottom* aligns the bottom of the image with the bottom of the text and *absbottom* aligns the bottom of the image with the bottom of the largest item.

📖 HTML script A.8

```
<HTML>
<HEAD>
<TITLE>My first home page</TITLE>
</HEAD>
<BODY BGCOLOR="#ffffff">
<IMG SRC ="a.gif" ALIGN=texttop>pple<P>
<IMG SRC ="a.gif" ALIGN=top>pple<P>
<IMG SRC ="a.gif" ALIGN=middle>pple<P>
<IMG SRC ="a.gif" ALIGN=bottom>pple<P>
<IMG SRC ="a.gif" ALIGN=baseline>pple<P>
<IMG SRC ="a.gif" ALIGN=absbottom>pple
</BODY>
</HTML>
```

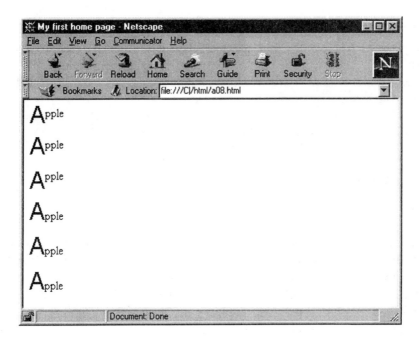

Figure A.8 WWW page showing image alignment

A.7 Horizontal lines

A horizontal line can be added with the <HR> tag. Most browsers allow extra parameters, such as:

SIZE= *n* – which defines that the height of the rule is *n* pixels.
WIDTH=*w* – which defines that the width of the rule is *w* pixels or as a percentage.
ALIGN=*direction* – where direction refers to the alignment of the rule. Valid options for *direction* are *left*, *right* or *center*.
NOSHADE – which defines that the line should be solid with no shading.

HTML script A.9 gives some example horizontal lines and Figure A.9 shows an example output.

📖 HTML script A.9

```
<HTML><HEAD><TITLE>My first home page</TITLE></HEAD>
<BODY BGCOLOR="#ffffff">
<IMG SRC ="a.gif">pple<P>
<HR>
<IMG SRC ="a.gif">pple<P>
```

```
<HR WIDTH=50% ALIGN=CENTER>
<IMG SRC ="a.gif">pple<P>
<HR SIZE=10 NOSHADE>
</BODY></HTML>
```

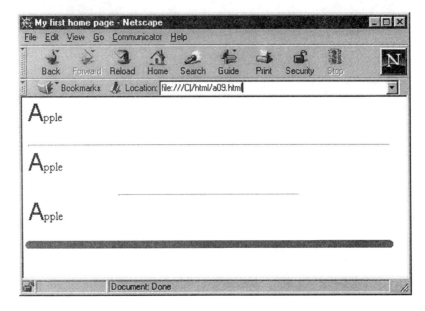

Figure A.9 WWW page showing horizontal lines

A.8   Exercises

A.8.1   The home page for this book can be found at the URL:

http://www.eece.napier.ac.uk/~bill_b/java.hmtl

Access this page and follow any links it contains.

A.8.2   If possible, create a WWW page with the following blinking text:

This is some blinking text

A.8.3   The last part of the server name normally gives an indication of the country where the server is located (for example www.fredco.co.uk is located in the UK). Determine which countries use the following country names:

(a) de   (b) nl   (c) it   (d) se   (e) dk   (f) sg
(g) ca   (h) ch   (i) tr   (j) jp   (k) au

Determine some other country identifier names.

A.8.4 Determine the HTML colour represented for the following:

(a) red   (b) green
(c) blue   (d) white
(e) black

A.8.5 Determine the HTML for the background, text and link colour:

(a) `<BODY BKCOLOR="#00FF00" "TEXT=#FF0000"`
                    `"LINK=#0000FF">`
(b) `<BODY BKCOLOR="#DC640D" "TEXT=#777777"`
                    `"LINK=#009DBE">`

A.8.6 Determine the error in the following HTML script:

📖 HTML script A.10

```
<HTML>
<HEAD>
<TITLE>Fred's page</TITLE>
</HEAD>
<BODY BGCOLOR="#FFFFFF">
<H1>List 1</H1>
<OL>
<LI>Part 1
<LI>Part 2
<LI>Part 3
<H1>List 2</H1>
<UL>
<LI>Section 1
<LI>Section 2
<LI>Section 3
</UL>
</BODY>
</HTML>
```

B Further HTML

B.1 Introduction

Appendix A introduced HTML; this chapter discusses some of HTML's more advanced features. HTML differs from compiled languages, such as C and Pascal, in that the HTML text file is interpreted by an interpreter (the browser) while languages such as C and Pascal must be precompiled before they can be run. HTML thus has the advantage that it does not matter if it is the operating system, the browser type or the computer type that reads the HTML file, as the file does not contain any computer specific code. The main disadvantage of interpreted files is that the interpreter does less error checking as it must produce fast results.

The basic pages on the WWW are likely to evolve around HTML and while HTML can be produced manually with a text editor, it is likely that, in the coming years, there will be an increase in the amount of graphically-based tools that will automatically produce HTML files. Although these tools are graphics-based they still produce standard HTML text files. Thus a knowledge of HTML is important as it defines the basic specification for the presentation of WWW pages.

B.2 Anchors

An anchor allows users to jump from a reference in a WWW page to another anchor point within the page. The standard format is:

`<A NAME="anchor name">`

where *anchor name* is the name of the section which is referenced. The `</A>` tag defines the end of an anchor name. A link is specified by:

`<A HREF="#anchor name">`

followed by the `</A>` tag. HTML script B.1 shows a sample script with four anchors and Figure B.1 shows a sample output. When the user selects one of the references, the browser automatically jumps to that anchor. Figure B.2

224

shows the output screen when the user selects the `#Token` reference. Anchors are typically used when an HTML page is long or when a backwards or forwards reference occurs (such as a reference within a published paper).

📖 HTML script B.1

```
<HTML>
<HEAD>
<TITLE>Sample page</TITLE>
</HEAD>
<BODY BGCOLOR="#FFFFFF">
<H2>Select which network technology you wish information:</H2>
<P><A HREF="#Ethernet">Ethernet</A></P>
<P><A HREF="#Token">Token Ring</A></P>
<P><A HREF="#FDDI">FDDI</A></P>
<P><A HREF="#ATM">ATM</A></P>
<H2><A NAME="Ethernet">Ethernet</A></H2>
Ethernet is a popular LAN which works at 10Mbps.
<H2><A NAME="Token">Token Ring</A></H2>
Token ring is a ring based network which operates
at 4 or 16Mbps.
<H2><A NAME="FDDI">FDDI</A></H2>
FDDI is a popular LAN technology which uses a ring of
fibre optic cable and operates at 100Mbps.
<H2><A NAME="ATM">ATM</A></H2>
ATM is a ring based network which operates at 155Mbps.
</BODY></HTML>
```

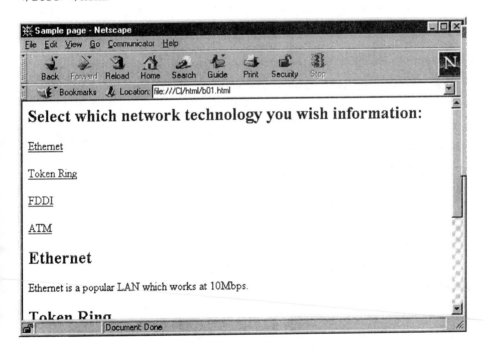

Figure B.1 Example window with references

Further HTML 225

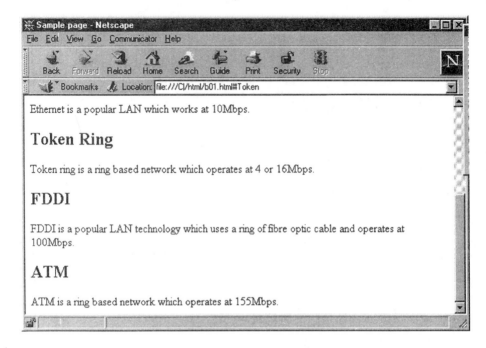

Figure B.2 Example window with references

B.3 Tables

Tables are one of the best methods to display complex information in a simple way. Unfortunately, in HTML they are relatively complicated to set up. The start of a table is defined with the <TABLE> tag and the end of a table by </TABLE>. A row is defined between the <TR> and </TR>, while a table header is defined between <TH> and </TH>. A regular table entry is defined between <TD> and </TD>. HTML script B.2 shows an example of a table with links to other HTML pages. The BORDER=n option has been added to the <TABLE> tag to define the thickness of the table border (in pixels). In this case the border size has a thickness of 10 pixels.

📖 HTML script B.2

```
<HTML><HEAD>
<TITLE> Fred Bloggs</TITLE></HEAD>
<BODY TEXT="#000000" BGCOLOR="#FFFFFF">
<H1>Fred Bloggs Home Page</H1>
I'm Fred Bloggs. Below is a tables of links.<HR><P>
<TABLE BORDER=10>
<TR>
  <TD><B>General</B></TD>
  <TD><A HREF="res.html">Research</TD>
```

```
<TD><A HREF="cv.html">CV</TD>
<TD><A HREF="paper.html">Papers Published</TD>
</TR>
<TR>
 <TD><B>HTML Tutorials</B></TD>
 <TD><A HREF="intro.html">Tutorial 1</TD>
 <TD><A HREF="inter.html">Tutorial 2</TD>
 <TD><A HREF="adv.html">Tutorial 3</TD>
</TR>
<TR>
 <TD><B>Java Tutorials</B></TD>
 <TD><A HREF="java1.html">Tutorial 1</TD>
 <TD><A HREF="java2.html">Tutorial 2</TD>
 <TD><A HREF="java3.html">Tutorial 3</TD>
</TR>
</TABLE></BODY></HTML>
```

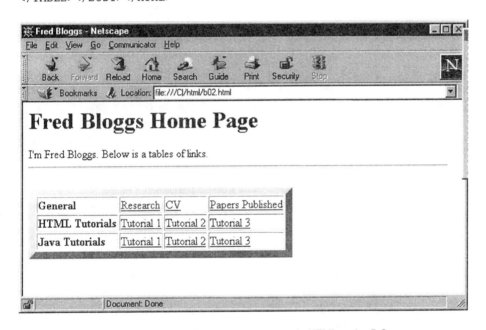

Figure B.3 Example window from example HTML script B.2

Other options in the <TABLE> tag are:

- WIDTH=x, HEIGHT=y – defines the size of the table with respect to the full window size. The parameters x and y are either absolute values in pixels for the height and width of the table or are percentages of the full window size.
- CELLSPACING=n – defines the number of pixels desired between each cell where n is the number of pixels (note that the default cell spacing is 2 pixels).

An individual cell can be modified by adding options to the <TH> or <TD> tag.

These include:

- WIDTH=*x*, HEIGHT=*y* – defines the size of the table with respect to the table size. The parameters *x* and *y* are either absolute values in pixels for the height and width of the table or are percentages of the table size.
- COLSPAN=*n* – defines the number of columns the cell should span.
- ROWSPAN=*n* – defines the number of rows the cell should span.
- ALIGN=*direction* – defines how the cell's contents are aligned horizontally. Valid options are *left*, *center* or *right*.
- VALIGN=*direction* – defines how the cell's contents are aligned vertically. Valid options are *top*, *middle* or *baseline*.
- NOWRAP – informs the browser to keep the text on a single line (that is, with no line breaks).

HTML script B.3 shows an example use of some of the options in the <TABLE> and <TD> options. In this case the text within each row is centre aligned. On the second row the second and third cells are merged using the COLSPAN=2 option. The first cell of the second and third rows have also been merged using the ROWSPAN=2 option. Figure B.4 shows an example output. The table width has been increased to 90% of the full window, with a width of 50%.

📖 HTML script B.3

```
<HTML><HEAD><TITLE> Fred Bloggs</TITLE></HEAD>
<BODY TEXT="#000000" BGCOLOR="#FFFFFF">
<H1>Fred Bloggs Home Page</H1>
I'm Fred Bloggs. Below is a table of links.
<HR>
<P>
<TABLE BORDER=10 WIDTH=90% LENGTH=50%>
<TR>
  <TD><B>General</B></TD>
  <TD><A HREF="res.html">Research</TD>
  <TD><A HREF="cv.html">CV</TD>
  <TD><A HREF="paper.html">Papers Published</TD>
  <TD></TD>
</TR>
<TR>
  <TD ROWSPAN=2><B>HTML/Java Tutorials</B></TD>
  <TD><A HREF="intro.html">Tutorial 1</TD>
  <TD COLSPAN=2><A HREF="inter.html">Tutorial 2</TD>
</TR>
<TR>
  <TD><A HREF="java1.html">Tutorial 1</TD>
  <TD><A HREF="java2.html">Tutorial 2</TD>
  <TD><A HREF="java3.html">Tutorial 3</TD>
</TR>
</TABLE>
</BODY></HTML>
```

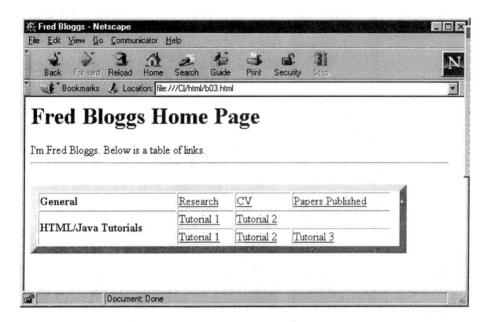

Figure B.4 Example window from example script B.3

B.4 CGI scripts

CGI (Common Gateway Interface) scripts are normally written in either C, Visual Basic or Perl and are compiled to produce an executable program. They can also come precompiled or in the form of a batch file. Perl has the advantage in that it is a script that can be easily run on any computer, while a precompiled C or Visual Basic program requires to be precompiled for the server computer.

CGI scripts allow the user to interact with the server and store and request data. They are often used in conjunction with forms and allow an HTML document to analyse, parse and store information received from a form. On most UNIX-type systems the default directory for CGI scripts is cgi-bin.

B.5 Forms

Forms are excellent methods of gathering data and can be used in conjunction with CGI scripts to collect data for future use.

A form is identified between the <FORM> and </FORM> tags. The method used to get the data from the form is defined with the METHOD="POST". The ACTION option defines the URL script to be run when the form is submitted. Data input is specified by the <INPUT TYPE> tag. HTML script B.4 form has the following parts:

- <form action="/cgi-bin/AnyForm2" method="POST"> — which defines the start of a form and when the "submit" option is selected the cgi script /cgi-bin/AnyForm2 will be automatically run.
- <input type="submit" value="Send Feedback"> — which causes the program defined in the action option in the <form> tag to be run. The button on the form will contain the text "Send Feedback", see Figure B.5 for a sample output screen.
- <input type="reset" value="Reset Form"> — which resets the data in the form. The button on the form will contain the text "Reset Form", see Figure B.5 for a sample output screen.
- <input type="hidden" name="AnyFormTo" value= "f.bloggs @toytown.ac.uk"> — which passes a value of f.bloggs@toytown.ac.uk which has the parameter name of "AnyFormTo". The program AnyForm2 takes this parameter and automatically sends it to the email address defined in the value (that is, f.bloggs@toytown.ac.uk).
- <input type="hidden" name="AnyFormSubject" value="Feedback form"> — which passes a value of Feedback form which has the parameter name of "AnyFormSubject". The program AnyForm2 takes this parameter and adds the text "Feedback form" in the text sent to the email recipient (in this case, f.bloggs@toytown.ac.uk).
- Surname <input name="Surname"> — which defines a text input and assigns this input to the parameter name Surname.
- <textarea name="Address" rows=2 cols=40> </textarea> — which defines a text input area which has two rows and has a width of 40 characters. The thumb bars appear at the right-hand side of the form if the text area exceeds more than 2 rows, see Figure B.5.

📖 HTML script B.4

```
<HTML>
<HEAD>
<TITLE>Example form</TITLE>
</HEAD>
<H1><CENTER>Example form</CENTER></H1><P>
<form action="/cgi-bin/AnyForm2" method="POST">
<input type="hidden" name="AnyFormTo" value="f.bloggs@toytown.ac.uk"
<input type="hidden" name="AnyFormSubject" value="Feedback form">
Surname <input name="Surname">
First Name/Names <input name="First Name"><P>
Address (including country)<P>
<textarea name="Address" rows=2 cols=40></textarea><P>
Business Phone <input name="Business Phone">
```

```
Place of study (or company) <input name="Study"><P>
E-mail    <input name="E-mail">
Fax Number <input name="Fax Number"><P>
<input type="submit" value="Send Feedback">
<input type="reset" value="Reset Form">
</Form><HTML>
```

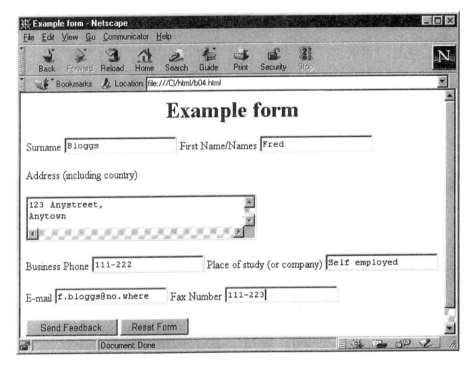

Figure B.5 Example window showing an example form

In this case the recipient (f.bloggs@toytown.ac.uk) will receive an email
with the contents:

```
Anyform Subject=Example form
Surname=Bloggs
First name=Fred
Address=123 Anystreet, Anytown
Business Phone=111-222
Place of study (or company)=Self employed
Email= f.bloggs@nowhere
Fax Number=111-2223
```

The extra options to the <input> tag are size="*n*", where *n* is the width of the
input box in characters, and maxlength="*m*", where *m* is the maximum number of characters that can be entered, in characters. For example:

```
<input type="text"  size="15" maxlength="10">
```

defines that the input type is text, the width of the box is 15 characters and the maximum length of input is 10 characters.

B.5.1 Input types

The type options to the `<input>` tag are defined in Table B.1. HTML script B.5 gives a few examples of input types and Figure B.6 shows a sample output.

Table B.1 Input type options

TYPE=	Description	Options
`"text"`	The input is normal text.	NAME="*nm*" where *nm* is the name that will be sent to the server when the text is entered. SIZE="*n*" where *n* is the desired box width in characters. SIZE="*m*" where *m* is the maximum number of input characters.
`"password"`	The input is a password which will be displayed with *s. For example if the user inputs a 4-letter password then only **** will be displayed.	SIZE="*n*" where *n* is the desired box width in characters. SIZE="*m*" where *m* is the maximum number of input characters.
`"radio"`	The input takes the form of a radio button (such as ⊙ or O). They are used to allow the user to select a single option from a list of options.	NAME="*radname*" where *radname* defines the name of the button. VALUE="*val*" where *val* is the data that will be sent to the server when the button is selected. CHECKED is used to specify that the button is initially set.
`"checkbox"`	The input takes the form of a checkbox (such as ⊠ or ☐). They are used to allow the user to select several options from a list of options.	NAME="*chkname*" where *chkname* defines the common name for all the checkbox options. VALUE="*defval*" where *defval* defines the name of the option. CHECKED is used to specify that the button is initially set.

HTML script B.5

```
<HTML><HEAD>
<TITLE>Example form</TITLE> </HEAD>
<FORM METHOD="Post" >
<H2>Enter type of network:</H2><P>
<INPUT TYPE="radio" NAME="network" VALUE="ethernet" CHECKED>Ethernet
<INPUT TYPE="radio" NAME="network" VALUE="token"> Token Ring
<INPUT TYPE="radio" NAME="network" VALUE="fddi" >FDDI
<INPUT TYPE="radio" NAME="network" VALUE="atm" >ATM
<H2>Enter usage:</H2><P>
<INPUT TYPE="checkbox" NAME="usage" VALUE="multi" >Multimedia
<INPUT TYPE="checkbox" NAME="usage" VALUE="word" >Word Processing
<INPUT TYPE="checkbox" NAME="usage" VALUE="spread" >Spread Sheets
<P>Enter Password<INPUT TYPE="password" NAME="passwd" SIZE="10">
</FORM></HTML>
```

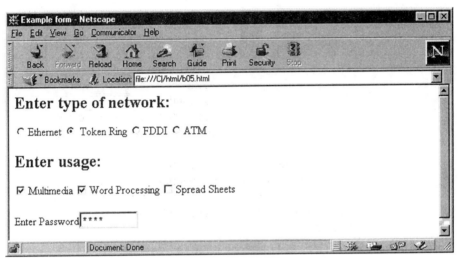

Figure B.6 Example window with different input options

B.5.2 Menus

Menus are a convenient method of selecting from multiple options. The
<SELECT> tag is used to define the start of a list of menu options and the
</SELECT> tag defines the end. Menu elements are then defined with the
<OPTION> tag. The options defined within the <SELECT> are:

- NAME="*name*" – which defines that *name* is the variable name of the menu.
  This is used when the data is collected by the server.
- SIZE="*n*" – which defines the number of options which are displayed in
  the menu.

HTML script B.6 shows an example of a menu. The additional options to the
<OPTION> tag are:

- SELECTED – which defines the default selected option.
- VALUE="*val*" – where *val* defines the name of the data when it is collected by the server.

📖 HTML script B.6

```
<HTML><HEAD><TITLE>Example form</TITLE> </HEAD>
<FORM METHOD="Post" >
Enter type of network:
<select Name="network" size="1">
<option>Ethernet
<option SELECTED>Token Ring
<option>FDDI
<option>ATM
</select>
</FORM></HTML>
```

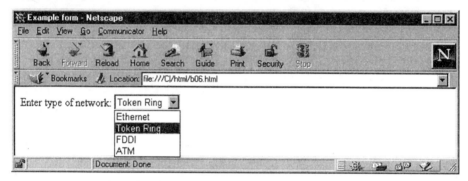

Figure B.7 Example window showing an example form

B.6   Multimedia

If the browser cannot handle all the file types it may call on other application helpers to process the file. This allows other 'third-party' programs to integrate into the browser. Figure B.8 shows an example of the configuration of the helper programs. The options in this case are:

- View in browser.
- Save to disk.
- Unknown: prompt user.
- Launch an application (such as an audio playback program or MPEG viewer).

For certain applications the user can select as to whether the browser processes the file or another application program processes it. Helper programs make upgrades in helper applications relatively simple and also allow new file types to be added with an application helper. Typically when a program is installed which can be used with a browser it will prompt the user to automatically update the helper application list so that it can handle the given file type(s).

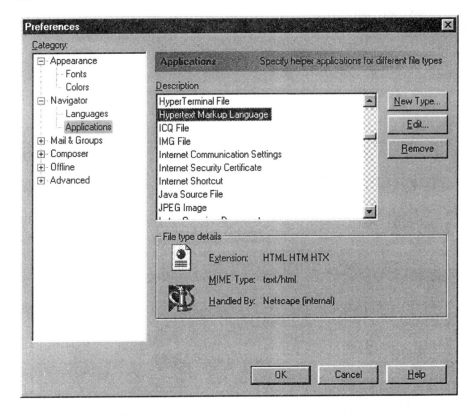

Figure B.8 Example window showing preferences

Each file type is defined by the file extension, such as .ps for postscript files, .exe for a binary executable file, and so on. These file extensions have been standardised in MIME (Multipurpose Internet Mail Extensions) specfication. Table B.2 shows some typical file extensions.

Table B.2 Input type options

Mime type	Extension	Typical action
application/octet-stream	exe, bin	Save
application/postscript	ps, ai, eps	Ask user
application/x-compress	Z	Compress program
application/x-gzip	gz	GZIP compress program
application/x-javascript	js, mocha	Ask user
application/x-msvideo	avi	Audio player

Table B.2 Input type options (cont.)

Mime type	Extension	Typical action
application/x-perl	pl	Save
application/x-tar	tar	Save
application/x-zip-compressed	zip	ZIP program
audio/basic	au, snd	Audio player
image/gif	gif	Browser
image/jpeg	jpeg, jpg, jpe	Browser
image/tiff	tif, tiff	Graphics viewer
image/x-MS-bmp	bmp	Graphics viewer
text/html	htm, html	Browser
text/plain	text, txt	Browser
video/mpeg	mpeg, mpg, mpe, mpv, vbs, mpegv	Video player
video/quicktime	qt, mov, moov	Video player

B.7 Exercises

B.7.1 Construct a WWW with anchor points for the following terms:

Select the network you wish to find out about:

Ethernet
Token ring
FDDI

Ethernet

Ethernet is the most widely used networking technology used in LAN (Local Area Network). In itself it cannot make a network and needs some other protocol such as TCP/IP or SPX/IPX to allow nodes to communicate. Unfortunately, Ethernet in its standard form does not cope well with heavy traffic. Its has many advantages, though, including:

- Networks are easy to plan and cheap to install.
- Network components are cheap and well supported.
- It is well-proven technology which is fairly robust and reliable.
- Simple to add and delete computers on the network.
- Supported by most software and hardware systems.

Token ring

Token ring networks were developed by several manufacturers, the most prevalent being the IBM Token Ring. Token ring networks cope well with high network traffic loadings. They were at one time extremely popular but their popularity has since been overtaken by Ethernet. Token ring networks have, in the past, suffered from network management problems and poor network fault tolerance.

Token ring networks are well suited to situations which have large amounts of traffic and also work well with most traffic loadings. They are not suited to large networks or networks with physically remote stations. Their main advantage is that they cope better with high traffic rates than Ethernet, but require a great deal of maintenance especially when faults occur or when new equipment is added to or removed from the network. Many of these problems have now been overcome by MAUs (multi-station access units), which are similar to the hubs used in Ethernet.

FDDI

A token-passing mechanism allows orderly access to a network. Apart from token ring the most commonly used token-passing network is the Fiber Distributed Data Interchange (FDDI) standard. This operates at 100 Mbps and, to overcome the problems of line breaks, has two concentric token rings. Fibre optic cables have a much high specification over copper cables and allow extremely long interconnection lengths. The maximum circumference of the ring is 100 km (62 miles), with a maximum 2 km between stations (in FDDI nodes are also known as stations). It is thus an excellent mechanism for connecting interconnecting networks over a city or a campus. Up to 500 stations can connect to each ring with a maximum of 1,000 stations for the complete network. Each station connected to the FDDI highway can be a normal station or a bridge to a conventional local area network, such as Ethernet or token ring.

B.7.2   Construct a WWW glossary page with the following terms:

Address	A unique label for the location of data or the identity of a communications device.
Address Resolution Protocol (ARP)	A TCP/IP process which maps an IP address to an Ethernet address.
American National Standards Institute (ANSI)	ANSI is a non-profit organization which is made up of expert committees that publish standards for national industries.

American Standard Code for Information Interchange (ASCII)	An ANSI-defined character alphabet which has since been adopted as a standard international alphabet for the interchange of characters.
Amplitude modulation (AM)	Information is contained in the amplitude of a carrier.
Amplitude-Shift Keying (ASK)	Uses two, or more, amplitudes to represent binary digits. Typically used to transmit binary data over speech-limited channels.
Application layer	The highest layer of the OSI model.
Asynchronous transmission	Transmission where individual characters are sent one by one. Normally each character is delimited by a start and stop bit. With asynchronous communication the transmitter and receiver only have to be roughly synchronized.

B.7.3 Construct a WWW page which can be used to enter a person's CV (note, use a form). The basic fields should be:

Name:
Address:
Email address:
Telephone number:
Experience:
Interests:
Any other information:

B.7.4 Write an HTML script which displays the following timetable.

	9–11	11–1	1–3	3–5
Monday	Data Comms		Networking	
Tuesday	Software Systems		Networking	Data Comms
Wednesday	Networking	FREE	Java	FREE
Thursday	Software Systems	C++	Networking	FREE
Friday	FREE		Networking	

B.7.5 Design your own home page with a basic user home page (index.html) which contains links to a basic CV page (for example, it could be named cv.html) and a page which lists your main interests (myinter.html). Design one of the home pages with a list of links and another with a table of links. If possible incorporate graphics files into the pages.

C HTML Reference

C.1 Introduction

C.1.1 Data Characters

Characters which are not markup text are mapped directly to strings of data characters. An ampersand followed by a character reference or a number value can be used to define a character. Table C.1 defines these characters (the equivalent ampersand character reference is given in brackets). For example:

```
Fred&#174&ampBert&iquest
```

will be displayed as:

```
Fred®&Bert¿
```

An ampersand is only recognised as markup when it is followed by a letter or a '#' and a digit:

```
Fred & Bert
```

will be displayed as:

```
Fred & Bert
```

In the HTML document character set only three control characters are allowed: Horizontal Tab, Carriage Return, and Line Feed (code positions 9, 13, and 10).

Table C.1 Character mappings

&#00-&#08	Unused	&#09	Horizontal tab
&#10	Line feed	&#11,&#12	Unused
&#13	Carriage return	&#14-&#31	Unused
&#32	Space	&#33	Exclamation mark
&#34	Quotation mark (&quot)	&#35	Number sign
&#36	Dollar sign	&#37	Percent sign
&#38	Ampersand (&amp)	&#39	Apostrophe

&#40	Left parenthesis	&#41	Right parenthesis
&#42	Asterisk	&#43	Plus sign
&#44	Comma	&#45	Hyphen
&#46	Period (fullstop)	&#47	Solidus
&#48-&#57	Digits 0-9	&#58	Colon
&#59	Semi-colon	&#60	Less than (&lt)
&#61	Equals sign	&#62	Greater than (&gt)
&#63	Question mark	&#64	Commercial at
&#65-&#90	Letters A-Z	&#91	Left square bracket
&#92	Reverse solidus (\)	&#93	Right square bracket
&#94	Caret	&#95	Underscore
&#96	Acute accent	&#97-&#122	Letters a-z
&#123	Left curly brace	&#124	Vertical bar
&#125	Right curly brace	&#126	Tilde
&#127-&#159	Unused		
	Non-breaking space ( )		
&#161	Inverted exclamation, ¡ (&iexcl)		
&#162	Cent sign ¢ (&cent)		
&#163	Pound sterling £ (&pound)		
&#164	General currency sign, ¤ (&curren)		
&#165	Yen sign, ¥ (&yen)		
&#166	Broken vertical bar, ¦ (&brvbar)		
&#167	Section sign, § (&sect)		
&#168	Umlaut, ¨ (&uml)		
&#169	Copyright, © (&copy)		
&#170	Feminine ordinal, ª (&ordf)		
&#171	Left angle quote, « (&laquo)		
&#172	Not sign, ¬ (&not)		
&#173	Soft hyphen, - (&shy)		
&#174	Registered trademark, ® (&reg)		
&#175	Macron accent, ¯ (&macr)		
&#176	Degree sign, ° (&deg)		
&#177	Plus or minus, ± (&plusmn)		
&#178	Superscript two, ² (&sup2)		
&#179	Superscript three, ³ (&sup3)		
&#180	Acute accent, ´ (&acute)		
&#181	Micro sign, µ (&micro)		
&#182	Paragraph sign, ¶ (&para)		
&#183	Middle dot, · (&middot)		
&#184	Cedilla, ¸ (&cedil)		
&#185	Superscript one, ¹ (&sup1)		
&#186	Masculine ordinal, º (&ordm)		
&#187	Right angle quote, » (&raquo)		
&#188	Fraction one-fourth, ¼ (&frac14)		
&#189	Fraction one-half, ½ (&frac12)		
&#190	Fraction three-fourths, ¾ (&frac34)		
&#191	Inverted question mark, ¿ (&iquest)		

&#192	Capital A, grave accent, À (&Agrave)
&#193	Capital A, acute accent, Á (&Aacute)
&#194	Capital A, circumflex accent, Â (&Acirc)
&#195	Capital A, tilde, Ã (&Atilde)
&#196	Capital A, dieresis, Ä (&Auml)
&#197	Capital A, ring, Å (&Aring)
&#198	Capital AE dipthong, Æ (&AElig)
&#199	Capital C, cedilla, Ç (&Ccedil)
&#200	Capital E, grave accent, È (&Egrave)
&#201	Capital E, acute accent, É (&Eacute)
&#202	Capital E, circumflex accent, Ê (&Ecirc)
&#203	Capital E, dieresis, Ë (&Euml)
&#204	Capital I, grave accent, Ì (&Igrave)
&#205	Capital I, acute accent, Í (&Iacute)
&#206	Capital I, circumflex accent, Î (&Icirc)
&#207	Capital I, dieresis, Ï (&Iuml)
&#208	Capital Eth, Icelandic, Ð (&ETH)
&#209	Capital N, tilde, Ñ (&Ntilde)
&#210	Capital O, grave accent, Ò (&Ograve)
&#211	Capital O, acute accent, Ó (&Oacute)
&#212	Capital O, circumflex accent, Ô (&Ocirc)
&#213	Capital O, tilde, Õ (&Otilde)
&#214	Capital O, dieresis, Ö (&Ouml)
&#215	Multiply sign, × (&times)
&#216	Capital O, slash, Ø (&Oslash)
&#217	Capital U, grave accent, Ù (&Ugrave)
&#218	Capital U, acute accent, Ú (&Uacute)
&#219	Capital U, circumflex accent, Û (&Ucirc)
&#220	Capital U, dieresis or umlaut mark, Ü (&Uuml)
&#221	Capital Y, acute accent, Ý (&Yacute)
&#222	Capital THORN, Icelandic, Þ (&THORN)
&#223	Small sharp s, German, ß (&szlig)
&#224	Small a, grave accent, à (&agrave)
&#225	Small a, acute accent, á (&aacute)
&#226	Small a, circumflex accent, â (&acirc)
&#227	Small a, tilde, ã (&atilde)
&#228	Small a, dieresis or umlaut mark, ä (&auml)
&#229	Small a, ring, å (&aring)
&#230	Small ae dipthong, æ (&aelig)
&#231	Small c, cedilla, ç (&ccedil)
&#232	Small e, grave accent, è (&egrave)
&#233	Small e, acute accent, é (&eacute)
&#234	Small e, circumflex accent, ê (&ecirc)
&#235	Small e, dieresis or umlaut mark, ë (&euml)
&#236	Small i, grave accent, ì (&igrave)
&#237	Small i, acute accent, í (&iacute)
&#238	Small i, circumflex accent, î (&icirc)

&#239	Small i, dieresis or umlaut mark, ï (&iuml)
&#240	Small eth, Icelandic, ð (&eth)
&#241	Small n, tilde, ñ (&ntilde)
&#242	Small o, grave accent, ò (&ograve)
&#243	Small o, acute accent, ó (&oacute)
&#244	Small o, circumflex accent, ô (&ocirc)
&#245	Small o, tilde, õ (&otilde)
&#246	Small o, dieresis or umlaut mark, ö (&ouml)
&#247	Division sign, ÷ (&divide)
&#248	Small o, slash, ø (&oslash)
&#249	Small u, grave accent, ù (&ugrave)
&#250	Small u, acute accent, ú (&uacute)
&#251	Small u, circumflex accent, û (&ucirc)
&#252	Small u, dieresis or umlaut mark, ü (&uuml)
&#253	Small y, acute accent, ý (&yacute)
&#254	Small thorn, Icelandic, þ (&thorn),
&#255	Small y, dieresis or umlaut mark, ÿ (&yuml)

C.1.2 Tags

Tags are used to delimit elements such as headings, paragraphs, lists, character highlighting and links. Normally an HTML element consists of a start tag, which gives the element name and attributes, followed by the content and then the end tag. A start tag is defined between a '<' and '>', and end tags between a '</' and '>'. For example to display text as bold:

```
<B>Header Level 1</B>
```

Some HTML elements only require a single start tag, these include:

</BR> Line break.   </P> Paragraph.

</LI> List Item.   </DT> Definition term.

</DD> Definition description.

Element content is a sequence of data character strings and nested elements. Some elements, such as anchors, cannot be nested.

C.1.3 Names

Names consist of a letter followed by letters, digits, periods or hyphens (normally limited to 72 characters). Entity names are case sensitive, but element and attribute names are not. For example:

'<FONT>', '<Font>', and '<font>'

are equivalent, but

'&lt' is different from '&LT'.

Start tags always begin directly after the opening delimiter ('<').

C.1.4 Attributes

In a start tag, white space and attributes are allowed between the element name and the closing delimiter. Attributes typically consist of an attribute name, an equal sign, and a value, which can be:

- A string literal, delimited by single quotes or double quotes and not containing any occurrences of the delimiting character.
- A name token (a sequence of letters, digits, periods, or hyphens). Name tokens are not case sensitive.

C.1.5 Comments

Comments are defined with a '<!' and end with a '>'. Each comment starts with '--' and includes all text up to and including the next occurrence of '--'. When defining a comment, white space is allowed after each comment, but not before the first comment. The entire comment declaration is ignored.

```
<!DOCTYPE HTML PUBLIC "-//IETF//DTD HTML 2.0//EN">
<HEAD>
<TITLE>Comment Document</TITLE>
<!-- Comment field 1 -->
<!-- Comment field 2 -->
<!>
</HEAD>
<BODY>
```

C.1.6 HTML Public Text Identifiers

Documents that conform to the HTML 2.0 specification can include the following line at the start of the document:

```
<!DOCTYPE HTML PUBLIC "-//IETF//DTD HTML 2.0//EN">
```

C.2   Document structure and block structuring

An HTML document is a tree of elements, including a head and body, headings, paragraphs, lists, and so on. These include:

<HTML>   Document element. Consists of a head and a body. The head contains the title and optional elements, and the body is the main text consisting of paragraphs, lists and other elements.

`<HEAD>`	Head element. An unordered collection of information about the document.
`<TITLE>`	Title. Identifies the contents of the document in a global context.
`<BASE>`	Base address. Provides a base address for interpreting relative URLs when the document is read out of context.
`<ISINDEX>`	Keyword index. Indicates that the user agent should allow the user to search an index by giving keywords.
`<LINK>`	Link. Represents a hyperlink (*see* Hyperlinks) and has the same attributes as the `<A>` element.
`<META>`	Associated meta-information. A container for identifying specialised document meta-information.
`<BODY>`	Body element. Contains the text flow of the document, including headings, paragraphs, lists, etc.
`<H1>...<H6>`	Headings. The six heading elements, `<H1>` to `<H6>` identify section headings. Typical renderings are:
	H1 Bold, very-large centred font. One or two blank lines above and below.
	H2 Bold, large flush-left font. One or two blank lines above and below.
	H3 Italic, large font, slightly indented from the left margin. One or two blank lines above and below.
	H4 Bold, normal font, indented more than H3. One blank line above and below.
	H5 Italic, normal font, indented as H4. One blank line above.
	H6 Bold, indented same as normal text, more than H5. One blank line above.
`<P>`	Paragraph. Indicates a paragraph. Typically, paragraphs are surrounded by a vertical space of one line or half a line. The first line in a paragraph is indented in some cases.
`<PRE>`	Preformatted text. Represents a character cell block of text and can be used to define monospaced font. It may be used with the optional `WIDTH` attribute, which specifies the maximum number of characters for a line.
`<ADDRESS>`	Address. Contains information such as address, signature and authorship. It is often used at the beginning or end of the body of a document.
`<BLOCKQUOTE>`	Block quote. Contains text quoted from another source. A typical rendering is a slight extra left and right indent, and/or italic font, and typically provides space above and below the quote.
`<UL>, <LI>`	Unordered list. `<UL>` represents a list of items and is typically rendered as a bulleted list. The content of a `<UL>` element is a sequence of `<LI>` elements.
`<OL>`	Ordered list. `<OL>` represents an ordered list of items which are sorted by sequence or order of importance and is typically rendered as a numbered list. The content of a `<OL>` element is a sequence of `<LI>` elements.
`<DIR>`	Directory list. `<DIR>` is similar to the `<UL>` element and represents a

list of short items. The content of a `<DIR>` element is a sequence of `<LI>` elements.

`<MENU>` Menu list. `<MENU>` is a list of items with typically one line per item. It is typically more compact than an unordered list. The content of a `<MENU>` element is a sequence of `<LI>` elements.

`<DL>`, `<DT>`, `<DD>` Definition list. Lists terms and corresponding definitions. Definition lists are typically formatted with the term flush-left and the definition, formatted paragraph style, indented after the term. The content of a `<DL>` element is a sequence of `<DT>` elements and/or `<DD>` elements, usually in pairs.

`<CITE>` Citation. `<CITE>` is used to indicate the title of a book or other citation. It is typically rendered as italics.

`<CODE>` Code. `<CODE>` indicates an example of code and is typically rendered in a monospaced font. It is intended for short words or phrases of code.

`<EM>` Emphasis. `<EM>` indicates an emphasised phrase and is typically rendered as italics.

`<KBD>` Typed text. `<KBD>` indicates text typed by a user and is typically rendered in a monospaced font.

`<SAMP>` Literal characters. `<SAMP>` indicates a sequence of literal characters and is typically rendered in a monospaced font.

`<STRONG>` Strong emphasis. `<STRONG>` indicates strong emphasis and is typically rendered in bold.

`<VAR>` Placeholder variable. `<VAR>` indicates a placeholder variable and is typically rendered as italic.

`<B>` Bold. `<B>` indicates bold text.

`<I>` Italic. `<I>` indicates italic text.

`<TT>` Teletype. `<TT>` indicates teletype (monospaced) text.

`<A>` Anchor. The `<A>` element indicates a hyperlink. Attributes of the `<A>` element are:

HREF   URI of the head anchor of a hyperlink.

NAME   Name of the anchor.

TITLE   Advisory title of the destination resource.

REL   The REL attribute gives the relationship(s) described by the hyperlink.

REV   Same as the REL attribute, but the semantics of the relationship are in the reverse direction.

URN   Specifies a preferred, more persistent identifier for the head anchor of the hyperlink.

METHODS Specifies methods to be used in accessing the destination, as a whitespace-separated list of names.

`<BR>` Line break. `<BR>` specifies a line break between words.

`<HR>` Horizontal rule. `<HR>` is a divider between sections of text and is typically a full width horizontal rule.

`<IMG>` Image. `<IMG>` refers to an image or icon. Attributes are:

ALIGN   alignment of the image with respect to the text baseline:

- 'TOP' specifies that the top of the image aligns with the tallest item on the line containing the image.
- 'MIDDLE' specifies that the centre of the image aligns with the baseline of the line containing the image.
- 'BOTTOM' specifies that the bottom of the image aligns with the baseline of the line containing the image.

ALT   Text to use in place of the referenced image resource.
ISMAP   Indicates an image map.
SRC   Specifies the URL of the image resource.

Java Reference

D.1 Package java.applet

D.1.1 Class java.applet.Applet

The `Applet` class is a superclass of any applet. It provides a standard interface between applets and their environment. The following are defined:

```
// Constructors
public Applet();

// Methods
public void destroy();
public AppletContext getAppletContext();
public String getAppletInfo();
public AudioClip getAudioClip(URL url);
public AudioClip getAudioClip(URL url, String name);
public URL getCodeBase();
public URL getDocumentBase();
public Image getImage(URL url);
public Image getImage(URL url, String name);
public String getLocale();                              // Java 1.1
public String getParameter(String name);
public String[][] getParameterInfo();
public void init();
public boolean isActive();
public void play(URL url);
public void play(URL url, String name);
public void resize(Dimension d);
public void resize(int width, int height);
public final void setStub(AppletStub stub);
public void showStatus(String msg);
public void start();
public void stop();
```

D.1.2 Interface java.applet.AppletContext

The `AppletContext` interface corresponds to the applet's environment. The following are defined:

```
// Methods
public abstract Applet getApplet(String name);
public abstract Enumeration getApplets();
public abstract AudioClip getAudioClip(URL url);
public abstract Image getImage(URL url);
public abstract void showDocument(URL url);
public abstract void showDocument(URL url, String target);
public abstract void showStatus(String status);
```

D.1.3 Interface java.applet.AppletStub

The AppletStub interface acts as the interface between the applet and the browser environment or applet viewer environment. The following are defined:

```
// Methods
public abstract void appletResize(int width, int height);
public abstract AppletContext getAppletContext();
public abstract URL getCodeBase();
public abstract URL getDocumentBase();
public abstract String getParameter(String name);
public abstract boolean isActive();
```

D.1.4 Interface java.applet.AudioClip

The AudioClip interface is a simple abstraction for playing a sound clip. Multiple AudioClip items can be playing at the same time, and the resulting sound is mixed together to produce a composite. The following are defined:

```
// Methods
public abstract void loop();
public abstract void play();
public abstract void stop();
```

D.2 Package java.awt

D.2.1 Class java.awt.BorderLayout

The BorderLayout class contains members named "North", "South", "East", "West", and "Center". These are laid out with a given size and constraints. The "North" and "South" components can be stretched horizontally and the "East" and "West" components can be stretched vertically. The "Center" component can be stretched horizontally and vertically. The following are defined:

```
// Constructors
public BorderLayout();
public BorderLayout(int hgap, int vgap);
// Constants
public static final String CENTER;                              // Java 1.1
public static final String EAST;                                // Java 1.1
public static final String NORTH;                               // Java 1.1
public static final String SOUTH;                               // Java 1.1
public static final String WEST;                                // Java 1.1
// Methods
public void addLayoutComponent(Component comp, Object obj);      // Java 1.1
public void addLayoutComponent(String name, Component comp);     // Java 1.0
public int getHgap();                                           // Java 1.1
public float getLayoutAlignmentX(Container parent);             // Java 1.1
public float getLayoutAlignmentY(Container parent);             // Java 1.1
public int getVgap();                                          // Java 1.1
public void invalidateLayout(Container target);                // Java 1.1
public void layoutContainer(Container target);
public Dimension maximumLayoutSize(Container target);          // Java 1.1
```

```
public Dimension minimumLayoutSize(Container target);
public Dimension preferredLayoutSize(Container target);
public void removeLayoutComponent(Component comp);
public int setHgap();                                        // Java 1.1
public int setVgap();                                        // Java 1.1
public String toString();
```

D.2.2 Class java.awt.Button

The Button class creates labelled buttons, which can have an associated action when pushed. Three typical actions are: normal, when it has the input focus (the darkening of the outline lets the user know that this is an active object) and when the user clicks the mouse over the button. The following are defined:

```
// Constructors
public Button();
public Button(String label);

// Methods
public synchronized void addActionListener(ActionListern l); // Java 1.1
public void addNotify();
public String getActionCommand();                            // Java 1.1
public String getLabel();
protected String paramString();
public synchronized void removeActionListener(ActionListener l);
                                                             // Java 1.1
public setActionCommand(String command);                     // Java 1.1
public void setLabel(String label);
```

D.2.3 Class java.awt.Checkbox

The Checkbox class contains a checkbox which has an on/off state. The following are defined:

```
// Constructors
public Checkbox();
public Checkbox(String label);
public Checkbox(String label, boolean state);                // Java 1.1
public Checkbox(String label, boolean state, Checkbox group);// Java 1.1
public Checkbox(String label, CheckboxGroup group, boolean state);

// Methods
public synchronized void addItemListener(ItemListener l);    // Java 1.1
public void addNotify();
public CheckboxGroup getCheckboxGroup();
public String getLabel();
public boolean getState();
public Object[] getSelectedObject();                         // Java 1.1
protected String paramString();
public synchronized void removeItemListener(ItemListener l); // Java 1.1
public void setCheckboxGroup(CheckboxGroup g);
public void setLabel(String label);
public void setState(boolean state);
```

D.2.4 Class java.awt.CheckboxGroup

The CheckGroup class groups a number of checkbox buttons. Only one of the checkboxes can be true (on) at a time. When one button is made true (on) the others will become false (off). The following are defined:

```
// Constructors
public CheckboxGroup();

// Methods
public Checkbox getCurrent();                              // Java 1.0
public Checkbox getSelectedCurrent();                     // Java 1.1
public void setCurrent(Checkbox box);                     // Java 1.0
public void setSelectedCheckbox(Checkbox box);            // Java 1.1
public String toString();
```

D.2.5 Class java.awt.CheckboxMenuItem

The CheckboxMenuItem class allows for a checkbox that can be included in a menu. The following are defined:

```
// Constructors
public CheckboxMenuItem();                                // Java 1.1
public CheckboxMenuItem(String label);
public CheckboxMenuItem(String label, boolean state);     // Java 1.1

// Methods
public synchronized void addItemListener(ItemListener l);   // Java 1.1
public void addNotify();
public boolean getState();
public synchronized Object[] getSelectObjects();          // Java 1.1
public String paramString();
public synchronized void removeItemListener(ItemListener l); // Java 1.1
public void setState(boolean t);
```

D.2.6 Class java.awt.Choice

The Choice class allows for a pop-up menu. The following are defined:

```
// Constructors
public Choice();

// Methods
public synchronized add(String item);                     // Java 1.1
public void addItem(String item);
public synchronized void addItemListener(ItemListener l);  // Java 1.1
public void addNotify();
public int countItems();                                  // Java 1.0
public String getItem(int index);
public String getItemCount();                             // Java 1.1
public int getSelectedIndex();
public String getSelectedItem();
protected String paramString();
public synchronized Object[] getSelectedObjects();        // Java 1.1
public synchronized void insert(String item, int index);  // Java 1.1
public synchronized void remove(String item);             // Java 1.1
public synchronized void remove(int position);            // Java 1.1
public synchronized void removeAll();                     // Java 1.1
public synchronized void removeItemListener(ItemListener l); // Java 1.1
public void select(int pos);
public void select(String str);
```

D.2.7 Class java.awt.Color

This Color class supports the RGB colour format. A colour is represented by a 24-bit value of which the red, green and blue components are represented by an 8-bit value (0 to 255). The minimum intensity is 0, and the maximum is 255. The following are defined:

```
// Constants
public final static Color black, blue, cyan, darkGray, gray, green;
public final static Color lightGray, magenta, orange, pink, red;
public final static Color white, yellow;

// Constructors
public Color(float r, float g, float b);
public Color(int rgb);
public Color(int r, int g, int b);

// Methods
public Color brighter();
public Color darker();
public static Color decode (Strimg nm);                     // Java 1.1
public boolean equals(Object obj);
public int getBlue();
public static Color getColor(String nm);
public static Color getColor(String nm, Color v);
public static Color getColor(String nm, int v);
public int getGreen();
public static Color getHSBColor(float h, float s, float b);
public int getRed();
public int getRGB();
public int hashCode();
public static int HSBtoRGB(float hue, float saturation,float brightness);
public static float[] RGBtoHSB(int r, int g, int b, float hsbvals[]);
public String toString();
```

D.2.8 Class java.awt.Component

The Component class is the abstract superclass for many of the Abstract Window Toolkit classes. The following are defined:

```
// Constants
public static final float BOTTOM_ALIGNMENT, CENTER_ALIGNMENT;
public static final float LEFT_ALIGNMENT, RIGHT_ALIGNMENT;
public static final float TOP_ALIGNMENT;

// Methods
public boolean action(Event evt, Object what);              // Java 1.0
public synchronized void add(PopupMenu popup);              // Java 1.1
public synchronized void addComponentListener(ComponentListener l);
                                                            // Java 1.1
public synchronized void addFocusListener(FocusListener l);  // Java 1.1
public synchronized void addKeyListener(KeyListener l);      // Java 1.1
public synchronized void addMouseListener(MouseListener l);  // Java 1.1
public synchronized void addMouseMotionListener(
        MouseMotionListener l);                             // Java 1.1
public void addNotify();
public Rectangle bounds();                                  // Java 1.0
public int checkImage(Image image, ImageObserver observer);
public int checkImage(Image image, int width, int height,
        ImageObserver observer);
public boolean contains(int x, int y);                     // Java 1.1
public boolean contains(Point p);                          // Java 1.1
public Image createImage(ImageProducer producer);
public Image createImage(int width, int height);
public void deliverEvent(Event evt);                       // Java 1.0
```

```
public void disable();                                              // Java 1.0
public final void displayEvent(AWTEvent e);                         // Java 1.1
public void doLayout();                                             // Java 1.1
public void enable();                                               // Java 1.0
public void enable(boolean cond);                                   // Java 1.0
public float getAlignmentX();                                       // Java 1.1
public float getAlignmentY();                                       // Java 1.1
public Color getBackground();
public Rectangle getBounds();                                       // Java 1.1
public ColorModel getColorModel();
public Component getComponentAt(int x, int y);                      // Java 1.1
public Component getComponentAt(Point p);                           // Java 1.1
public Cursor getCursor();                                          // Java 1.1
public Font getFont();
public FontMetrics getFontMetrics(Font font);
public Color getForeground();
public Graphics getGraphics();
public Locale getLocale();                                          // Java 1.1
public Point getLocation();                                         // Java 1.1
public Point getLocationOnScreen();                                 // Java 1.1
public Dimension getMaximumSize();                                  // Java 1.1
public Dimension getMinimumSize();                                  // Java 1.1
public Container getParent();
public ComponentPeer getPeer();                                     // Java 1.0
public Dimension getPreferredSize();                               // Java 1.1
public Dimension getSize();                                         // Java 1.1
public Toolkit getToolkit();
public final Object getTreeLock();                                  // Java 1.1
public boolean gotFocus(Event evt, Object what);                    // Java 1.0
public boolean handleEvent(Event evt);                              // Java 1.0
public void hide();                                                 // Java 1.0
public boolean imageUpdate(Image img, int flags, int x, int y,
            int w, int h);
public boolean inside(int x, int y);                                // Java 1.0
public void invalidate();
public boolean isEnabled();
public boolean isFocusTransversable();                              // Java 1.1
public boolean isShowing();
public boolean isValid();
public boolean isVisible();
public boolean keyDown(Event evt, int key);                         // Java 1.0
public boolean keyUp(Event evt, int key);                           // Java 1.0
public void layout();                                               // Java 1.0
public void list();
public void list(PrintStream out);
public void list(PrintStream out, int indent);
public void list(PrintStream out);                                  // Java 1.1
public Component locate(int x, int y);                              // Java 1.0
public Point location();                                            // Java 1.0
public boolean lostFocus(Event evt, Object what);                   // Java 1.0
public Dimension minimumSize();                                     // Java 1.0
public boolean mouseDown(Event evt, int x, int y);                  // Java 1.0
public boolean mouseDrag(Event evt, int x, int y);                  // Java 1.0
public boolean mouseEnter(Event evt, int x, int y);                 // Java 1.0
public boolean mouseExit(Event evt, int x, int y);                  // Java 1.0
public boolean mouseMove(Event evt, int x, int y);                  // Java 1.0
public boolean mouseUp(Event evt, int x, int y);                    // Java 1.0
public void move(int x, int y);                                     // Java 1.0
public void nextFocus();                                            // Java 1.0
public void paint(Graphics g);
public void paintAll(Graphics g);
```

```
protected String paramString();
public boolean postEvent(Event evt);                        // Java 1.0
public Dimension preferredSize();                           // Java 1.0
public boolean prepareImage(Image image, ImageObserver observer);
public prepareImage(Image image, int width, int height,
        ImageObserver observer);
public void print(Graphics g);
public void printAll(Graphics g);
public synchronized void remove(MenuComponent popup);       // Java 1.1
public synchronized void removeComponentListener(ComponentListener l);
                                                            // Java 1.1
public synchronized void removeFocusListener(FocusListener l);
                                                            // Java 1.1
public synchronized void removeKeyListener(KeyListener l);  // Java 1.1
public synchronized void removeMouseListener(MouseListener l);
                                                            // Java 1.1
public synchronized void removeMouseMotionListener(
        MouseMotionListener l);                             // Java 1.1
public void removeNotify();
public void repaint();
public void repaint(int x, int y, int width, int height);
public void repaint(long tm);
public void repaint(long tm, int x, int y, int width, int height);
public void requestFocus();
public void reshape(int x, int y, int width, int height);  // Java 1.0
public void resize(Dimension d);                           // Java 1.0
public void resize(int width, int height);                 // Java 1.0
public void setBackground(Color c);
public void setBounds(int x, int y, int width, int height); // Java 1.1
public void setBounds(Rectangle r);                        // Java 1.1
public synchronized void setCursor(Cursor cursor);         // Java 1.1
public void setEnabled(boolean b);                         // Java 1.1
public void setFont(Font f);
public void setForeground(Color c);
public void setLocale(Locale l);                           // Java 1.1
public void setLocation(int x, int y);                     // Java 1.1
public void setLocation(Point p);                          // Java 1.1
public void setName(String name);                          // Java 1.1
public void setSize(int width, int height);                // Java 1.1
public void setSize(Dimension d);                          // Java 1.1
public void setVisible(boolean b);                         // Java 1.1
public void show();                                        // Java 1.0
public void show(boolean cond);                            // Java 1.0
public Dimension size();                                   // Java 1.0
public String toString();
public void transferFocus();                               // Java 1.1
public void update(Graphics g);
public void validate();
```

D.2.9 Class java.awt.Container

The Container class is the abstract superclass representing all components that can hold other components. The following are defined:

```
// Methods
public Component add(Component comp);
public Component add(Component comp, int pos);
public Component add(String name, Component comp);
public void add(Component comp, Object constraints);       // Java 1.1
public void add(Component comp, Object constraints, int index);
                                                            // Java 1.1
```

```
public void addContainerListener(ContainerListener l);         // Java 1.1
public void addNotify();
public int countComponents();                                  // Java 1.0
public void deliverEvent(Event evt);                           // Java 1.0
public void doLayout();                                        // Java 1.1
public void getAlignmentX();                                   // Java 1.1
public void getAlignmentY();                                   // Java 1.1
public Component getComponent(int n);
public Component getComponentAt(int x, int y);                 // Java 1.1
public Component getComponentAt(Point p);                      // Java 1.1
public int getComponentCount();                                // Java 1.1
public Component[] getComponents();
public getInsets();                                            // Java 1.1
public LayoutManager getLayout();
public Dimension getMaximumSize();                             // Java 1.1
public Dimension getMinimumSize();                             // Java 1.1
public Dimension getPreferredSize();                           // Java 1.1
public Insets insets();                                        // Java 1.0
public void invalidate();                                      // Java 1.1
pubic boolean isAncestorOf(Component c);                       // Java 1.1
public void layout();                                          // Java 1.0
public void list(PrintStream out, int indent);
public void list(PrintWriter out, int indent);                // Java 1.1
public Component locate(int x, int y);                         // Java 1.0
public Dimension minimumSize();                                // Java 1.0
public void paintComponents(Graphics g);
protected String paramString();
public Dimension preferredSize();                              // Java 1.0
public void print(Graphics g);                                 // Java 1.1
public void printComponents(Graphics g);
public void remove(int index);                                 // Java 1.1
public void remove(Component comp);
public void removeAll();
public void removeContainerListener(ContainerListener l);      // Java 1.1
public void removeNotify();
public void setLayout(LayoutManager mgr);
public void validate();
```

D.2.10   Class *java.awt.Cursor*

The Cursor class represents a mouse cursor. The following are defined:

```
// Constructors
public Cursor(int type);                                       // Java 1.1

// Constants
public static final int DEFAULT_CURSOR;                        // Java 1.1
public static final int CROSSHAIR_CURSOR, HAND_CURSOR;         // Java 1.1
public static final int MOVE_CURSOR;                           // Java 1.1
public static final int TEXT_CURSOR, WAIT_CURSOR;              // Java 1.1
public static final int N_RESIZE_CURSOR, S_RESIZE_CURSOR;      // Java 1.1
public static final int E_RESIZE_CURSOR, W_RESIZE_CURSOR;      // Java 1.1
public static final int NE_RESIZE_CURSOR, NW_RESIZE_CURSOR;    // Java 1.1
public static final int SE_RESIZE_CURSOR, SW_RESIZE_CURSOR;    // Java 1.1

// Methods
public static Cursor getDefaultCursor();                       // Java 1.1
public static Cursor getPredefinedCursor();                    // Java 1.1
```

D.2.11 Class java.awt.Dialog

The `Dialog` class supports a dialog window, in which a user can enter data. Dialog windows are invisible until the show method is used. The following are defined:

```
// Constructors
public Dialog(Frame parent);                                    // Java 1.1
public Dialog(Frame parent, boolean modal);
public Dialog(Frame parent, String title);                      // Java 1.1
public Dialog(Frame parent, String title, boolean modal);

// Methods
public void addNotify();
public String getTitle();
public boolean isModal();
public boolean isResizable();
public void setModal(boolean b);                                // Java 1.1
protected String paramString();
public void setResizable(boolean resizable);
public void setTitle(String title);
public void show();                                             // Java 1.1
```

D.2.12 Class java.awt.Dimension

The `Dimension` class contains the width and height of a component in an object. The following are defined:

```
// Fields
public int height;
public int width;

// Constructors
public Dimension();
public Dimension(Dimension d);
public Dimension(int width, int height);

// Methods
public boolean equals(Object obj);                             // Java 1.1
public Dimension getSize();                                    // Java 1.1
public void setSize(Dimension d);                             // Java 1.1
public void setSize(int width, int height);                  // Java 1.1
public String toString();
```

D.2.13 Class java.awt.Event

The `Event` class encapsulates user events from the GUI. The following are defined:

```
// Fields
public Object arg;
public int clickCount;
public Event evt;
public int id;
public int key;
public int modifiers;
public Object target;
public long when;
public int x;
public int y;

// possible values for the id field
```

```
public final static int ACTION_EVENT, GOT_FOCUS;
public final static int KEY_ACTION, KEY_ACTION_RELEASE;
public final static int KEY_PRESS, KEY_RELEASE;
public final static int LIST_DESELECT, LIST_SELECT;
public final static int LOAD_FILE, LOST_FOCUS;
public final static int MOUSE_DOWN, MOUSE_DRAG;
public final static int MOUSE_ENTER, MOUSE_EXIT;
public final static int MOUSE_MOVE, MOUSE_UP;
public final static int SAVE_FILE, SCROLL_ABSOLUTE;
public final static int SCROLL_BEGIN, SCROLL_END;             // Java 1.1
public final static int SCROLL_LINE_DOWN, SCROLL_LINE_UP;
public final static int SCROLL_PAGE_DOWN, SCROLL_PAGE_UP;
public final static int WINDOW_DEICONIFY, WINDOW_DESTROY;
public final static int WINDOW_EXPOSE, WINDOW_ICONIFY;
public final static int WINDOW_MOVED;

// possible values for the key field when the
// action is KEY_ACTION or KEY_ACTION_RELEASE
public final static int DOWN, END;
public final static int F1, F2, F3, F4, F5, F6, F7, F8, F9, F10, F11, F12
public final static int HOME, LEFT, PGDN, PGUP, RIGHT, UP;
public final static int INSERT, DELETE;                      // Java 1.1
public final static int BACK_SPACE, ENTER;                   // Java 1.1
public final static int TAB, ESCAPE;                         // Java 1.1
public final static int CAPS_LOCK, NUM_LOCK;                 // Java 1.1
public final static int SCROLL_LOCK, PAUSE;                  // Java 1.1
public final static int PRINT_SCREEN;                        // Java 1.1

// possible masks for the modifiers field
public final static int ALT_MASK;
public final static int CTRL_MASK;
public final static int META_MASK;
public final static int SHIFT_MASK;

// Constructors
public Event(Object target, int id, Object arg);
public Event(Object target, long when, int id,
        int x, int y, int key, int modifiers);
public Event(Object target, long when, int id,
        int x, int y, int key, int modifiers, Object arg);

// Methods
public boolean controlDown();
public boolean metaDown();
protected String paramString();
public boolean shiftDown();
public String toString();
public void translate(int dX, int dY);
```

D.2.14   Class java.awt.FileDialog

The FileDialog class displays a dialog window. The following are defined:

```
// Fields
public final static int LOAD, SAVE;

// Constructors
public FileDialog(Frame parent);                             // Java 1.1
public FileDialog(Frame parent, String title);
public FileDialog(Frame parent, String title, int mode);
// Methods
public void addNotify();
```

```
public String getDirectory();
public String getFile();
public FilenameFilter getFilenameFilter();
public int getMode();
protected String paramString();
public void setDirectory(String dir);
public void setFile(String file);
public void setFilenameFilter(FilenameFilter filter);
```

D.2.15   Class java.awt.FlowLayout

The FlowLayout class arranges components from left to right. The following are defined:

```
// Fields
public final static int CENTER, LEFT, RIGHT;

// Constructors
public FlowLayout();
public FlowLayout(int align);
public FlowLayout(int align, int hgap, int vgap);

// Methods
public void addLayoutComponent(String name, Component comp);
public int getAlignment();                                     // Java 1.1
public int getHgap();                                          // Java 1.1
public int getVgap();                                          // Java 1.1
public void layoutContainer(Container target);
public Dimension minimumLayoutSize(Container target);
public Dimension preferredLayoutSize(Container target);
public void removeLayoutComponent(Component comp);
public void setAlignment(int align);                           // Java 1.1
public void setHgap(int hgap);                                 // Java 1.1
public void setVgap(int vgap);                                 // Java 1.1
public String toString();
```

D.2.16   Class java.awt.Font

The Font class represents fonts. The following are defined:

```
// Fields
protected String name;
protected int size;
protected int style;

// style has the following bit masks
public final static int BOLD, ITALIC, PLAIN;

// Constructors
public Font(String name, int style, int size);

// Methods
public static Font decode(String str);                         // Java 1.1
public boolean equals(Object obj);
public String getFamily();
public static Font getFont(String nm);
public static Font getFont(String nm, Font font);
public String getName();
public int getSize();
public int getStyle();
public FontPeer getPeer();                                     // Java 1.1
```

```
public int hashCode();
public boolean isBold();
public boolean isItalic();
public boolean isPlain();
public String toString();
```

D.2.17   Class java.awt.FontMetrics

The `FontMetrics` class provides information about the rendering of a particular font. The following are defined:

```
// Fields
protected Font font;

// Constructors
protected FontMetrics(Font font);

// Methods
public int bytesWidth(byte data[], int off, int len);
public int charsWidth(char data[], int off, int len);
public int charWidth(char ch);
public int charWidth(int ch);
public int getAscent();
public int getDescent();
public Font getFont();
public int getHeight();
public int getLeading();
public int getMaxAdvance();
public int getMaxAscent();
public int getMaxDescent();                              // Java 1.0
public int[] getWidths();
public int stringWidth(String str);
public String toString();
```

D.2.18   Class java.awt.Frame

The `Frame` class contains information on the top-level window. The following are defined:

```
// possible cursor types for the setCursor method
public final static int CROSSHAIR_CURSOR, DEFAULT_CURSOR;
public final static int E_RESIZE_CURSOR, HAND_CURSOR;
public final static int MOVE_CURSOR, N_RESIZE_CURSOR;
public final static int NE_RESIZE_CURSOR, NW_RESIZE_CURSOR;
public final static int S_RESIZE_CURSOR, SE_RESIZE_CURSOR;
public final static int SW_RESIZE_CURSOR, TEXT_CURSOR;
public final static int W_RESIZE_CURSOR, WAIT_CURSOR;
// Constructors
public Frame();
public Frame(String title);
// Methods
public void addNotify();
public void dispose();
public int getCursorType();                              // Java 1.0
public Image getIconImage();
public MenuBar getMenuBar();
public String getTitle();
public boolean isResizable();
protected String paramString();
public void remove(MenuComponent m);
public void setCursor(int cursorType);                   // Java 1.0
```

```
public void setIconImage(Image image);
public void setMenuBar(MenuBar mb);
public void setResizable(boolean resizable);
public void setTitle(String title);
```

D.2.19   Class java.awt.Graphics

The Graphics class is an abstract class for all graphics contexts. This allows an application to draw onto components or onto off-screen images. The following are defined:

```
// Constructors
protected Graphics();

// Methods
public abstract void clearRect(int x, int y, int width, int height);
public abstract void clipRect(int x, int y, int width, int height);
public abstract void copyArea(int x, int y, int width, int height,
             int dx, int dy);
public abstract Graphics create();
public Graphics create(int x, int y, int width, int height);
public abstract void dispose();
public void draw3DRect(int x, int y, int width, int height,
             boolean raised);
public abstract void drawArc(int x, int y, int width, int height,
             int startAngle, int arcAngle);
public void drawBytes(byte data[], int offset, int length, int x, int y);
public void drawChars(char data[], int offset, int length, int x, int y);
public abstract boolean drawImage(Image img, int x, int y, Color bgcolor,
             ImageObserver observer);
public abstract boolean drawImage(Image img, int x, int y,
             ImageObserver observer);
public abstract boolean drawImage(Image img, int x, int y, int width,
             int height, Color bgcolor, ImageObserver observer);
public abstract boolean drawImage(Image img, int x, int y, int width,
int height, ImageObserver observer);
public abstract boolean drawImage(Image img, int x, int y, int width,
int height, Color bgcolor, ImageObserver observer);         // Java 1.1
public abstract void drawLine(int x1, int y1, int x2, int y2);
public abstract void drawOval(int x, int y,int width, int height);
public abstract void drawPolygon(int xPoints[], int yPoints[],
             int nPoints);
public void drawPolygon(Polygon p);
public abstract void drawPolyline(int xPoints[], int yPoints[],
             int nPoints);                                    // Java 1.1
public void drawRect(int x, int y, int width, int height);
public abstract void drawRoundRect(int x, int y, int width,
  int height, int arcWidth, int arcHeight);
public abstract void drawString(String str, int x, int y);
public void fill3DRect(int x, int y, int width, int height,
             boolean raised);
public abstract void fillArc(int x, int y, int width, int height,
             int startAngle int arcAngle);
public abstract void fillOval(int x, int y, int width, int height);
public abstract void fillPolygon(int xPoints[], int yPoints[],
             int nPoints);
public void fillPolygon(Polygon p);
public abstract void fillRect(int x, int y, int width, int height);
public abstract void fillRoundRect(int x, int y, int width, int height,
             int arcWidth, int arcHeight);
public void finalize();
public abstract Shape getClip();                             // Java 1.1
public abstract Rectangle getClipBounds();                   // Java 1.1
```

```
public abstract Rectangle getClipRect();                          // Java 1.0
public abstract Color getColor();
public abstract Font getFont();
public FontMetrics getFontMetrics();
public abstract FontMetrics getFontMetrics(Font f);
public abstract void setClip(int x, int y, int width, int height);
                                                                   // Java 1.1
public abstract void setClip(Shape clip);                          // Java 1.1
public abstract void setColor(Color c);
public abstract void setFont(Font font);
public abstract void setPaintMode();
public abstract void setXORMode(Color c1);
public String toString();
public abstract void translate(int x, int y);
```

D.2.20   Class java.awt.Image

The Image abstract class is the superclass of all classes that represents graphical images.

```
// Constants
public static final int SCALE_AREA_AVERAGING, SCALE_DEFAULT;
public static final int SCALE_FAST, SCALE_REPLICATE;
public static final int SCALE_SMOOTH;

// Fields
public final static Object UndefinedProperty;

// Constructors
public Image();

// Methods
public abstract void flush();
public abstract Graphics getGraphics();
public abstract int getHeight(ImageObserver observer);
public abstract Object getProperty(String name, ImageObserver observer);
public Image getScaledInstance(int width, int height, int hints);
                                                                   // Java 1.1
public abstract ImageProducer getSource();
public abstract int getWidth(ImageObserver observer)
```

D.2.21   Class java.awt.Insets

The Insets object represents borders of a container and specifies the space that should be left around the edges of a container. The following are defined:

```
// Fields
public int bottom, left;
public int right, top;
// Constructors
public Insets(int top, int left, int bottom, int right);

// Methods
public Object clone();
public boolean equals(Object obj);                                // Java 1.1
public String toString();
```

D.2.22   Class java.awt.Label

The label class is a component for placing text in a container. The following are defined:

```
// Fields
public final static int CENTER, LEFT, RIGHT;

// Constructors
public Label();
public Label(String label);
public Label(String label, int alignment);

// Methods
public void addNotify();
public int getAlignment();
public String getText();
protected String paramString();
public void setAlignment(int alignment);
public void setText(String label);
```

D.2.23   Class *java.awt.List*

The List object can be used to produce a scrolling list of text items. It can be set up so that the user can either pick one or many items. The following are defined:

```
// Constructors
public List();
public List(int rows);                                          // Java 1.1
public List(int rows, boolean multipleSelections);

// Methods
public void add(String item);                                   // Java 1.1
public void addActionListener(ActionListener l);                // Java 1.1
public void addItem(String item);
public void addItem(String item, int index);
public synchronized void addItemListener(ItemListener l);       // Java 1.1
public void addNotify();
public boolean allowsMultipleSelections();                      // Java 1.0
public void clear();                                            // Java 1.0
public int countItems();                                        // Java 1.0
public void delItem(int position);
public void delItems(int start, int end);                       // Java 1.0
public void deselect(int index);
public String getItem(int index);
public int getItemCount();                                      // Java 1.1
public synchronized String[] getItems();                        // Java 1.1
public Dimension getMinimumSize(int rows);                      // Java 1.1
public Dimension getMinimumSize();                              // Java 1.1
public Dimension getPreferredSize(int rows);                    // Java 1.1
public Dimension getPreferredSize();                            // Java 1.1
public int getRows();
public int getSelectedIndex();
public int[] getSelectedIndexes();
public String getSelectedItem();
public String[] getSelectedItems();
public Object[] getSelectedObjects();                           // Java 1.1
public int getVisibleIndex();
public boolean isIndexSelected(int index);                      // Java 1.1
public MultipleMode();                                          // Java 1.1
public boolean isSelected(int index);                          // Java 1.0
public void makeVisible(int index);
public Dimension minimumSize();                                 // Java 1.0
public Dimension minimumSize(int rows);                         // Java 1.0
protected String paramString();
public Dimension preferredSize();                               // Java 1.0
```

```
public Dimension preferredSize(int rows);              // Java 1.0
public synchronized void remove(String item);          // Java 1.1
public synchronized void remove(int position);         // Java 1.1
public synchronized void removeActionListener(ActionListener l);
                                                        // Java 1.1
public synchronized void removeAll();                   // Java 1.1
public synchronized void removeItemListener(ItemListener l); // Java 1.1
public void removeNotify();
public void replaceItem(String newValue, int index);
public void select(int index);
public synchronized void setMultipleMode(boolean b);   // Java 1.1
public void setMultipleSelections(boolean v);
```

D.2.24 Class *java.awt.MediaTracker*

The MediaTracker class contains a number of media objects, such as images and audio. The following are defined:

```
// Fields
public final static int ABORTED, COMPLETE;
public final static int ERRORED, LOADING;

// Constructors
public MediaTracker(Component comp);

// Methods
public void addImage(Image image, int id);
public void addImage(Image image, int id, int w, int h);
public boolean checkAll();
public boolean checkAll(boolean load);
public boolean checkID(int id);
public boolean checkID(int id, boolean load);
public Object[] getErrorsAny();
public Object[] getErrorsID(int id);
public boolean isErrorAny();
public boolean isErrorID(int id);
public synchronized removeImage(Image image);          // Java 1.1
public synchronized removeImage(Image image, int id);  // Java 1.1
public synchronized removeImage(Image image, int id, int width, int height);
                                                        // Java 1.1
public int statusAll(boolean load);
public int statusID(int id, boolean load);
public void waitForAll();
public boolean waitForAll(long ms);
public void waitForID(int id);
public boolean waitForID(int id, long ms);
```

D.2.25 Class *java.awt.Menu*

The Menu object contains a pull-down component for a menu bar. The following are defined:

```
// Constructors
public Menu();                                          // Java 1.1
public Menu(String label);
public Menu(String label, boolean tearOff);

// Methods
public MenuItem add(MenuItem mi);
public void add(String label);
public void addNotify();
```

```
public void addSeparator();
public int countItems();
public MenuItem getItem(int index);
public int getItemCount();                                    // Java 1.1
public synchronized void Insert(MenuItem menuitem, int index);// Java 1.1
public void InsertSepatator(int index);                       // Java 1.1
public boolean isTearOff();
public void remove(int index);
public void remove(MenuComponent item);
public synchronized void removeAll();                         // Java 1.1
public void removeNotify();
```

D.2.26   Class *java.awt.MenuBar*

The MenuBar object contains a menu bar which is bound to a frame. The following are defined:

```
// Constructors
public MenuBar();

// Methods
public Menu add(Menu m);
public void addNotify();
public int countMenus();
public void deleteShortCut(MenuShortCut s);                   // Java 1.1
public Menu getHelpMenu();
public Menu getMenu(int i);
public int getMenuCount();                                    // Java 1.1
public MenuItem getShortcutMenuItem(MenuShortcut s);          // Java 1.1
public void remove(int index);
public void remove(MenuComponent m);
public void removeNotify();
public void setHelpMenu(Menu m);
public synchronized Enumeration shortcuts();                  // Java 1.1
```

D.2.27   Class *java.awt.MenuComponent*

The MenuComponent abstract class is the superclass of all menu-related components. The following are defined:

```
// Constructors
public MenuComponent();

// Methods
public final void dispatchEvent(AWTEvent e);                 // Java 1.1
public Font getFont();
public String getName();                                     // Java 1.1
public MenuContainer getParent();
public MenuComponentPeer getPeer();                          // Java 1.0
protected String paramString();
public boolean postEvent(Event evt);
public void removeNotify();
public void setFont(Font f);
public void setName(String name);                            // Java 1.1
public String toString();
```

D.2.28   Class *java.awt.MenuItem*

The MenuItem class contains all menu items. The following are defined:

```
// Constructors
public MenuItem();                                            // Java 1.1
public MenuItem(String label);
public MenuItem(String label, MenuShortcut s);               // Java 1.1

// Methods
public void addActionListener(ActionListener l);            // Java 1.1
public void addNotify();
public void deleteShortcut();                                // Java 1.1
public void disable();                                       // Java 1.0
public void enable();                                        // Java 1.0
public void enable(boolean cond);                            // Java 1.0
public String getLabel();
public MenuShortcut getShortcut();                           // Java 1.1
public boolean isEnabled();
public String paramString();
public synchronized void removeActionListener(ActionListener l);
                                                             // Java 1.1
public void setActionCommand(String command);               // Java 1.1
public synchronized void setEnabled(boolean b);             // Java 1.1
public void setLabel(String label);
public void setShortcut(MenuShortcut s);                     // Java 1.1
```

D.2.29   Class *java.awt.MenuShortcut*

The MenuShortcut class has been added with Java 1.1. It represents a keystroke used to select a MenuItem. The following are defined:

```
// Constructors
public MenuShortcut(int key);                                // Java 1.1
public MenuShortcut(int key, boolean useShiftModifier);      // Java 1.1

// Methods
public boolean equals(MenuShortcut s);                       // Java 1.1
public int getKey();                                         // Java 1.1
public String toString();                                    // Java 1.1
public boolean usesShiftModifier();                          // Java 1.1
```

D.2.30   Class *java.awt.Panel*

The Panel class provides space into which an application can attach a component. The following are defined:

```
// Constructors
public Panel();
public Panel(LayoutManger layout);                           // Java 1.1

// Methods
public void addNotify();
```

D.2.31   Class *java.awt.Point*

The Point class represents an (x, y) co-ordinate. The following are defined:

```
// Fields
public int x;
public int y;

// Constructors
public Point();                                              // Java 1.1
public Point(Point p);                                       // Java 1.1
```

```
public Point(int x, int y);

// Methods
public boolean equals(Object obj);
public Point getLocation();                                    // Java 1.1
public int hashCode();
public void move(int x, int y);
public void setLocation(Point p);                              // Java 1.1
public void setLocation(int x, int y);                         // Java 1.1
public String toString();
public void translate(int dx, int dy);
```

D.2.32   Class *java.awt.Polygon*

The Polygon class consists of an array of (x, y), which define the sides of a polygon. The following are defined:

```
// Fields
public int npoints, xpoints[],ypoints[];

// Constructors
public Polygon();
public Polygon(int xpoints[], int ypoints[], int npoints);

// Methods
public void addPoint(int x, int y);
public boolean contains(Point p);                              // Java 1.1
public boolean contains(int x, int y);                         // Java 1.1
public Rectangle getBoundingBox();                             // Java 1.0
public Rectangle getBounds();                                  // Java 1.1
public boolean inside(int x, int y);                           // Java 1.0
```

D.2.33   Class *java.awt.PopupMenu*

The PopupMenu class has been added with Java 1.1. It represetns a pop-up menu rather than a pull-down menu. The following are defined:

```
// Constructors
public PopupMenu();                                            // Java 1.1
public PopupMenu(String label);                                // Java 1.1

// Methods
public synchronized void addNotify();                          // Java 1.1
public void show(Component origin, int x, int y);              // Java 1.1
```

D.2.34   Class *java.awt.Rectangle*

The Rectangle class defines an area defined by its top-left (x, y) co-ordinate, its width and its height. The following are defined:

```
// Fields
public int height, width, x, y;

// Constructors
public Rectangle();
public Rectangle(Rectangle r);                                 // Java 1.1
public Rectangle(Dimension d);
public Rectangle(int width, int height);
public Rectangle(int x, int y, int width, int height);
public Rectangle(Point p);
public Rectangle(Point p, Dimension d);
```

```
// Methods
public void add(int newx, int newy);
public void add(Point pt);
public void add(Rectangle r);
public boolean contains(Point p);                              // Java 1.1
public boolean contains(int x, int y);                         // Java 1.1
public boolean equals(Object obj);
public Rectangle getBounds();                                  // Java 1.1
public Point getLocation();                                    // Java 1.1
public Dimension getSize();                                    // Java 1.1
public void grow(int h, int v);
public int hashCode();
public boolean inside(int x, int y);                           // Java 1.0
public Rectangle intersection(Rectangle r);
public boolean intersects(Rectangle r);
public boolean isEmpty();
public void move(int x, int y);                                // Java 1.0
public void reshape(int x, int y, int width, int height);      // Java 1.0
public void resize(int width, int height);                     // Java 1.0
public void setBounds(Rectangle r);                            // Java 1.1
public void setBounds(int x, int y, int width, int height);    // Java 1.1
public void setLocation(Point p);                              // Java 1.1
public void setLocation(int x, int y);                         // Java 1.1
public void setSize(Dimension d);                              // Java 1.1
public void setSize(int x, int y);                             // Java 1.1
public String toString();
public void translate(int dx, int dy);
public Rectangle union(Rectangle r);
```

D.2.35   Class *java.awt.Scrollbar*

The Scrollbar class is a convenient means of allowing a user to select from a range of values. The following are defined:

```
// Fields
public final static int HORIZONTAL, VERTICAL;

// Constructors
public Scrollbar();
public Scrollbar(int orientation);
public Scrollbar(int orientation, int value, int visible, int minimum,
          int maximum);

// Methods
public synchronized void addAdjustmenuListener(AdjustmentListener l);
                                                               // Java 1.1
public void addNotify();
public int getBlockIncrement();                                // Java 1.1
public int getLineIncrement();                                 // Java 1.0
public int getMaximum();
public int getMinimum();
public int getOrientation();
public int getPageIncrement();                                 // Java 1.0
public int getUnitIncrement();                                 // Java 1.1
public int getValue();
public int getVisible();                                       // Java 1.0
protected String paramString();
public void setLineIncrement(int l);                           // Java 1.0
public synchronized void setMaximum(int max);                  // Java 1.1
public synchronized void setMinimum(int min);                  // Java 1.1
public synchronized void setOrientation(int orien);            // Java 1.1
```

```
public void setPageIncrement(int l);                              // Java 1.0
public void setValue(int value);
public void setValues(int value, int visible, int minimum, int maximum);
public void setVisibleAmount(int am);                             // Java 1.1
```

D.2.36 Class *java.awt.TextArea*

The TextArea class allows for a multi-line area for displaying text. The following are
defined:

```
// Constructors
public TextArea();
public TextArea(int rows, int cols);
public TextArea(String text);
public TextArea(String text, int rows, int cols);
public TextArea(String text, int rows, int cols, int scrollbars);
                                                                 // Java 1.1
// Constants
public static final int SCROLLBARS_BOTH;                         // Java 1.1
public static final int SCROLLBARS_HORIZONTAL_ONLY;              // Java 1.1
public static final int SCROLLBARS_NONE;                         // Java 1.1
public static final int SCROLLBARS_VERTICAL_ONLY;                // Java 1.1

// Methods
public void addNotify();
public synchronized void append(String str);                     // Java 1.1
public void appendText(String str);                              // Java 1.0
public int getColumns();
public Dimension getMinimumSize(int rows, int cols);             // Java 1.1
public Dimension getMinimumSize();                               // Java 1.1
public Dimension getPreferredSize(int rows, int cols);           // Java 1.1
public Dimension getPreferredSize();                             // Java 1.1
public int getRows();
public int getScrollbarVisibility();                             // Java 1.1
public void insertText(String str, int pos);                     // Java 1.1
public Dimension minimumSize();                                  // Java 1.0
public Dimension minimumSize(int rows, int cols);                // Java 1.0
protected String paramString();
public Dimension preferredSize();                                // Java 1.0
public Dimension preferredSize(int rows, int cols);              // Java 1.0
public void replaceText(String str, int start, int end);         // Java 1.0
public void setColumns(int cols);                                // Java 1.1
public void setRows(int rows);                                   // Java 1.1
```

D.2.37 Class *java.awt.TextComponent*

The TextComponent class is the superclass of any component that allows the editing
of some text. The following are defined:

```
// Methods
public void addTextListener(TextListener l);                     // Java 1.1
public int getCaretPosition();                                   // Java 1.1
public String getSelectedText();
public int getSelectionEnd();
public int getSelectionStart();
public String getText();
public boolean isEditable();
protected String paramString();
public void removeNotify();
public void removeTextListener(TextListener l);                  // Java 1.1
```

```
public void select(int selStart, int selEnd);
public void selectAll();
public void setCaretPosition(int position);              // Java 1.1
public void setEditable(boolean t);
public synchronized void setSelectionEnd(int selectionEnd);   // Java 1.1
public synchronized void setSelectionStart(int selectionStart);  // Java 1.1
public void setText(String t);
```

D.2.38   Class *java.awt.TextField*

The TextField class is a component that presents the user with a single editable line of text. The following are defined:

```
// Constructors
public TextField();
public TextField(int cols);
public TextField(String text);
public TextField(String text, int cols);

// Methods
public synchronized void addActionListener(ActionListener l); // Java 1.1
public void addNotify();
public boolean echoCharIsSet();
public int getColumns();
public char getEchoChar();
public Dimension getMinimumSize(int cols);              // Java 1.1
public Dimension getMinimumSize();                      // Java 1.1
public Dimension getPreferredSize(int cols);            // Java 1.1
public Dimension getPreferredSize();                    // Java 1.1
public Dimension minimumSize();                         // Java 1.0
public Dimension minimumSize(int cols);                 // Java 1.0
protected String paramString();
public Dimension preferredSize();                       // Java 1.0
public Dimension preferredSize(int cols);               // Java 1.0
public void setColumns(int cols);                       // Java 1.1
public void setEchoChar(char c);                        // Java 1.1
public void setEchoCharacter(char c);                   // Java 1.0
```

D.2.39   Class *java.awt.Toolkit*

The Toolkit class is the abstract superclass of all actual implementations of the Abstract Window Toolkit. The following are defined:

```
// Constructors
public Toolkit();

// Methods
public abstract int beep();                             // Java 1.1
public abstract int checkImage(Image image, int width,
          int height, ImageObserver observer);
public abstract Image createImage(ImageProducer producer);
public Image createImage(byte[] imagedatea);            // Java 1.1
public Image createImage(byte[] imagedata, int imageoffset,
          int imagelength);                             // Java 1.1
public abstract ColorModel getColorModel();
public static Toolkit getDefaultToolkit();
public abstract String[] getFontList();
public abstract FontMetrics getFontMetrics(Font font);
public abstract Image getImage(String filename);
public abstract Image getImage(URL url);
public int getMenuShortcutKeyMask();                    // Java 1.1
```

```
public abstract PrintJob getPrintJob(Frame frame, String jobtitle,
        Properties props);                                    // Java 1.1
public abstract int getScreenResolution();
public abstract Dimension getScreenSize();
public abstract Clipboard getSystemClipbaord();               // Java 1.1
public abstract EventQueue getSystemEventQueue();             // Java 1.1
public abstract boolean prepareImage(Image image, int width,
        int height, ImageObserver observer);
public abstract void sync();
```

D.2.40 Class *java.awt.Window*

The `Window` class is the top-level window; it has no borders and no menu bar. The following are defined:

```
// Constructors
public Window(Frame parent);
// Methods
public void addNotify();
public synchronized void addWindowListener(WindowListener l); // Java 1.1
public void dispose();
public Component getFocusOwner();                             // Java 1.1
public Locale getLocale();                                    // Java 1.1
public Toolkit getToolkit();
public final String getWarningString();
public boolean isShowing();                                   // Java 1.1
public void pack();
public postEvent(Event e);                                    // Java 1.1
public synchronized void removeWindowListener(WindowListener l);
public void show();
public void toBack();
public void toFront();
```

D.3 Package java.awt.datatransfer

D.3.1 Class *java.awt.datatransfer.Clipboard*

The `Clipboard` class has been added with Java 1.1. It represents a clipboard onto which data can be transferred using cut-and-paste techniques. The following are defined:

```
// Constructors
public Clipboard(String name);                               // Java 1.1

// Methods
public synchronized Transferable getContents(Object requestor);
                                                             // Java 1.1
public String getName();                                     // Java 1.1
public synchronized void setContents(Transferable contents,
        Clipboard owner);                                    // Java 1.1
```

D.4.1 Class *java.awt.event.ActionEvent*

The `ActionEvent` class has been added with Java 1.1. It occurs when a event happens for a `Button`, `List`, `MenuItem` or `TextField`. The following are defined:

```
// Constructors
public ActionEvent(Object src, String cmd);              // Java 1.1

// Methods
public String getActionCommand();                        // Java 1.1
public int getModifiers();                               // Java 1.1
public int paramString();                                // Java 1.1
```

D.4.2 Interface *java.awt.event.ActionListener*

The `ActionListener` interface has been added with Java 1.1. It defines the method which is called by an `ActionEvent`. The following is defined:

```
public void actionPerformed(ActionEvent e);              // Java 1.1
```

D.4.3 Class *java.awt.event.AdjustmentEvent*

The `AdjustmentEvent` class has been added with Java 1.1. It occurs when a event happens for a `Scrollbar`. The following are defined:

```
// Constructors
public AdjustmentEvent(Object src, int id, int type, int value);
                                                         //Java 1.1

// Methods
public Adjustable getAdjustable();                       // Java 1.1
public int getAdjustmentType();                          // Java 1.1
public int getValue();                                   // Java 1.1
public String paramString();                             // Java 1.1
```

D.4.4 Class *java.awt.event.AdjustmentListener*

The `AdjustmentListener` interface has been added with Java 1.1. It defines the method which is called by an `AdjustmentEvent`. The following is defined:

```
public void adjustmentValueChanged(AdjustmentEvent e);   // Java 1.1
```

D.4.5 Class *java.awt.event.ComponentEvent*

The `ComponentEvent` class has been added with Java 1.1. It occurs when a event happens for a `Component`. The following are defined:

```
// Constructors
public ComponentEvent(Object src, int id, int type, int value);

// Methods
public Component getComponent();                         // Java 1.1
public String paramString();                             // Java 1.1
```

D.4.6 Class *java.awt.event.ComponentListener*

The `ComponentListener` interface has been added with Java 1.1. It defines the method which is called by a `ComponentEvent`. The following are defined:

```
public void componentHidden(ComponentEvent e);      // Java 1.1
public void componentMoved(ComponentEvent e);       // Java 1.1
public void componentResized(ComponentEvent e);     // Java 1.1
public void componentShown(ComponentEvent e);       // Java 1.1
```

D.4.7 Class *java.awt.event.ContainerEvent*

The `ComponentEvent` class has been added with Java 1.1. It occurs when a event happens for a `Container`. The following are defined:

```
// Constructors
public ContainerEvent(Component src, int id, Compoent child);

// Methods
public Component getChild();                         // Java 1.1
public Component getContainer();                     // Java 1.1
public String paramString();                         // Java 1.1
```

D.4.8 Class *java.awt.event.ContainerListener*

The `ContainerListener` interface has been added with Java 1.1. It defines the method which is called by a `ContainerEvent`. The following are defined:

```
public void componentAdded(ComponentEvent e);       // Java 1.1
public void componentRemoved(ComponentEvent e);     // Java 1.1
```

D.4.9 Class *java.awt.event.ItemEvent*

The `ItemEvent` class has been added with Java 1.1. It occurs when a event happens for a `Container`. The following are defined:

```
// Constructors
public ItemEvent(ItemSelectable src, int id, Object item,
            int stateChanged);                       // Java 1.1

// Methods
public Object getItem();                             // Java 1.1
public ItemSelectable getItemSelectable();           // Java 1.1
public int getStateChange();                         // Java 1.1
public String paramString();                         // Java 1.1
```

D.4.10 Class *java.awt.event.ItemListener*

The `ItemListener` interface has been added with Java 1.1. It defines the method which is called by an `ItemEvent`. The following is defined:

```
public void itemStateChanged(ItemEvent e);          // Java 1.1
```

D.4.11 Class *java.awt.event.KeyEvent*

The `KeyEvent` class has been added with Java 1.1. It occurs when a event happens for a keypress. The following are defined:

```
// Constructors
public KeyEvent(Component src, int id, long when, int modifiers,
         int keyCode, char keyChar);                          // Java 1.1

// Constants
public static final int KEY_LAST, KEY_PRESSED, KEY_RELEASED, KEY_TYPED;
         // Undefined Key and Character (Java 1.1)
public static final int VK_UNDEFINED, CHAR_UNDEFINED;
         // Alphanumeric keys (Java 1.1)
public static final int VK_A, VK_B, VK_C, VK_D, VK_E, VK_F, VK_G, VK_H;
public static final int VK_I, VK_J, VK_K, VK_L, VK_M, VK_N, VK_O, VK_P;
public static final int VK_Q, VK_R, VK_S, VK_T, VK_U, VK_V, VK_W, VK_X;
public static final int VK_Y, VK_Z;
public static final int VK_SPACE;
public static final int VK_0, VK_1, VK_2, VK_3, VK_4, VK_5, VK_6, VK_7;
public static final int VK_8, VK_9;
public static final int VK_NUMPAD0, VK_NUMPAD1, VK_NUMPAD2, VK_NUMPAD3;
public static final int VK_NUMPAD4, VK_NUMPAD5, VK_NUMPAD6, VK_NUMPAD7;
public static final int VK_NUMPAD8, VK_NUMPAD9;
         // Control keys (Java 1.1)
public static final int VK_BACK_SPACE, VK_ENTER, VK_ESCAPE, VK_TAB;
         // Modifier keys (Java 1.1)
public static final int VK_ALT, VK_CAPS_LOCK, VK_CONTROL, VK_META, VK_SHIFT;
         // Function keys (Java 1.1)
public static final int VK_F0, VK_F1, VK_F2, VK_F3, VK_F4, VK_F5, VK_F6;
public static final int VK_F7, VK_F8, VK_F9;
public static final int VK_PRINTSCREEN, VK_SCROLL_LOCK, VK_PAUSE;
public static final int VK_PAGE_DOWN, VK_PAGE_UP;
public static final int VK_DOWN, VK_UP, VK_RIGHT, VK_LEFT;
public static final int VK_END, VK_HOME, VK_ACCEPT, VK_NUM_LOCK, VK_CANCEL;
public static final int VK_CLEAR, VK_CONVERT, VK_FINAL, VK_HELP;
public static final int VK_KANA, VK_KANJI, VK_MODECHANGE, VK_NONCONVERT;
         // Punctuation keys (Java 1.1)
public static final int VK_ADD, VK_BACK_QUOTE, VK_BACK_SLASH;
public static final int VK_CLOSE_BRACKET, VK_COMMA, VK_DECIMAL;
public static final int VK_DIVIDE, VK_EQUALS, VK_MULTIPLY;
public static final int VK_OPEN_BRACKET, VK_PERIOD, VK_QUOTE;
public static final int VK_SEMICOLON, VK_SEPARATER, VK_SLASH;
public static final int VK_SUBTRACT;

// Methods
public void getKeyChar();                                     // Java 1.1
public int getKeyCode();                                      // Java 1.1
public boolean isActionKey();                                 // Java 1.1
public String paramString();                                  // Java 1.1
public void setKeyChar(char keyChar);                         // Java 1.1
public void setKeyCode(int keyCode);                          // Java 1.1
public void setModifiers(int modifiers);                      // Java 1.1
```

D.4.12 Class *java.awt.event.KeyListener*

The KeyListener interface has been added with Java 1.1. It defines the method
which is called by a KeyEvent. The following is defined:

```
public void keyPressed(KeyEvent e);                           // Java 1.1
public void keyReleased(KeyEvent e);                          // Java 1.1
public void keyTyped(KeyEvent e);                             // Java 1.1
```

D.4.13 Class *java.awt.event.MouseEvent*

The MouseEvent class has been added with Java 1.1. It occurs when a event happens for a `MouseEvent`. The following are defined:

```
// Constructors
public MouseEvent(Component src, int id, long when, int modifiers, int x,
          int y, intclickCount, boolean popupTrigger);      // Java 1.1

// Constants
public static final int MOUSE_CLICKED, MOUSE_DRAGGED;
public static final int MOUSE_ENTERED, MOUSE_EXITED;
public static final int MOUSE_FIRST, MOUSE_LAST;
public static final int MOUSE_MOVED, MOUSE_PRESSED;
public static final int MOUSE_RELEASED;


// Methods
public int getClickCount();                                 // Java 1.1
public Point getPoint();                                    // Java 1.1
public int getX();                                          // Java 1.1
public int getY();                                          // Java 1.1
public boolean isPopupTrigger();                            // Java 1.1
public String paramString();                                // Java 1.1
public synchronized void translatePoint(int x, int y);      // Java 1.1
```

D.4.14 Class *java.awt.event.MouseListener*

The `MouseListener` interface has been added with Java 1.1. It defines the method which is called by a mouse click event. The following are defined:

```
public void mouseClicked(MouseEvent e);                     // Java 1.1
public void mouseEntered(MouseEvent e);                     // Java 1.1
public void mouseExited(MouseEvent e);                      // Java 1.1
public void mousePressed(MouseEvent e);                     // Java 1.1
public void mouseReleased(MouseEvent e);                    // Java 1.1
```

D.4.15 Class *java.awt.event.MouseMouseListener*

The `MouseMouseListener` interface has been added with Java 1.1. It defines the method which is called by a mouse drag or move event. The following are defined:

```
public void mouseDragged(MouseEvent e);                     // Java 1.1
public void mouseMoved(MouseEvent e);                       // Java 1.1
```

D.4.16 Class *java.awt.eventTextEvent*

The `TextEvent` class has been added with Java 1.1. It occurs when a event happens for an event within `TextField`, `TextArea` or other `TextComponent`. The following are defined:

```
// Constructors
public TextEvent(Object src, int id);                       // Java 1.1

// Constants
public static final int TEXT_FIRST, TEXT_LAST;
public static final int TEXT_VALUE_CHANGED;

// Methods
public String paramString();                                // Java 1.1
```

D.4.17   Class *java.awt.event.TextListener*

The `TextListener` interface has been added with Java 1.1. It defines the method which is called by a `TextEvent`. The following is defined:

```
public void textValueChanged(TextEvent e);                    // Java 1.1
```

D.4.18   Class *java.awt.eventWindowEvent*

The `WindowEvent` class has been added with Java 1.1. It occurs when an event happens within a `Window` object. The following are defined:

```
// Constructors
public WindowEvent(Window src, int id);                       // Java 1.1

// Constants
public static final int WINDOW_ACTIVATED, WINDOW_CLOSED;
public static final int WINDOW_CLOSING, WINDOW_DEACTIVATED;
public static final int WINDOW_DEICONIFIED, WINDOW_FIRST;
public static final int WINDOW_ICONIFIED, WINDOW_LAST;
public static final int WINDOW_OPENED;


// Methods
public Window getWindow();                                    // Java 1.1
public String paramString();                                  // Java 1.1
```

D.4.19   Class *java.awt.event.WindowListener*

The `WindowListener` interface has been added with Java 1.1. It defines the method which is called by an `WindowEvent`. The following are defined:

```
public void windowActivated(WindowEvent e);                   // Java 1.1
public void windowClosed(WindowEvent e);                      // Java 1.1
public void windowDeactivated(WindowEvent e);                 // Java 1.1
public void windowDeiconified(WindowEvent e);                 // Java 1.1
public void windowIconified(WindowEvent e);                   // Java 1.1
public void windowOpened(WindowEvent e);                      // Java 1.1
```

D.5   Package java.awt.image

This package has been added with Java 1.1 and supports image processing classes.

D.6   Package java.io

D.6.1 Class *java.io.BufferedOutputStream*

The `BufferedOutputStream` implements a buffered output stream. These streams allow the program to write to an input device without having to worry about the interfacing method. The following are defined:

```
// Fields
protected byte buf[];
protected int count;

// Constructors
public BufferedOutputStream(OutputStream out);
public BufferedOutputStream(OutputStream out, int size);

// Methods
public void flush();
public void write(byte b[], int off, int len);
public void write(int b);
```

D.6.2 Class *java.io.BufferedReader*

The BufferReader class has been added with Java 1.1. It represents a buffered character input stream. The following are defined:

```
// Constructors
public BufferedReader(Reader in, int sz);                        // Java 1.1
public BufferedReader(Reader in);                                // Java 1.1

// Methods
public void close() throws IOException;                          // Java 1.1
public void mark(int readAheadLimit) throws IOException;         // Java 1.1
public boolean markSupported() throws IOException;               // Java 1.1
public int read() throws IOException;                            // Java 1.1
public int read(char [] cbuf, int off, int len) throws IOException;
                                                                 // Java 1.1
public String readLine() throws IOException;                     // Java 1.1
public boolean ready() throws IOException;                       // Java 1.1
public void reset() throws IOException;                          // Java 1.1
public long skip(long n) throws IOException;                     // Java 1.1
```

D.6.3 Class *java.io.BufferedWriter*

The BufferWriter class has been added with Java 1.1. It represents a buffered character output stream. The following are defined:

```
// Constrsuctors
public BufferedWriter(Writer out, int sz);                       // Java 1.1
public BufferedWriter(Writer in);                                // Java 1.1

// Methods
public void close() throws IOException;                          // Java 1.1
public void flush() throws IOException;                          // Java 1.1
public void newLine() throws IOException;                        // Java 1.1
public void write(int c) throws IOException;                     // Java 1.1
public void write(char [] cbuf, int off, int len) throws IOException;
                                                                 // Java 1.1
```

D.6.4 Class *java.io.ByteArrayInputStream*

The ByteArrayInputStream class supports input from a byte array. The following are defined:

```
// Fields
protected byte buf[];
protected int count;
protected int mark;                                              // Java 1.1
```

```
protected int pos;

// Constructors
public ByteArrayInputStream(byte buf[]);
public ByteArrayInputStream(byte buf[], int offset, int length);

// Methods
public int available();
public void mark(int markpos);                                    // Java 1.1
public boolean markSupported();                                   // Java 1.1
public int read();
public int read(byte b[], int off, int len);
public void reset();
public long skip(long n);
```

D.6.5 Class *java.io.ByteArrayOutputStream*

The ByteArrayOutputStream class allows supports output to a byte array. The following are defined:

```
// Fields
protected byte buf[];
protected int count;

// Constructors
public ByteArrayOutputStream();
public ByteArrayOutputStream(int size);

// Methods
public void reset();
public int size();
public byte[] toByteArray();
public String toString();
public String toString(int hibyte);                              // Java 1.0
public String toString(String enc);                              // Java 1.1
public void write(byte b[], int off, int len);
public void write(int b);
public void writeTo(OutputStream out);
```

D.6.6 Interface *java.io.DataInput*

The DataInput interface gives support for streams to read in a machine-independent way. The following are defined:

```
// Methods
public abstract boolean readBoolean();
public abstract byte readByte();
public abstract char readChar();
public abstract double readDouble();
public abstract float readFloat();
public abstract void readFully(byte b[]);
public abstract void readFully(byte b[], int off, int len);
public abstract int readInt();
public abstract String readLine();
public abstract long readLong();
public abstract short readShort();
public abstract int readUnsignedByte();
public abstract int readUnsignedShort();
public abstract String readUTF();
public abstract int skipBytes(int n);
```

D.6.7 Class *java.io.DataInputStream*

The `DataInputStream` class allows an application to read data in a machine-independent way. It uses standard Unicode strings which conforms to the UTF-81 specification. The following are defined:

```
// Constructors
public DataInputStream(InputStream in);

// Methods
public final int read(byte b[]);
public final int read(byte b[], int off, int len);
public final boolean readBoolean();
public final byte readByte();
public final char readChar();
public final double readDouble();
public final float readFloat();
public final void readFully(byte b[]);
public final void readFully(byte b[], int off, int len);
public final int readInt();
public final String readLine();                          // Java 1.0
public final long readLong();
public final short readShort();
public final int readUnsignedByte();
public final int readUnsignedShort();
public final String readUTF();
public final static String readUTF(DataInput in);
public final int skipBytes(int n);
```

D.6.8 Interface *java.io.DataOutput*

The `DataOutput` interface gives support for streams to write in a machine-independent way. The following are defined:

```
// Methods
public abstract void write(byte b[]);
public abstract void write(byte b[], int off, int len);
public abstract void write(int b);
public abstract void writeBoolean(boolean v);
public abstract void writeByte(int v);
public abstract void writeBytes(String s);
public abstract void writeChar(int v);
public abstract void writeChars(String s);
public abstract void writeDouble(double v);
public abstract void writeFloat(float v);
public abstract void writeInt(int v);
public abstract void writeLong(long v);
public abstract void writeShort(int v);
public abstract void writeUTF(String str);
```

D.6.9 Class *java.io.DataOutputStream*

The `DataOutputStream` class allows an application to write data in a machine-independent way. It uses standard Unicode strings which conforms to the UTF-81 specification. The following are defined:

```
// Fields
protected int written;
// Constructors
```

```
public DataOutputStream(OutputStream out);

// Methods
public void flush();
public final int size();
public void write(byte b[], int off, int len);
public void write(int b);
public final void writeBoolean(boolean v);
public final void writeByte(int v);
public final void writeBytes(String s);
public final void writeChar(int v);
public final void writeChars(String s);
public final void writeDouble(double v);
public final void writeFloat(float v);
public final void writeInt(int v);
public final void writeLong(long v);
public final void writeShort(int v);
public final void writeUTF(String str);
```

D.6.10   Class *java.io.EOFException*

Exception that identifies that the end-of-file has been reached unexpectedly during input. The following are defined:

```
// Constructors
public EOFException();
public EOFException(String s);
```

D.6.11   Class *java.io.File*

The File class implements the file manipulation operations in an operating system independent way. The following are defined:

```
// Fields
public final static String pathSeparator;
public final static char pathSeparatorChar;
public final static String separator;
public final static char separatorChar;

// Constructors
public File(File dir, String name);
public File(String path);
public File(String path, String name);

// Methods
public boolean canRead();
public boolean canWrite();
public boolean delete();
public boolean equals(Object obj);
public boolean exists();
public String getAbsolutePath();
public String getCanonicalPath();                              // Java 1.1
public String getName();
public String getParent();
public String getPath();
public int hashCode();
public boolean isAbsolute();
public boolean isDirectory();
public boolean isFile();
public long lastModified();
public long length();
```

```
public String[] list();
public String[] list(FilenameFilter filter);
public boolean mkdir();
public boolean mkdirs();
public boolean renameTo(File dest);
public String toString();
```

D.6.12   Class *java.io.FileDescriptor*

The FileDescriptor class provides a way to cope with opening files or sockets. The following are defined:

```
// Fields
public final static FileDescriptor err, in, out;

// Constructors
public FileDescriptor();

// Methods
public void sync();                                    // Java 1.1
public boolean valid();
```

D.6.13   Class *java.io.FileInputStream*

The FileInputStream class provides supports for an input file. The following are defined:

```
// Constructors
public FileInputStream(File file);
public FileInputStream(FileDescriptor fdObj);
public FileInputStream(String name);

// Methods
public int available();
public void close();
protected void finalize();
public final FileDescriptor getFD();
public int read();
public int read(byte b[]);
public int read(byte b[], int off, int len);
public long skip(long n);
```

D.6.14   Interface *java.io.FilenameFilter*

The FilenameFile interface is used to filter filenames. The following is defined:

```
// Methods
public abstract boolean accept(File dir, String name);
```

D.6.15   Class *java.io.FileNotFoundException*

Exception that identifies that a file could not be found. The following are defined:

```
// Constructors
public FileNotFoundException();
public FileNotFoundException(String s);
```

D.6.16   Class *java.io.FileOutputStream*

The FileOutputStream class provides supports for an output file. The following are defined:

```
// Constructors
public FileOutputStream(File file);
public FileOutputStream(String name, boolean append);          // Java 1.1
public FileOutputStream(FileDescriptor fdObj);
public FileOutputStream(String name);

// Methods
public void close();
protected void finalize();
public final FileDescriptor getFD();
public void write(byte b[]);
public void write(byte b[], int off, int len);
public void write(int b);
```

D.6.17   Class *java.io.FilterInputStream*

The FilterInputStream class is the superclass of all classes that filter input streams. The following are defined:

```
// Fields
protected InputStream in;

// Constructors
protected FilterInputStream(InputStream in);

// Methods
public int available();
public void close();
public void mark(int readlimit);
public boolean markSupported();
public int read();
public int read(byte b[]);
public int read(byte b[], int off, int len);
public void reset();
public long skip(long n);
```

D.6.18   Class *java.io.FilterOutputStream*

The FilterOutputStream class is the superclass of all classes that filter output streams. The following are defined:

```
// Fields
protected OutputStream out;

// Constructors
public FilterOutputStream(OutputStream out);

// Methods
public void close();
public void flush();
public void write(byte b[]);
public void write(byte b[], int off, int len);
public void write(int b);
```

D.6.19   Class *java.io.InputStream*

The InputStream class is the superclass of all classes representing an input stream of bytes. The following are defined:

```
// Constructors
public InputStream();

// Methods
public int available();
public void close();
public void mark(int readlimit);
public boolean markSupported();
public abstract int read();
public int read(byte b[]);
public int read(byte b[], int off, int len);
public void reset();
public long skip(long n);
```

D.6.20 Class *java.io.InterruptedIOException*

Exception that identifies that an I/O operation has been interrupted. The following are defined:

```
// Fields
public int bytesTransferred;

// Constructors
public InterruptedIOException();
public InterruptedIOException(String s);
```

D.6.21 Class *java.io.IOException*

Exception that identifies that an I/O exception has occurred. The following are defined:

```
// Constructors
public IOException();
public IOException(String s);
```

D.6.22 Class *java.io.LineNumberInputStream*

The LineNumberInputStream class provides support for the current line number in an input stream. Each line is delimited by either a carriage return character ('\r'), newline character ('\n') or both together. The following are defined:

```
// Constructors
public LineNumberInputStream(InputStream in);

// Methods
public int available();
public int getLineNumber();
public void mark(int readlimit);
public int read();
public int read(byte b[], int off, int len);
public void reset();
public void setLineNumber(int lineNumber);
public long skip(long n);
```

D.6.23 Class *java.io.OutputStream*

The InputStream class is the superclass of all classes representing an output stream of bytes. The following are defined:

```
// Constructors
public OutputStream();

// Methods
public void close();
public void flush();
public void write(byte b[]);
public void write(byte b[], int off, int len);
public abstract void write(int b);
```

D.6.24 Class *java.io.PipedInputStream*

The PipedInputStream class provides support for pipelined input communications. The following are defined:

```
// Constructors
public PipedInputStream();
public PipedInputStream(PipedOutputStream src);

// Methods
public void close();
public void connect(PipedOutputStream src);
public int read();
public int read(byte b[], int off, int len);
```

D.6.25 Class *java.io.PipedOutputStream*

The PipedOutputStream class provides support for pipelined output communications. The following are defined:

```
// Constructors
public PipedOutputStream();
public PipedOutputStream(PipedInputStream snk);

// Methods
public void close();
public void connect(PipedInputStream snk);
public void write(byte b[], int off, int len);
public void write(int b);
```

D.6.26 Class *java.io.PrintStream*

The PrintStream class provides support for output print streams. The following are defined:

```
// Constructors
public PrintStream(OutputStream out);                        // Java 1.0
public PrintStream(OutputStream out, boolean autoflush);     // Java 1.0

// Methods
public boolean checkError();
public void close();
public void flush();
public void print(boolean b);
public void print(char c);
public void print(char s[]);
public void print(double d);
public void print(float f);
public void print(int i);
```

```
public void print(long l);
public void print(Object obj);
public void print(String s);
public void println();
public void println(boolean b);
public void println(char c);
public void println(char s[]);
public void println(double d);
public void println(float f);
public void println(int i);
public void println(long l);
public void println(Object obj);
public void println(String s);
public void write(byte b[], int off, int len);
public void write(int b);
```

D.6.27 Class *java.io.PushbackInputStream*

The PushbackInputStream class provides support to put bytes back into an input stream. The following are defined:

```
// Fields
protected int pushBack;

// Constructors
public PushbackInputStream(InputStream in);

// Methods
public int available();
public boolean markSupported();
public int read();
public int read(byte bytes[], int offset, int length);
public void unread(int ch);
```

D.6.28 Class *java.io.RandomAccessFile*

The RandomAccessFile class support reading and writing from a random access file. The following are defined:

```
// Constructors
public RandomAccessFile(File file, String mode);
public RandomAccessFile(String name, String mode);

// Methods
public void close();
public final FileDescriptor getFD();
public long getFilePointer();
public long length();
public int read();
public int read(byte b[]);
public int read(byte b[], int off, int len);
public final boolean readBoolean();
public final byte readByte();
public final char readChar();
public final double readDouble();
public final float readFloat();
public final void readFully(byte b[]);
public final void readFully(byte b[], int off, int len);
public final int readInt();
public final String readLine();
public final long readLong();
```

```
public final short readShort();
public final int readUnsignedByte();
public final int readUnsignedShort();
public final String readUTF();
public void seek(long pos);
public int skipBytes(int n);
public void write(byte b[]);
public void write(byte b[], int off, int len);
public void write(int b);
public final void writeBoolean(boolean v);
public final void writeByte(int v);
public final void writeBytes(String s);
public final void writeChar(int v);
public final void writeChars(String s);
public final void writeDouble(double v);
public final void writeFloat(float v);
public final void writeInt(int v);
public final void writeLong(long v);
public final void writeShort(int v);
public final void writeUTF(String str);
```

D.6.29   Class *java.io.SequenceInputStream*

The SequenceInputStream supports the combination of several input streams into a
single input stream. The following are defined:

```
// Constructors
public SequenceInputStream(Enumeration e);
public SequenceInputStream(InputStream s1, InputStream s2);

// Methods
public void avialable();                                    // Java 1.1
public void close();
public int read();
public int read(byte buf[], int pos, int len);
```

D.6.30   Class *java.io.StreamTokenizer*

The StreamTokenizer class splits an input stream into tokens. These tokens can be
defined by number, quotes strings or comment styles. The following are defined:

```
// Fields
public double nval;
public String sval;
public int ttype;

// possible values for the ttype field
public final static int TT_EOF, TT_EOL, TT_NUMBER, TT_WORD;

// Constructors
public StreamTokenizer(InputStream I);

// Methods
public void commentChar(int ch);
public void eolIsSignificant(boolean flag);
public int lineno();
public void lowerCaseMode(boolean fl);
public int nextToken();
public void ordinaryChar(int ch);
public void ordinaryChars(int low, int hi);
public void parseNumbers();
```

```
public void pushBack();
public void quoteChar(int ch);
public void resetSyntax();
public void whitespaceChars(int low, int hi);
public void slashStarComments(boolean flag);
public String toString();
public void whitespaceChars(int low, int hi);
public void wordChars(int low, int hi);
```

D.6.31   Class *java.io.StringBufferInputStream*

The StringBufferInputStream class supports stream input buffers. The following are defined:

```
// Fields
protected String buffer;
protected int count, pos;

// Constructors
public StringBufferInputStream(String s);

// Methods
public int available();
public int read();
public int read(byte b[], int off, int len);
public void reset();
public long skip(long n);
```

D.6.32   Class *java.io.UTFDataFormatException*

Exception that identifies that a malformed UTF-8 string has been read in a data input stream. The following are defined:

```
// Constructors
public UTFDataFormatException();
public UTFDataFormatException(String s);
```

D.7   Package java.lang

D.7.1 Class *java.lang.ArithmeticException*

Exception that is thrown when an exceptional arithmetic condition has occurred, such as a division-by-zero or a square root of a negative number. The following are defined:

```
// Constructors
public ArithmeticException();
public ArithmeticException(String s);
```

D.7.2 Class *java.lang.ArrayIndexOutOfBoundsException*

Exception that is thrown when an illegal index term in an array has been accessed. The following are defined:

```
// Constructors
```

```
public ArrayIndexOutOfBoundsException();
public ArrayIndexOutOfBoundsException(int index);
public ArrayIndexOutOfBoundsException(String s);
```

D.7.3 Class *java.lang.ArrayStoreException*

Exception that is thrown when the wrong type of object is stored in an array of objects. The following are defined:

```
// Constructors
public ArrayStoreException();
public ArrayStoreException(String s);
```

D.7.4 Class *java.lang.Boolean*

The Boolean class implements the primitive type boolean of an object. Other methods are included for a converting a boolean to a String and vice versa. The following are defined:

```
public final static Boolean FALSE, TRUE;
public final static Boolean TYPE;                            // Java 1.1


// Constructors
public Boolean(boolean value);
public Boolean(String s);

// Methods
public boolean booleanValue();
public boolean equals(Object obj);
public static boolean getBoolean(String name);
public int hashCode();
public String toString();
public static Boolean valueOf(String s);
```

D.7.5 Class *java.lang.Character*

The Character class implements the primitive type character of an object. Other methods are defined for determining the type of a character, and converting characters from uppercase to lowercase and vice versa. The following are defined:

```
// Constants
public final static int MAX_RADIX, MAX_VALUE;
public final static int MIN_RADIX, MIN_VALUE;
public final static int TYPE;                                // Java 1.1
            // Character type constants
public final static byte COMBINING_SPACE_MARK;               // Java 1.1
public final static byte CONNECTOR_PUNCUATION, CONTROL;       // Java 1.1
public final static byte CURRENCY_SYMBOL, DASH_PUNCTUATION;   // Java 1.1
public final static byte DIGIT_NUMBER, ENCLOSING_MARK;        // Java 1.1
public final static byte END_PUNCTUATION, FORMAT;             // Java 1.1
public final static byte LETTER_NUMBER, LINE_SEPERATOR;       // Java 1.1
public final static byte LOWERCASE_LETTER, MATH_SYMBOL;       // Java 1.1
public final static byte MODIFIER_LETTER, MODIFIER_SYMBOL;    // Java 1.1
public final static byte NON_SPACING_MARK, OTHER_LETTER;      // Java 1.1
public final static byte OTHER_NUMBER, OTHER_PUNCTUATION;     // Java 1.1
public final static byte OTHER_SYMBOL, PARAGRAPH_SEPARATOR;   // Java 1.1
public final static byte PRIVATE_USE, SPACE_SEPARATOR;        // Java 1.1
public final static byte START_PUNCTUATION, SURROGATE;        // Java 1.1
```

```
public final static byte TITLECASE_LETTER, UNASSIGNED;        // Java 1.1
public final static byte UPPERCASE_LETTER;                     // Java 1.1

// Constructors
public Character(char value);

// Methods
public char charValue();
public static int digit(char ch, int radix);
public boolean equals(Object obj);
public static char forDigit(int digit, int radix);
public static char getNumericValue(char ch);                   // Java 1.1
public static char getType(char ch);                           // Java 1.1
public static boolean isDefined(char ch);
public static boolean isDigit(char ch);
public static boolean isISOControl(char ch);                   // Java 1.1
public static boolean isIdentifierIgnoreable(char ch);         // Java 1.1
public static boolean isJavaIndentierPart(char ch);            // Java 1.1
public static boolean isJavaIndentierStart(char ch);           // Java 1.1
public static boolean isJavaLetter(char ch);                   // Java 1.0
public static boolean isJavaLetterOrDigit(char ch);            // Java 1.0
public static boolean isLetter(char ch);
public static boolean isLetterOrDigit(char ch);
public static boolean isLowerCase(char ch);
public static boolean isSpace(char ch);                        // Java 1.0
public static boolean isSpaceChar(char ch);                    // Java 1.0
public static boolean isTitleCase(char ch);
public static boolean isUnicodeIdentifierPart(char ch);        // Java 1.1
public static boolean isUnicodeIdentifierStart(char ch);       // Java 1.1
public static boolean isUpperCase(char ch);
public static boolean isWhitespace(char ch);                   // Java 1.1
public static char toLowerCase(char ch);
public String toString();
public static char toTitleCase(char ch);
public static char toUpperCase(char ch);
```

D.7.6 Class *java.lang.*Class

The Class class implements the class Class and interfaces in a running Java application. The following are defined:

```
// Methods
public static Class forName(String className);
public ClassLoader getClassLoader();
public Class[] getInterfaces();
public String getName();
public Class getSuperclass();
public boolean isInterface();
public Object newInstance();
public String toString();
```

D.7.7 Class *java.lang.*ClassCastException

Exception that is thrown when an object is casted to a subclass which it is not an instance. The following are defined:

```
// Constructors
public ClassCastException();
public ClassCastException(String s);
```

D.7.8 Class *java.lang.Compiler*

The Compiler class supports Java-to-native-code compilers and related services. The following are defined:

```
// Methods
public static Object command(Object any);
public static boolean compileClass(Class clazz);
public static boolean compileClasses(String string);
public static void disable();
public static void enable();
```

D.7.9 Class *java.lang.Double*

The Double class implements the primitive type double of an object. Other methods are included for a converting a double to a String and vice versa. The following are defined:

```
// Fields
public final static double MAX_VALUE, MIN_VALUE;
public final static double NaN, NEGATIVE_INFINITY, POSITIVE_INFINITY;
public final static double TYPE;                          // Java 1.1

// Constructors
public Double(double value);
public Double(String s);

// Methods
public static long doubleToLongBits(double value);
public double doubleValue();
public boolean equals(Object obj);
public float floatValue();
public int hashCode();
public int intValue();
public boolean isInfinite();
public static boolean isInfinite(double v);
public boolean isNaN();
public static boolean isNaN(double v);
public static double longBitsToDouble(long bits);
public long longValue();
public String toString();
public static String toString(double d);
public static Double valueOf(String s);
```

D.7.10 Class *java.lang.Error*

Exception that is thrown when there are serious problems that a reasonable application should not try to catch. The following are defined:

```
// Constructors
public Error();
public Error(String s);
```

D.7.11 Class *java.lang.Exception*

Exception that is thrown that indicates conditions that a reasonable application might want to catch.

```
// Constructors
```

```
public Exception();
public Exception(String s);
```

D.7.12   Class *java.lang.Float*

The `Float` class implements the primitive type float of an object. Other methods are included for a converting a float to a String and vice versa. The following are defined:

```
// Fields
public final static float MAX_VALUE MIN_VALUE;
public final static float NaN, NEGATIVE_INFINITY, POSITIVE_INFINITY;
public final static float TYPE;                          // Java 1.1

// Constructors
public Float(double value);
public Float(float value);
public Float(String s);

// Methods
public double doubleValue();
public boolean equals(Object obj);
public static int floatToIntBits(float value);
public float floatValue();
public int hashCode();
public static float intBitsToFloat(int bits);
public int intValue();
public boolean isInfinite();
public static boolean isInfinite(float v);
public boolean isNaN();
public static boolean isNaN(float v);
public long longValue();
public String toString();
public static String toString(float f);
public static Float valueOf(String s);
```

D.7.13   Class *java.lang.IllegalAccessError*

Exception that is thrown when an application attempts to access or modify a field, or to call a method that it does not have access to. The following are defined:

```
// Constructors
public IllegalAccessError();
public IllegalAccessError(String s);
```

D.7.14   Class *java.lang.IllegalArgumentException*

Exception that is thrown when a method has been passed an illegal or inappropriate argument. The following are defined:

```
// Constructors
public IllegalArgumentException();
public IllegalArgumentException(String s);
```

D.7.15   Class *java.lang.IllegalThreadStateException*

Exception that is thrown to indicate that a thread is not in an appropriate state for the requested operation. The following are defined:

```
// Constructors
public IllegalThreadStateException();
```

```
public IllegalThreadStateException(String s);
```

D.7.16   Class *java.lang.IndexOutOfBoundsException*

Exception that is thrown to indicate that an index term is out of range. The following are defined:

```
// Constructors
public IndexOutOfBoundsException();
public IndexOutOfBoundsException(String s);
```

D.7.17   Class *java.lang.Integer*

The `Integer` class implements the primitive type integer of an object. Other methods are included for a converting a integer to a String and vice versa. The following are defined:

```
// Fields
public final static int MAX_VALUE, MIN_VALUE;
public final static int TYPE;                              // Java 1.1

// Constructors
public Integer(int value);
public Integer(String s);

// Methods
public Integer decode(String nm);                          // Java 1.1
public double doubleValue();
public boolean equals(Object obj);
public float floatValue();
public static Integer getInteger(String nm);
public static Integer getInteger(String nm, int val);
public static Integer getInteger(String nm, Integer val);
public int hashCode();
public int intValue();
public long longValue();
public static int parseInt(String s);
public static int parseInt(String s, int radix);
public static String toBinaryString(int i);
public static String toHexString(int i);
public static String toOctalString(int i);
public String toString();
public static String toString(int i);
public static String toString(int i, int radix);
public static Integer valueOf(String s);
public static Integer valueOf(String s, int radix);
```

D.7.18   Class *java.lang.InternalError*

Exception that is thrown when an unexpected internal error has occurs. The following are defined:

```
// Constructors
public InternalError();
public InternalError(String s);
```

D.7.19   Class *java.lang.InterruptedException*

Exception that is thrown when a thread is waiting, sleeping, or otherwise paused for a long time and another thread interrupts it using the interrupt method in class Thread.

The following are defined:

```
// Constructors
public InterruptedException();
public InterruptedException(String s);
```

D.7.20   Class *java.lang.Long*

The Long class implements the primitive type long of an object. Other methods are included for a converting a long to a String and vice versa. The following are defined:

```
// Fields
public final static long MAX_VALUE, MIN_VALUE;
public final static long TYPE;                           // Java 1.1

// Constructors
public Long(long value);
public Long(String s);

// Methods
public double doubleValue();
public boolean equals(Object obj);
public float floatValue();
public static Long getLong(String nm);
public static Long getLong(String nm, long val);
public static Long getLong(String nm, Long val);
public int hashCode();
public int intValue();
public long longValue();
public static long parseLong(String s);
public static long parseLong(String s, int radix);
public static String toBinaryString(long i);
public static String toHexString(long i);
public static String toOctalString(long i);
public String toString();
public static String toString(long i);
public static String toString(long i, int radix);
public static Long valueOf(String s);
public static Long valueOf(String s, int radix);
```

D.7.21   Class *java.lang.Math*

The Math class contains methods to perform basic mathematical operations. The following are defined:

```
// Fields
public final static double E;
public final static double PI;

// Methods
public static double abs(double a);
public static float abs(float a);
public static int abs(int a);
public static long abs(long a);
public static double acos(double a);
public static double asin(double a);
public static double atan(double a);
public static double atan2(double a, double b);
public static double ceil(double a);
public static double cos(double a);
```

```
public static double exp(double a);
public static double floor(double a);
public static double IEEEremainder(double f1, double f2);
public static double log(double a);
public static double max(double a, double b);
public static float max(float a, float b);
public static int max(int a, int b);
public static long max(long a, long b);
public static double min(double a, double b);
public static float min(float a, float b);
public static int min(int a, int b);
public static long min(long a, long b);
public static double pow(double a, double b);
public static double random();
public static double rint(double a);
public static long round(double a);
public static int round(float a);
public static double sin(double a);
public static double sqrt(double a);
public static double tan(double a);
```

D.7.22   Class *java.lang.NegativeArraySizeException*

Exception that is thrown when an array is created with a negative size.

```
// Constructors
public NegativeArraySizeException();
public NegativeArraySizeException(String s);
```

D.7.23   Class *java.lang.NullPointerException*

Exception that is thrown when an application attempts to use a null pointer. The following are defined:

```
// Constructors
public NullPointerException();
public NullPointerException(String s);
```

D.7.24   Class *java.lang.Number*

The Number class contains the superclass of classes for float, double, integer and long. It can be used to convert values into int, long, float or double. The following are defined:

```
// Methods
public abstract double doubleValue();
public abstract float floatValue();
public abstract int intValue();
public abstract long longValue();
```

D.7.25   Class *java.lang.NumberFormatException*

Exception that is thrown when an application attempts to convert a string to one of the numeric types, but that the string does not have the appropriate format.

```
// Constructors
public NumberFormatException();
public NumberFormatException(String s);
```

D.7.26 Class *java.lang.Object*

The `Object` class contains the root of the class hierarchy. The following are defined:

```
// Constructors
public Object();

// Methods
protected Object clone();
public boolean equals(Object obj);
protected void finalize();
public final Class getClass();
public int hashCode();
public final void notify();
public final void notifyAll();
public String toString();
public final void wait();
public final void wait(long timeout);
public final void wait(long timeout, int nanos);
```

D.7.27 Class *java.lang.OutOfMemoryError*

Exception that is thrown when an application runs out of memory. The following are defined:

```
// Constructors
public OutOfMemoryError();
public OutOfMemoryError(String s);
```

D.7.28 Class *java.lang.Process*

The `Process` class contains methods which are used to control the process. The following are defined:

```
// Constructors
public Process();
// Methods
public abstract void destroy();
public abstract int exitValue();
public abstract InputStream getErrorStream();
public abstract InputStream getInputStream();
public abstract OutputStream getOutputStream();
public abstract int waitFor();
```

D.7.29 Class *java.lang.Runtime*

The `Runtime` class allows the application to interface with the environment in which it is running. The following are defined:

```
// Methods
public Process exec(String command);
public Process exec(String command, String envp[]);
public Process exec(String cmdarray[]);
public Process exec(String cmdarray[], String envp[]);
public void exit(int status);
public long freeMemory();
public void gc();
public InputStream getLocalizedInputStream(InputStream in);   // Java 1.0
public OutputStream getLocalizedOutputStream(OutputStream out);
                                                             // Java 1.0
```

```
public static Runtime getRuntime();
public void load(String filename);
public void loadLibrary(String libname);
public void runFinalization();
public long totalMemory();
public void traceInstructions(boolean on);
public void traceMethodCalls(boolean on);
```

D.7.30   Class *java.lang.SecurityManager*

The `SecurityManager` class is an abstract class that allows applications to determine if it is safe to execute a given operation. The following are defined:

```
// Fields
 protected boolean inCheck;

// Constructors
 protected SecurityManager();

// Methods
public void checkAccept(String host, int port);
public void checkAccess(Thread g);
public void checkAccess(ThreadGroup g);
public void checkConnect(String host, int port);
public void checkConnect(String host, int port, Object context);
public void checkCreateClassLoader();
public void checkDelete(String file);
public void checkExec(String cmd);
public void checkExit(int status);
public void checkLink(String lib);
public void checkListen(int port);
public void checkPackageAccess(String pkg);
public void checkPackageDefinition(String pkg);
public void checkPropertiesAccess();
public void checkPropertyAccess(String key);
public void checkRead(FileDescriptor fd);
public void checkRead(String file);
public void checkRead(String file, Object context);
public void checkSetFactory();
public boolean checkTopLevelWindow(Object window);
public void checkWrite(FileDescriptor fd);
public void checkWrite(String file);
protected int classDepth(String name);
protected int classLoaderDepth();
protected ClassLoader currentClassLoader();
protected Class[] getClassContext();
public boolean getInCheck();
public Object getSecurityContext();
protected boolean inClass(String name);
protected boolean inClassLoader();
```

D.7.31   Class *java.lang.StackOverflowError*

Exception that is thrown when a stack overflow occurs. The following are defined:

```
// Constructors
public StackOverflowError();
public StackOverflowError(String s);
```

D.7.32   Class *java.lang.String*

The `String` class represents character strings. As in C, a string is delimted by inverted commas. It contains string manipulation methods, such as `concat` (string concatenation), `equals` (if string is equal to), `toLowCase` (to convert a string to lowercase), and so on. The following are defined:

```
// Constructors
public String();
public String(byte ascii[], int hibyte);                            // Java 1.0
public String(byte ascii[], int hibyte, int offset, int count);
                                                                    // Java 1.0
public String(char value[]);
public String(char value[], int offset, int count);
public String(String value);
public String(StringBuffer buffer);
public String(byte ascii[], int offset, int length, String enc);
                                                                    // Java 1.1


// Methods
public char charAt(int index);
public int compareTo(String anotherString);
public String concat(String str);
public static String copyValueOf(char data[]);
public static String copyValueOf(char data[], int offset, unt count);
public boolean endsWith(String suffix);
public boolean equals(Object anObject);
public boolean equalsIgnoreCase(String anotherString);
public void getBytes(int srcBegin, int srcEnd, byte dst[], int dstBegin);
public void getChars(int srcBegin, int srcEnd, char dst[], int dstBegin);
public int hashCode();
public int indexOf(int ch);
public int indexOf(int ch, int fromIndex);
public int indexOf(String str);
public int indexOf(String str, int fromIndex);
public String intern();
public int lastIndexOf(int ch);
public int lastIndexOf(int ch, int fromIndex);
public int lastIndexOf(String str);
public int lastIndexOf(String str, int fromIndex);
public int length();
public boolean regionMatches(boolean ignoreCase, int toffset,
            String other, int ooffset, int len);
public boolean regionMatches(int toffset, String other,int offset, int len);
public String replace(char oldChar, char newChar);
public boolean startsWith(String prefix);
public boolean startsWith(String prefix, int toffset);
public String substring(int beginIndex);
public String substring(int beginIndex, int endIndex);
public char[] toCharArray();
public String toLowerCase();
public String toLowerCase(Locale locale);                           // Java 1.1

public String toString();
public String toUpperCase();
public String toUpperCase(Locale locale);                           // Java 1.1
public String trim();
public static String valueOf(boolean b);
public static String valueOf(char c);
public static String valueOf(char data[]);
```

```
public static String valueOf(char data[], int offset, int count);
public static String valueOf(double d);
public static String valueOf(float f);
public static String valueOf(int i);
public static String valueOf(long l);
public static String valueOf(Object obj);
```

D.7.33   Class *java.lang.StringBuffer*

The `StringBuffer` class implements a string buffer. The following are defined:

```
// Constructors
public StringBuffer();
public StringBuffer(int length);
public StringBuffer(String str);
// Methods
public StringBuffer append(boolean b);
public StringBuffer append(char c);
public StringBuffer append(char str[]);
public StringBuffer append(char str[], int offset, int len);
public StringBuffer append(double d);
public StringBuffer append(float f);
public StringBuffer append(int i);
public StringBuffer append(long l);
public StringBuffer append(Object obj);
public StringBuffer append(String str);
public int capacity();
public char charAt(int index);
public void ensureCapacity(int minimumCapacity);
public void getChars(int srcBegin, int srcEnd, char dst[], int dstBegin);
public StringBuffer insert(int offset, boolean b);
public StringBuffer insert(int offset, char c);
public StringBuffer insert(int offset, char str[]);
public StringBuffer insert(int offset, double d);
public StringBuffer insert(int offset, float f);
public StringBuffer insert(int offset, int i);
public StringBuffer insert(int offset, long l);
public StringBuffer insert(int offset, Object obj);
public StringBuffer insert(int offset, String str);
public int length();
public StringBuffer reverse();
public void setCharAt(int index, char ch);
public void setLength(int newLength);
public String toString();
```

D.7.34   Class *java.lang.StringIndexOutOfBoundsException*

Exception that is thrown when a string is indexed with a negative value or a value which is greater than or equal to the size of the string. The following are defined:

```
// Constructors
public StringIndexOutOfBoundsException();
public StringIndexOutOfBoundsException(int index);
public StringIndexOutOfBoundsException(String s)
```

D.7.35   Class *java.lang.System*

The `System` class implements a number of system methods. The following are defined:

```
// Fields
public static PrintStream err, in, out;
// Methods
public static void arraycopy(Object src, int src_position,
            Object dst, int dst_position, int length);
public static long currentTimeMillis();
public static void exit(int status);
public static void gc();
public static Properties getProperties();
public static String getProperty(String key);
public static String getProperty(String key, String def);
public static SecurityManager getSecurityManager();
public static void load(String filename);
public static void loadLibrary(String libname);
public static void runFinalization();
public static void setProperties(Properties props);
public static void setSecurityManager(SecurityManager s);
```

D.7.36   Class *java.lang.Thread*

The Thread class implements one or more threads. The following are defined:

```
// Fields
public final static int MAX_PRIORITY, MIN_PRIORITY, NORM_PRIORITY;

// Constructors
public Thread();
public Thread(Runnable target);
public Thread(Runnable target, String name);
public Thread(String name);
public Thread(ThreadGroup group, Runnable target);
public Thread(ThreadGroup group, Runnable target, String name);
public Thread(ThreadGroup group, String name);

// Methods
public static int activeCount();
public void checkAccess();
public int countStackFrames();
public static Thread currentThread();
public void destroy();
public static void dumpStack();
public static int enumerate(Thread tarray[]);
public final String getName();
public final int getPriority();
public final ThreadGroup getThreadGroup();
public void interrupt();
public static boolean interrupted();
public final boolean isAlive();
public final boolean isDaemon();
public boolean isInterrupted();
public final void join();
public final void join(long millis);
public final void join(long millis, int nanos);
public final void resume();
public void run();
public final void setDaemon(boolean on);
public final void setName(String name);
public final void setPriority(int newPriority);
public static void sleep(long millis);
public static void sleep(long millis, int nanos)
public void start();
public final void stop();
```

```
public final void stop(Throwable obj);
public final void suspend();
public String toString();
public static void yield();
```

D.7.37   Class *java.lang.ThreadGroup*

The `ThreadGroup` class implements a set of threads. The following are defined:

```
// Constructors
public ThreadGroup(String name);
public ThreadGroup(ThreadGroup parent, String name);

// Methods
public int activeCount();
public int activeGroupCount();
public final void checkAccess();
public final void destroy();
public int enumerate(Thread list[]);
public int enumerate(Thread list[], boolean recurse);
public int enumerate(ThreadGroup list[]);
public int enumerate(ThreadGroup list[], boolean recurse);
public final int getMaxPriority();
public final String getName();
public final ThreadGroup getParent();
public final boolean isDaemon();
public void list();
public final boolean parentOf(ThreadGroup g);
public final void resume();
public final void setDaemon(boolean daemon);
public final void setMaxPriority(int pri);
public final void stop();
public final void suspend();
public String toString();
public void uncaughtException(Thread t, Throwable e);
```

D.7.38   Class *java.lang.Throwable*

The `Throwable` class is the superclass of all errors and exceptions in the Java language. The following are defined:

```
// Constructors
public Throwable();
public Throwable(String message);

// Methods
public Throwable fillInStackTrace();
public String getMessage();
public void printStackTrace();
public void printStackTrace(PrintStream s);
public String toString();
```

D.7.39   Class *java.lang.UnknownError*

Exception that is thrown when an unknown error occurs. The following are defined:

```
// Constructors
public UnknownError();
public UnknownError(String s);
```

D.8 Package java.net

D.8.1 Class java.net.DatagramPacket

The `DatagramPacket` class implements datagram packets. The following are defined:

```
// Constructors
public DatagramPacket(byte[] ibuf, int ilength);
public DatagraamPacket(byte[] ibuf, int ilength, inetAddress iadd,
          int iport);

// Methods
public synchronized InetAddress getAddress();
public synchronized byte[] getData();
public synchronized int getLength();
public synchronized int getPort();
public synchronized void setAddress(InetAddress iaddr);      // Java 1.1
public synchronized void setDate(byte[] ibuf);               // Java 1.1
public synchronized void setLength(int ilength);             // Java 1.1
public synchronized void setPort(int iport);                 // Java 1.1
```

D.8.2 Class java.net.InetAddress

The `InetAddress` class represents Internet addresses. The following are defined:

```
// Methods
public InetAddress[] getAllByName(String host);
public InetAddress getByName(String host);
public InetAddress getLocalHost(String host);
public boolean equals(Object obj);
public byte[] getAddress();
public String getHostAddress();
public String getHostName();
public int hashCode();
public boolean isMulticastAddress();                         // Java 1.1
public String toString();
```

D.8.3 Class java.net.ServerSocket

The `ServerSocket` class represents servers which listen for a connection from clients. The following are defined:

```
// Constructors
public ServerSocket(int port);
public ServerSocket(int port, int backlog);
public ServerSocket(int port, int backlog, InetAddress bindAddr);
                                                             // Java 1.1
// Methods
public Socket accept();
public void close();
public InetAddress getInetAddress();
public synchronized int getSoTimeout();                      // Java 1.1
public String toString();
```

D.8.4 Class java.net.Socket

The `Socket` class represents socket connections over a network. The following are defined:

```
// Constructors
public Socket(String host, int port);
public Socket(InetAddress addr, int port);
public Socket(InetAddress addr, int port, boolean stream);      // Java 1.0

public Socket(String host, int port, InetAddress addr, int localport);
                                                                // Java 1.1
public Socket(InetAddress addr, int port, InetAddress localAddress,
              int localport);                                   // Java 1.1

// Methods
public synchronized void close();
public InetAddress getInetAddress();
public InputStream getInputStream();
public InetAddress getLocalAddress();                           // Java 1.1
public int getLocalPort();
public OutputStream getOutputStream();
public int getPort();
public int getSoLinger();                                       // Java 1.1
public synchronized int getSoTimed();                           // Java 1.1
public boolean getTcpNoDelay();                                 // Java 1.1
public void setSoLinger(boolean on, int val);                  // Java 1.1
public synchronized void setSoTimed(int timeout);              // Java 1.1
public void setTcpNoDelay(boolean on);                          // Java 1.1
public String toString();
```

D.8.5 Class *java.net.SocketImpl*

The SocketImpl class represents socket connections over a network. The following are defined:

```
// Methods
public abstract void accept(SocketImpl s);
public abstract int available();
public abstract void bind(InetAddress host, int port);
public abstract void close();
public abstract void connect(String host, int port);
public abstract void connect(InetAddress addr, int port);
public abstract void create(boolean stream);
public FileDescriptor getFileDescriptor();
public InetAddress getInetAddress();
public abstract InetAddress getInputStream();
```

D.8.6 Class *java.net.URL*

The URL class represents Uniform Resource Locators. The following are defined:

```
// Constructors
public URL(String protocol, String host, int port, String file);
public URL(String protocol, String host, String file);
public URL(String spec);
public URL(URL context, String spec);

// Methods
public boolean equals(Object obj);
public final Object getContent();
public String getFile();
public String getHost();
public int getPort();
```

```
public String getProtocol();
public String getRef();
public int hashcode();
public URLConnection openConnection();
public final InputStream openStream();
public boolean sameFile(URL other);
public String toExternalForm();
public String toString();
```

D.9   Package java.utils

D.9.1 Class *java.utils.BitSet*

The BitSet class implements boolean operations. The following are defined:

```
// Constructors
public BitSet();
public BitSet(int nbits);

// Methods
public void and(BitSet set);
public void clear(int bit);
public Object clone();
public boolean equals(Object obj);
public boolean get(int bit);
public int hashCode();
public void or(BitSet set);
public void set(int bit);
public int size();
public String toString();
public void xor(BitSet set);
```

D.9.2 Class *java.utils.Calender*

The Calender class has been added with Java 1.1. It supports dates and times.

D.9.3 Class *java.utils.Date*

The Date class supports dates and times. The following are defined:

```
// Constructors
public Date();
public Date(int year, int month, int date);                          // Java 1.0
public Date(int year, int month, int date, int hrs, int min); // Java 1.0
public Date(int year, int month, int date, int hrs, int min, int sec);
                                                                     // Java 1.0
public Date(long date);                                              // Java 1.0
public Date(String s);                                              // Java 1.0

// Methods
public boolean after(Date when);
public boolean before(Date when);
public boolean equals(Object obj);
public int getDate();                                              // Java 1.0
public int getDay();                                               // Java 1.0
public int getHours();                                             // Java 1.0
```

```
public int getMinutes();                                          // Java 1.0
public int getMonth();                                            // Java 1.0
public int getSeconds();                                          // Java 1.0
public long getTime();
public int getTimezoneOffset();                                   // Java 1.0
public int getYear();                                             // Java 1.0
public int hashCode();
public static long parse(String s);
public void setDate(int date);                                    // Java 1.0
public void setHours(int hours);                                  // Java 1.0
public void setMinutes(int minutes);                              // Java 1.0
public void setMonth(int month);                                  // Java 1.0
public void setSeconds(int seconds);                              // Java 1.0
public void setTime(long time);
public void setYear(int year);                                    // Java 1.0
public String toGMTString();                                      // Java 1.0
public String toLocaleString();                                   // Java 1.0
public String toString();
public static long UTC(int year, int month, int date, int hrs, int min,
            int sec);                                             // Java 1.0
```

D.9.4 Class *java.utils.Dictionary*

The Dictionary class is the abstract parent of any class which maps keys to values.
The following are defined:

```
// Constructors
public Dictionary();

// Methods
public abstract Enumeration elements();
public abstract Object get(Object key);
public abstract boolean isEmpty();
public abstract Enumeration keys();
public abstract Object put(Object key, Object value);
public abstract Object remove(Object key);
public abstract int size();
```

D.9.5 Class *java.utils.EmptyStackException*

The EmptyStackException is thrown when the stack is empty. The following is
defined:

```
// Constructors
public EmptyStackException();
```

D.9.6 Class *java.utils.Hashtable*

This Hashtable class supports a hashtable which maps keys to values. The following
are defined:

```
// Constructors
public Hashtable();
public Hashtable(int initialCapacity);
public Hashtable(int initialCapacity, float loadFactor);
// Methods
public void clear();
public Object clone();
public boolean contains(Object value);
public boolean containsKey(Object key);
```

```
public Enumeration elements();
public Object get(Object key);
public boolean isEmpty();
public Enumeration keys();
public Object put(Object key, Object value);
protected void rehash();
public Object remove(Object key);
public int size();
public String toString();
```

D.9.7 Class *java.utils.NoSuchElementException*

The NoSuchElementException is thrown when there are no more elements in the enumeration. The following are defined:

```
// Constructors
public NoSuchElementException();
public NoSuchElementException(String s);
```

D.9.8 Class *java.utils.Observable*

The Observable class represents an observable object. The following are defined:

```
// Constructors
public Observable();

// Methods
public void addObserver(Observer o);
protected void clearChanged();
public int countObservers();
public void deleteObserver(Observer o);
public void deleteObservers();
public boolean hasChanged();
public void notifyObservers();
public void notifyObservers(Object arg);
protected void setChanged();
```

D.9.9 Class *java.utils.Properties*

The Properties class represents a persistent set of properties. The following are defined:

```
// Fields
protected Properties defaults;

// Constructors
public Properties();
public Properties(Properties defaults);

// Methods
public String getProperty(String key);
public String getProperty(String key, String defaultValue);
public void list(PrintStream out);
public void load(InputStream in);
public Enumeration propertyNames();
public void save(OutputStream out, String header);
```

D.9.10 Class *java.utils.Random*

The Random class implements pseudo-random generator functions. The following are defined:

```
// Constructors
public Random();
public Random(long seed);

// Methods
public double nextDouble();
public float nextFloat();
public double nextGaussian();
public int nextInt();
public long nextLong();
public void setSeed(long seed);
```

D.9.11   Class *java.utils.Stack*

The Stack class implements a last-in-first-out (LIFO) stack.

```
// Constructors
public Stack();

// Methods
public boolean empty();
public Object peek();
public Object pop();
public Object push(Object item);
public int search(Object o);
```

D.9.12   Class *java.utils.StringTokenizer*

The StringTokenizer class allows strings to be split into tokens. The following are defined:

```
// Constructors
public StringTokenizer(String str);
public StringTokenizer(String str, String delim);
public StringTokenizer(String str, String delim, boolean returnTokens);

// Methods
public int countTokens();
public boolean hasMoreElements();
public boolean hasMoreTokens();
public Object nextElement();
public String nextToken();
public String nextToken(String delim);
```

D.9.13   Class *java.utils.Vector*

The Vector class implements a growable array of objects. The following are defined:

```
// Fields
protected int capacityIncrement;
protected int elementCount;
protected Object elementData[];

// Constructors
public Vector();
public Vector(int initialCapacity);
public Vector(int initialCapacity, int capacityIncrement);
```

```
// Methods
public final void addElement(Object obj);
public final int capacity();
public Object clone();
public final boolean contains(Object elem);
public final void copyInto(Object anArray[]);
public final Object elementAt(int index);
public final Enumeration elements();
public final void ensureCapacity(int minCapacity)
public final Object firstElement();
public final int indexOf(Object elem);
public final int indexOf(Object elem, int index);
public final void insertElementAt(Object obj, int index);
public final boolean isEmpty();
public final Object lastElement();
public final int lastIndexOf(Object elem);
public final int lastIndexOf(Object elem, int index);
public final void removeAllElements();
public final boolean removeElement(Object obj);
public final void removeElementAt(int index);
public final void setElementAt(Object obj, int index);
public final void setSize(int newSize);
public final int size();
public final String toString();
public final void trimToSize();
```

Microsoft Java J++

E.1 Introduction

Microsoft Java J++ is one of the excellent development systems that can be used to develop Java programs and applets. It integrates well with other languages, such as Visual C++ and Visual Basic. Figure E.1 shows a sample selection from the New Option in the development system. The selected option is this case is for the Java Applet Wizard. This option allows the development system to create the outline of the Applet with all the required methods. The project name in this case is set to myfirst which has a special workspace directory below the c:\java\new directory.

Next, after the Applet Wizard has been selected the user (Figure E.2) is asked whether they are:

- Developing an Applet or an Applet and an Application.
- The name of the Applet class (by default it is the name of the project).
- Whether comments are to be included (with explanatory comments and TODO comments).

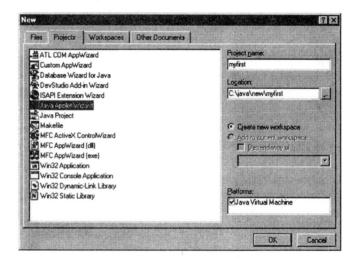

Figure E.1 New workspace options

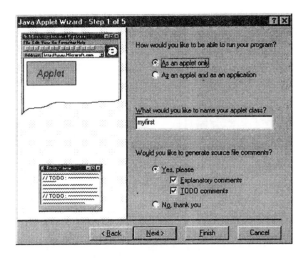

Figure E.2 New workspace options

Next (by selected the Next button) the user is asked whether an HTML file is to be created and the size of the applet. Figure E.3 shows example settings with an HTML file generated and an applet size of 320×240 pixels.

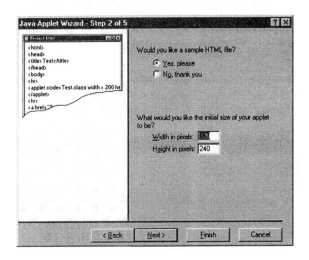

Figure E.3 New workspace options

After this the user is asked whether the Applet is multithreaded or not. The following section relates to a non multithreaded applet.

E.1.1 Adding mouse events

Figure E.4 shows the options for adding mouse events to the applet. In this case all the mouse events are selected, that is, mouseDown(), mouseUp(), mouseDrag(), mouseMove(), mouseEnter() and mouseExit().

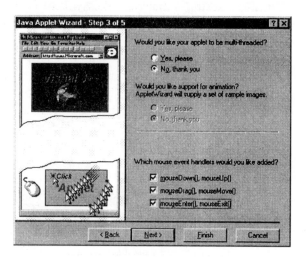

Figure E.4 Mouse event handlers

After this the applet information is displayed, as shown in Figure E.5.

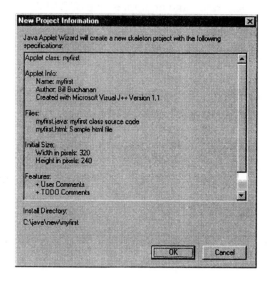

Figure E.5 Project information

Figure E.6 shows the resulting workspace. The Project Workspace window is to the left of the code window. It has three tab options:

- ClassView. Displays the classes and their members for all projects on the workspace. The folder name shown in bold type represents the default project configuration. The classes within the workspace can be viewed by expanding the project folder, then expanding a class displays the members

in that class. Double-clicking a member takes you to its location in the
source code. In Figure E.6 the applet code is viewed by first clicking on
myfirst classes and the myfirst (which is the only object in the myfirst
class).

- FileView. Displays the classes and their members for all projects on the
  workspace. Folder name which is shown in bold type represents the default project configuration. Expanding a project folder displays the classes
  included in that project. Then expanding a class displays the members in
  that class. Double-clicking a member shows the source code.
- InfoView. Shows help information.

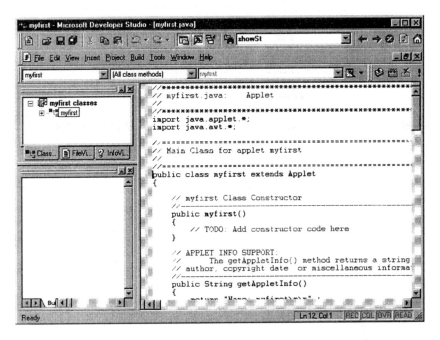

Figure E.6 Resulting workspace

Figure E.7 shows the result of clicking on the FileView tab and selecting the
HTML file from the source code option. The resulting HTML file is:

```
<html><head><title>myfirst
</title></head>
<body>
<hr>
<applet
    code=myfirst.class
    name=myfirst
    width=320
    height=240 >
</applet>
<hr>
<a href="myfirst.java">The source.</a>
</body></html>
```

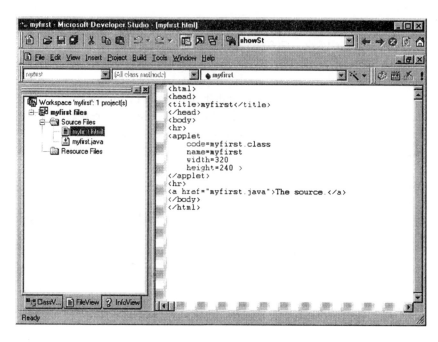

Figure E.7 HTML file viewing

The resulting Java applet code is as follows:

```
//************************************************************************
// myfirst.java:  Applet
//
//************************************************************************
import java.applet.*;
import java.awt.*;

//========================================================================
// Main Class for applet myfirst
//
//========================================================================
public class myfirst extends Applet
{

  // myfirst Class Constructor
  //----------------------------------------------------------------------
  public myfirst()
  {
      // TODO: Add constructor code here
  }

  // APPLET INFO SUPPORT:
  /  The getAppletInfo() method returns a string describing the applet's
  // author, copyright date, or miscellaneous information.
  //----------------------------------------------------------------------
  public String getAppletInfo()
  {
      return "Name: myfirst\r\n" +
             "Author: Bill Buchanan\r\n" +
             "Created with Microsoft Visual J++ Version 1.1";
  }
```

```
// The init() method is called by the AWT when an applet is first loaded or
// reloaded.  Override this method to perform whatever initialization your
// applet needs, such as initializing data structures, loading images or
// fonts, creating frame windows, setting the layout manager, or adding UI
// components.
//-----------------------------------------------------------------------
public void init()
{
 // If you use a ResourceWizard-generated "control creator" class to
 // arrange controls in your applet, you may want to call its
 // CreateControls() method from within this method. Remove the following
 // call to resize() before adding the call to CreateControls();
 // CreateControls() does its own resizing.
 //-----------------------------------------------------------------------
     resize(320, 240);

// TODO: Place additional initialization code here
}

// Place additional applet clean up code here.  destroy() is called when
// when you applet is terminating and being unloaded.
//-----------------------------------------------------------------------
public void destroy()
{
     // TODO: Place applet cleanup code here
}

// myfirst Paint Handler
//-----------------------------------------------------------------------
public void paint(Graphics g)
{
     g.drawString("Created with Microsoft Visual J++ Version 1.1", 10, 20);
}

//      The start() method is called when the page containing the applet
// first appears on the screen. The AppletWizard's initial implementation
// of this method starts execution of the applet's thread.
//-----------------------------------------------------------------------
public void start()
{
     // TODO: Place additional applet start code here
}

//      The stop() method is called when the page containing the applet is
// no longer on the screen. The AppletWizard's initial implementation of
// this method stops execution of the applet's thread.
//-----------------------------------------------------------------------
public void stop()
{
}

// MOUSE SUPPORT:
//      The mouseDown() method is called if the mouse button is pressed
// while the mouse cursor is over the applet's portion of the screen.
//-----------------------------------------------------------------------
public boolean mouseDown(Event evt, int x, int y)
{
     // TODO: Place applet mouseDown code here
     return true;
}

// MOUSE SUPPORT:
//      The mouseUp() method is called if the mouse button is released
// while the mouse cursor is over the applet's portion of the screen.
//-----------------------------------------------------------------------
public boolean mouseUp(Event evt, int x, int y)
```

```
{
    // TODO: Place applet mouseUp code here
    return true;
}

// MOUSE SUPPORT:
// The mouseDrag() method is called if the mouse cursor moves over the
// applet's portion of the screen while the mouse button is being held dow
//--------------------------------------------------------------------
public boolean mouseDrag(Event evt, int x, int y)
{
    // TODO: Place applet mouseDrag code here
    return true;
}

// MOUSE SUPPORT:
// The mouseMove() method is called if the mouse cursor moves over the
// applet's portion of the screen and the mouse button isn't being held d
//--------------------------------------------------------------------
public boolean mouseMove(Event evt, int x, int y)
{
    // TODO: Place applet mouseMove code here
    return true;
}

// MOUSE SUPPORT:
// The mouseEnter() method is called if the mouse cursor enters the
// applet's portion of the screen.
//--------------------------------------------------------------------
public boolean mouseEnter(Event evt, int x, int y)
{
    // TODO: Place applet mouseEnter code here
    return true;
}

// MOUSE SUPPORT:
// The mouseExit() method is called if the mouse cursor leaves the
// applet's portion of the screen.
//--------------------------------------------------------------------
public boolean mouseExit(Event evt, int x, int y)
{
    // TODO: Place applet mouseExit code here
    return true;
}
    // TODO: Place additional applet code here
}
```

Next the Build→Build option is selected. The applet is then compiled and an Output window is shown. This window is used to display compilation warnings and errors. The result from a Build is shown in Figure E.8.

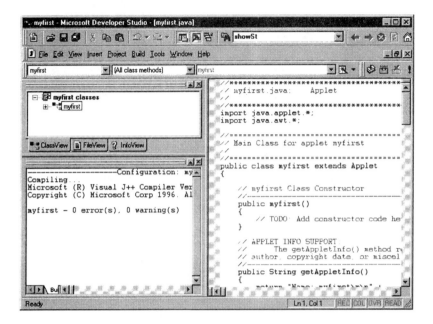

Figure E.8 New workspace options

Next the Build→Execute option is selected. The Browser is then called-up automatically and the Applet is run. The result from a Build is shown in Figure E.9.

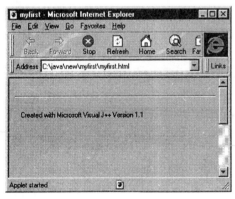

Figure E.9 Sample run

After the development is finished the workspace is then closed by selected the File→Close workspace option.

E.1.2 Adding multithreaded

If the multithreaded option (without animation mouse events) is selected then the window in Figure E.10 is shown. Figure E.11 shows the resulting information.

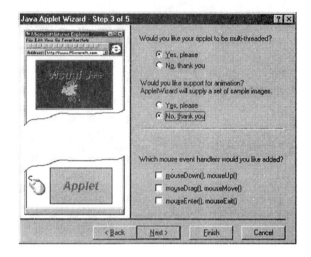

Figure E.10 Sample run

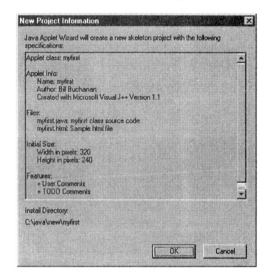

Figure E.11 Project information

The resulting applet code is as follows:

```
//****************************************************************************
// myfirst.java:  Applet
//
//****************************************************************************
import java.applet.*;
import java.awt.*;

//============================================================================
// Main Class for applet myfirst
//
//============================================================================
public class myfirst extends Applet implements Runnable
{
  // THREAD SUPPORT:
  //     m_myfirst   is the Thread object for the applet
  //-------------------------------------------------------------------------
  private Thread    m_myfirst = null;


  // myfirst Class Constructor
  //-------------------------------------------------------------------------
  public myfirst()
  {
      // TODO: Add constructor code here
  }

  // APPLET INFO SUPPORT:
  //     The getAppletInfo() method returns a string describing the applet's
  // author, copyright date, or miscellaneous information.
    //-------------------------------------------------------------------------
  public String getAppletInfo()
  {
      return "Name: myfirst\r\n" +
             "Author: Bill Buchanan\r\n" +
             "Created with Microsoft Visual J++ Version 1.1";
  }

  // The init() method is called by the AWT when an applet is first loaded or
  // reloaded.  Override this method to perform whatever initialization your
  // applet needs, such as initializing data structures, loading images or
  // fonts, creating frame windows, setting the layout manager, or adding UI
  // components.
    //-------------------------------------------------------------------------
  public void init()
  {
  // If you use a ResourceWizard-generated "control creator" class to
  // arrange controls in your applet, you may want to call its
  // CreateControls() method from within this method. Remove the following
  // call to resize() before adding the call to CreateControls();
  // CreateControls() does its own resizing.
    //-------------------------------------------------------------------------
      resize(320, 240);

  // TODO: Place additional initialization code here
  }

  // Place additional applet clean up code here.  destroy() is called when
  // when you applet is terminating and being unloaded.
  //-------------------------------------------------------------------------
  public void destroy()
  {
      // TODO: Place applet cleanup code here
  }

  // myfirst Paint Handler
  //-------------------------------------------------------------------------
```

```
public void paint(Graphics g)
{
    // TODO: Place applet paint code here
    g.drawString("Running: " + Math.random(), 10, 20);
}

//      The start() method is called when the page containing the applet
// first appears on the screen. The AppletWizard's initial implementation
// of this method starts execution of the applet's thread.
//----------------------------------------------------------------------
public void start()
{
    if (m_myfirst == null)
    {
        m_myfirst = new Thread(this);
        m_myfirst.start();
    }
    // TODO: Place additional applet start code here
}

//      The stop() method is called when the page containing the applet is
// no longer on the screen. The AppletWizard's initial implementation of
// this method stops execution of the applet's thread.
//----------------------------------------------------------------------
public void stop()
{
    if (m_myfirst != null)
    {
        m_myfirst.stop();
        m_myfirst = null;
    }

    // TODO: Place additional applet stop code here
}

// THREAD SUPPORT
//      The run() method is called when the applet's thread is started. If
// your applet performs any ongoing activities without waiting for user
// input, the code for implementing that behavior typically goes here. For
// example, for an applet that performs animation, the run() method contro
// the display of images.
//----------------------------------------------------------------------
public void run()
{
    while (true)
    {
        try
        {
            repaint();
            // TODO:  Add additional thread-specific code here
            Thread.sleep(50);
        }
        catch (InterruptedException e)
        {
            // TODO: Place exception-handling code here in case an
            //       InterruptedException is thrown by Thread.sleep(),
            //     meaning that another thread has interrupted this one
            stop();
        }
    }
}


// TODO: Place additional applet code here
}
```

Figure E.12 shows a sample run.

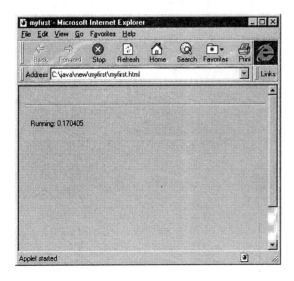

Figure E.12 Sample run

E.1.3 Animation

Figure E.13 shows the selected options for animation and the project information is shown in Figure E.14.

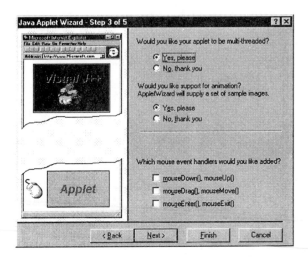

Figure E.13 Animation options

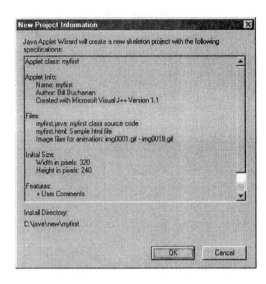

Figure E.14 Project information

The code produced is:

```
//************************************************************************
// myfirst.java: Applet
//
//************************************************************************
import java.applet.*;
import java.awt.*;

//========================================================================
// Main Class for applet myfirst
//
//========================================================================
public class myfirst extends Applet implements Runnable
{
  // THREAD SUPPORT:
  //    m_myfirst    is the Thread object for the applet
  //--------------------------------------------------------------------
  private Thread  m_myfirst = null;

  // ANIMATION SUPPORT:
  //    m_Graphics      used for storing the applet's Graphics context
  //    m_Images[]      the array of Image objects for the animation
  //    m_nCurrImage    the index of the next image to be displayed
  //    m_ImgWidth      width of each image
  //    m_ImgHeight     height of each image
  //    m_fAllLoaded    indicates whether all images have been loaded
  //    NUM_IMAGES      number of images used in the animation
  //--------------------------------------------------------------------
  private Graphics m_Graphics;
  private Image    m_Images[];
  private int      m_nCurrImage;
  private int      m_nImgWidth  = 0;
  private int      m_nImgHeight = 0;
  private boolean  m_fAllLoaded = false;
  private final int NUM_IMAGES = 18;

  // myfirst Class Constructor
  //--------------------------------------------------------------------
```

```
public myfirst()
{
    // TODO: Add constructor code here
}

// APPLET INFO SUPPORT:
//     The getAppletInfo() method returns a string describing the applet's
// author, copyright date, or miscellaneous information.
    //-----------------------------------------------------------------
public String getAppletInfo()
{
    return "Name: myfirst\r\n" +
           "Author: Bill Buchanan\r\n" +
           "Created with Microsoft Visual J++ Version 1.1";
}

// The init() method is called by the AWT when an applet is first loaded or
// reloaded.  Override this method to perform whatever initialization your
// applet needs, such as initializing data structures, loading images or
// fonts, creating frame windows, setting the layout manager, or adding UI
// components.
    //-----------------------------------------------------------------
public void init()
{
  // If you use a ResourceWizard-generated "control creator" class to
  // arrange controls in your applet, you may want to call its
  // CreateControls() method from within this method. Remove the following
  // call to resize() before adding the call to CreateControls();
  // CreateControls() does its own resizing.
  //-----------------------------------------------------------------
    resize(320, 240);

    // TODO: Place additional initialization code here
}

// Place additional applet clean up code here.  destroy() is called when
// when you applet is terminating and being unloaded.
//-----------------------------------------------------------------
public void destroy()
{
    // TODO: Place applet cleanup code here
}

    // ANIMATION SUPPORT:
    //     Draws the next image, if all images are currently loaded
    //-----------------------------------------------------------------
private void displayImage(Graphics g)
{
    if (!m_fAllLoaded)
       return;

    // Draw Image in center of applet
    //-----------------------------------------------------------------
    g.drawImage(m_Images[m_nCurrImage],
            (size().width - m_nImgWidth)  / 2,
            (size().height - m_nImgHeight) / 2, null);
}

// myfirst Paint Handler
//-----------------------------------------------------------------
public void paint(Graphics g)
{
    // ANIMATION SUPPORT:
    //     The following code displays a status message until all the
    // images are loaded. Then it calls displayImage to display the current
    // image.
```

```
//---------------------------------------------------------------------
if (m_fAllLoaded)
{
    Rectangle r = g.getClipRect();
    g.clearRect(r.x, r.y, r.width, r.height);
    displayImage(g);
}
else
    g.drawString("Loading images...", 10, 20);

// TODO: Place additional applet Paint code here
}
//     The start() method is called when the page containing the applet
// first appears on the screen. The AppletWizard's initial implementation
// of this method starts execution of the applet's thread.
//---------------------------------------------------------------------
public void start()
{
    if (m_myfirst == null)
    {
        m_myfirst = new Thread(this);
        m_myfirst.start();
    }
    // TODO: Place additional applet start code here
}

//     The stop() method is called when the page containing the applet is
// no longer on the screen. The AppletWizard's initial implementation of
// this method stops execution of the applet's thread.
//---------------------------------------------------------------------
public void stop()
{
    if (m_myfirst != null)
    {
        m_myfirst.stop();
        m_myfirst = null;
    }

    // TODO: Place additional applet stop code here
}

// THREAD SUPPORT
//     The run() method is called when the applet's thread is started. If
// your applet performs any ongoing activities without waiting for user
// input, the code for implementing that behavior typically goes here. For
// example, for an applet that performs animation, the run() method contro
// the display of images.
//---------------------------------------------------------------------
public void run()
{
    m_nCurrImage = 0;

    // If re-entering the page, then the images have already been loaded.
    // m_fAllLoaded == TRUE.
    //---------------------------------------------------------------------
    if (!m_fAllLoaded)
    {
        repaint();
        m_Graphics = getGraphics();
        m_Images   = new Image[NUM_IMAGES];

        // Load in all the images
        //---------------------------------------------------------------------
        MediaTracker tracker = new MediaTracker(this);
        String strImage;
```

```java
        // For each image in the animation, this method first constructs a
        // string containing the path to the image file; then it begins
        // loading the image into the m_Images array.  Note that the call to
        // getImage will return before the image is completely loaded.
        //-------------------------------------------------------------
        for (int i = 1; i <= NUM_IMAGES; i++)
        {
            // Build path to next image
            //---------------------------------------------------------
            strImage = "images/img00" + ((i < 10) ? "0" : "") + i + ".gif";
             m_Images[i-1] = getImage(getDocumentBase(), strImage);

                tracker.addImage(m_Images[i-1], 0);
        }

        // Wait until all images are fully loaded
        //-------------------------------------------------------------
        try
        {
            tracker.waitForAll();
            m_fAllLoaded = !tracker.isErrorAny();
        }
        catch (InterruptedException e)
        {
            // TODO: Place exception-handling code here in case an
            //       InterruptedException is thrown by Thread.sleep(),
            //       meaning that another thread has interrupted this one
        }

        if (!m_fAllLoaded)
        {
            stop();
            m_Graphics.drawString("Error loading images!", 10, 40);
            return;
        }
        // Assuming all images are same width and height.
        //-------------------------------------------------------------
         m_nImgWidth  = m_Images[0].getWidth(this);
         m_nImgHeight = m_Images[0].getHeight(this);
        }
    repaint();
    while (true)
    {
        try
        {
            // Draw next image in animation
            //---------------------------------------------------------
            displayImage(m_Graphics);
            m_nCurrImage++;
            if (m_nCurrImage == NUM_IMAGES)
                m_nCurrImage = 0;

            // TODO:  Add additional thread-specific code here
            Thread.sleep(50);
        }
        catch (InterruptedException e)
        {
            // TODO: Place exception-handling code here in case an
            //       InterruptedException is thrown by Thread.sleep(),
            //       meaning that another thread has interrupted this one
            stop();
        }
    }
}
// TODO: Place additional applet code here
}
```

Figure E.15 shows a sample run.

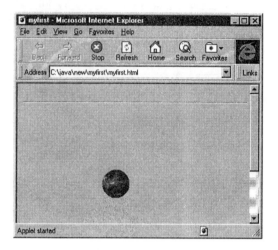

Figure E.15 Sample run

E.1.4 Development as an application and as an applet

The Java program can be developed as an application and as an applet (see Figure E.2). This option generates two code files: an applet and a frame, as shown in Figure E.16. This allows for the code to be run either as a frame or as an applet (if it is allowed).

Figure E.16 Frame workspace

The frame code is as follows:

```
//****************************************************************************
// myfirstFrame.java:
//
//****************************************************************************
import java.awt.*;

//============================================================================
// STANDALONE APPLICATION SUPPORT
// This frame class acts as a top-level window in which the applet appears
// when it's run as a standalone application.
//============================================================================
class myfirstFrame extends Frame
{
  // myfirstFrame constructor
  //-------------------------------------------------------------------------
  public myfirstFrame(String str)
  {
      // TODO: Add additional construction code here
      super (str);
  }

  // The handleEvent() method receives all events generated within the frame
  // window. You can use this method to respond to window events. To respond
  // to events generated by menus, buttons, etc. or other controls in the
  // frame window but not managed by the applet, override the window's
  // action() method.
  //-------------------------------------------------------------------------
  public boolean handleEvent(Event evt)
  {
      switch (evt.id)
      {
// Application shutdown (e.g. user chooses Close from the system menu).
//-------------------------------------------------------------
          case Event.WINDOW_DESTROY:
              // TODO: Place additional clean up code here
              dispose();
              System.exit(0);
              return true;

          default:
              return super.handleEvent(evt);
      }
  }
}
```

The generated applet code is as follows:

```
// myfirst.java:  Applet
//
//****************************************************************************
import java.applet.*;
import java.awt.*;
import myfirstFrame;

//============================================================================
// Main Class for applet myfirst
//
//============================================================================
public class myfirst extends Applet implements Runnable
{
  // THREAD SUPPORT:
```

```
//      m_myfirst   is the Thread object for the applet
//-----------------------------------------------------------------------
private Thread   m_myfirst = null;

// ANIMATION SUPPORT:
//      m_Graphics      used for storing the applet's Graphics context
//      m_Images[]      the array of Image objects for the animation
//      m_nCurrImage    the index of the next image to be displayed
//      m_ImgWidth      width of each image
//      m_ImgHeight     height of each image
//      m_fAllLoaded    indicates whether all images have been loaded
//      NUM_IMAGES      number of images used in the animation
//-----------------------------------------------------------------------
private Graphics m_Graphics;
private Image m_Images[];
private int    m_nCurrImage;
private int    m_nImgWidth  = 0;
private int    m_nImgHeight = 0;
private boolean  m_fAllLoaded = false;
private final int NUM_IMAGES = 18;

// STANDALONE APPLICATION SUPPORT:
//      m_fStandAlone will be set to true if applet is run standalone
//-----------------------------------------------------------------------
private boolean m_fStandAlone = false;

// STANDALONE APPLICATION SUPPORT
//   The main() method acts as the applet's entry point when it is run
// as a standalone application. It is ignored if the applet is run from
// within an HTML page.
//-----------------------------------------------------------------------
public static void main(String args[])
{
// Create Toplevel Window to contain applet myfirst
//-----------------------------------------------------------------
    myfirstFrame frame = new myfirstFrame("myfirst");

// Must show Frame before we size it so insets() will return valid values
//-----------------------------------------------------------------
    frame.show();
    frame.hide();
    frame.resize(frame.insets().left + frame.insets().right  + 320,
              frame.insets().top  + frame.insets().bottom + 240);

// The following code starts the applet running within the frame window.
// It also calls GetParameters() to retrieve parameter values from the
// command line, and sets m_fStandAlone to true to prevent init() from
// trying to get them from the HTML page.
//-----------------------------------------------------------------
    myfirst applet_myfirst = new myfirst();

    frame.add("Center", applet_myfirst);
    applet_myfirst.m_fStandAlone = true;
    applet_myfirst.init();
    applet_myfirst.start();
      frame.show();
}

// myfirst Class Constructor
//-----------------------------------------------------------------------
public myfirst()
{
    // TODO: Add constructor code here
}

// APPLET INFO SUPPORT:
```

```
//      The getAppletInfo() method returns a string describing the applet's
// author, copyright date, or miscellaneous information.
//----------------------------------------------------------------
public String getAppletInfo()
{
    return "Name: myfirst\r\n" +
           "Author: Bill Buchanan\r\n" +
           "Created with Microsoft Visual J++ Version 1.1";
}


// The init() method is called by the AWT when an applet is first loaded or
// reloaded.  Override this method to perform whatever initialization your
// applet needs, such as initializing data structures, loading images or
// fonts, creating frame windows, setting the layout manager, or adding UI
// components.
    //----------------------------------------------------------------
public void init()
{
        // If you use a ResourceWizard-generated "control creator" class to
        // arrange controls in your applet, you may want to call its
        // CreateControls() method from within this method. Remove the
        // following call to resize() before adding the call to
        // CreateControls();
        //----------------------------------------------------------------
    resize(320, 240);

        // TODO: Place additional initialization code here
}

// Place additional applet clean up code here.  destroy() is called when
// when you applet is terminating and being unloaded.
//----------------------------------------------------------------
public void destroy()
{
    // TODO: Place applet cleanup code here
}

    // ANIMATION SUPPORT:
    //      Draws the next image, if all images are currently loaded
    //----------------------------------------------------------------
private void displayImage(Graphics g)
{
    if (!m_fAllLoaded)
       return;

    // Draw Image in center of applet
    //----------------------------------------------------------------
    g.drawImage(m_Images[m_nCurrImage],
            (size().width  - m_nImgWidth)  / 2,
            (size().height - m_nImgHeight) / 2, null);
}

// myfirst Paint Handler
//----------------------------------------------------------------
public void paint(Graphics g)
{
// ANIMATION SUPPORT:
//   The following code displays a status message until all the images
// are loaded. Then it calls displayImage to display the current
// image.
//----------------------------------------------------------------
    if (m_fAllLoaded)
    {
        Rectangle r = g.getClipRect();
```

```
        g.clearRect(r.x, r.y, r.width, r.height);
        displayImage(g);
    }
    else
        g.drawString("Loading images...", 10, 20);

    // TODO: Place additional applet Paint code here
}

// The start() method is called when the page containing the applet
// first appears on the screen. The AppletWizard's initial implementation
// of this method starts execution of the applet's thread.
//-----------------------------------------------------------------------
public void start()
{
    if (m_myfirst == null)
    {
        m_myfirst = new Thread(this);
        m_myfirst.start();
    }
    // TODO: Place additional applet start code here
}

// The stop() method is called when the page containing the applet is
// no longer on the screen. The AppletWizard's initial implementation of
// this method stops execution of the applet's thread.
//-----------------------------------------------------------------------
public void stop()
{
    if (m_myfirst != null)
    {
        m_myfirst.stop();
        m_myfirst = null;
    }

    // TODO: Place additional applet stop code here
}

// THREAD SUPPORT
// The run() method is called when the applet's thread is started. If
// your applet performs any ongoing activities without waiting for user
// input, the code for implementing that behavior typically goes here.
// For example, for an applet that performs animation, the run() method
// controls the display of images.
//-----------------------------------------------------------------------
public void run()
{
    m_nCurrImage = 0;

    // If re-entering the page, then the images. have already been loaded.
    // m_fAllLoaded == TRUE.
    //-------------------------------------------------------------------
    if (!m_fAllLoaded)
    {
        repaint();
        m_Graphics = getGraphics();
        m_Images   = new Image[NUM_IMAGES];

        // Load in all the images
        //---------------------------------------------------------------
        MediaTracker tracker = new MediaTracker(this);
        String strImage;

        // For each image in the animation, this method first constructs a
        // string containing the path to the image file; then it begins
        // loading the image into the m_Images array.  Note that the call
```

```
    // to getImage will return before the image is completely loaded.
    //-------------------------------------------------------------
    for (int i = 1; i <= NUM_IMAGES; i++)
    {
        // Build path to next image
        //---------------------------------------------------------
        strImage = "images/img00" + ((i < 10) ? "0" : "") + i + ".gif";
        if (m_fStandAlone)
         m_Images[i-1] = Toolkit.getDefaultToolkit().getImage(strImage);
        else
         m_Images[i-1] = getImage(getDocumentBase(), strImage);

        tracker.addImage(m_Images[i-1], 0);
    }

    // Wait until all images are fully loaded
    //-------------------------------------------------------------
    try
    {
        tracker.waitForAll();
        m_fAllLoaded = !tracker.isErrorAny();
    }
    catch (InterruptedException e)
    {
        // TODO: Place exception-handling code here in case an
        //       InterruptedException is thrown by Thread.sleep(),
        //       meaning that another thread has interrupted this one
    }
    if (!m_fAllLoaded)
    {
        stop();
        m_Graphics.drawString("Error loading images!", 10, 40);
        return;
    }
    // Assuming all images are same width and height.
    //-------------------------------------------------------------
     m_nImgWidth  = m_Images[0].getWidth(this);
     m_nImgHeight = m_Images[0].getHeight(this);
    }
   repaint();

   while (true)
   {
       try
       {
           // Draw next image in animation
           //-------------------------------------------------------
           displayImage(m_Graphics);
           m_nCurrImage++;
           if (m_nCurrImage == NUM_IMAGES)
             m_nCurrImage = 0;

           // TODO:  Add additional thread-specific code here
           Thread.sleep(50);
       }
       catch (InterruptedException e)
       {
           // TODO: Place exception-handling code here in case an
           //       InterruptedException is thrown by Thread.sleep(),
           //       meaning that another thread has interrupted this one
           stop();
       }
   }
  }
 }
 // TODO: Place additional applet code here
}
```

E.1.5 Database wizard

Java J++ provides for a Database Wizard for Java. After selecting it from the New Project window, the user is prompted for the database which should be used. Figure E.17 shows that the user has selected the `shop.mdb` database. Next the user is asked which table in the database to use (in the case in Figure E.18 the Suppliers table is used). Next the user is asked which of the fields in the database are to be used (Figure E.19). Finally the user is asked to whether comments and TODOs should be added (Figure E.20). The finally information is then displayed (Figure E.21).

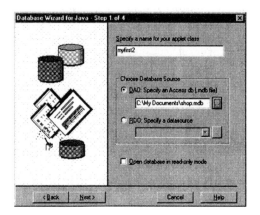

Figure E.17 Selection of database

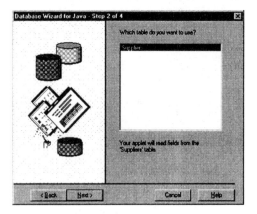

Figure E.18 Table in the database to use

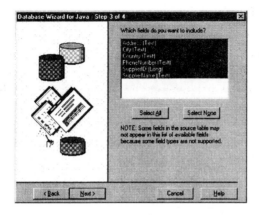

Figure E.19 Fields in the database to use

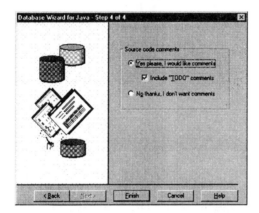

Figure E.20 Wizard prompt

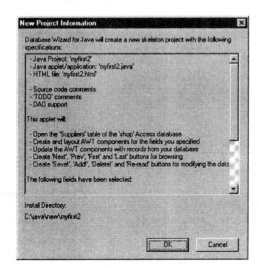

Figure E.21 Database information

Figure E.22 shows the completed code in the workspace. It shows that there are two Java code files: `Alert.java` and `myfirst2.java`, which contain four classes.

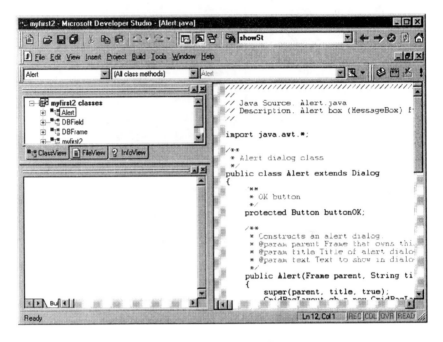

Figure E.22 Database workspace

The source code for `Alert.java` is:

```
///////////////////////////////////////////////////////////////////////////
//
// Java Source: Alert.java
// Description: Alert box (MessageBox) functionality

import java.awt.*;

/**
 * Alert dialog class
 */
public class Alert extends Dialog
{
    /**
     * OK button
     */
    protected Button buttonOK;

    /**
     * Constructs an alert dialog.
     * @param parent Frame that owns this dialog
     * @param title Title of alert dialog
     * @param text Text to show in dialog
     */
    public Alert(Frame parent, String title, String text)
    {
        super(parent, title, true);
```

```
        GridBagLayout gb = new GridBagLayout();
        setLayout(gb);
        GridBagConstraints c = new GridBagConstraints();
        c.gridx = 0;
        c.insets = new Insets(10, 10, 10, 10);
        Label l;
        add(l = new Label(text));
        gb.setConstraints(l, c);
        add(buttonOK = new Button("OK"));
        gb.setConstraints(buttonOK, c);
        setResizable(false);
        pack();
        Rectangle rcParent = parent.bounds();
        Dimension dAlert = size();
        move
        (
            rcParent.x + (rcParent.width - dAlert.width) / 2,
            rcParent.y + (rcParent.height - dAlert.height) / 2
        );
        show();
    }

    /**
     * This method is called when an action occurs inside this component.
     * @param e Event class with information about the action.
     * @param o Argument object.
     * @return True if the event was handled, false otherwise
     */
    public boolean action(Event e, Object o)
    {
        if (e.target == buttonOK)
        {
            dispose();
            return true;
        }
        return false;
    }
}
```

The source code for myfirst2.java is:

```
////////////////////////////////////////////////////////////////////////
//
// Java Source: myfirst2.java
// Description: Applet with DAO support for accessing the
//              "shop" database.
//

import java.applet.*;
import java.awt.*;
import java.util.*;

//----------------------------------------------------------------------
// DAO SUPPORT: Import the DAO 3.5 object library and the COM classes
//----------------------------------------------------------------------

// TODO: Run the "Type Library Wizard" on the DAO 3.5 object library!

import dao350.*;
import com.ms.com.*;
import Alert;

//----------------------------------------------------------------------
// DAO SUPPORT: Class that defines a database field
//----------------------------------------------------------------------
```

```
/**
 * Field class that defines the field's name and type as well as it's
 * attached Label and TextField components.
 */
class DBField
{
    /**
     * Name of field
     */
    String strName;

    /**
     * Type of field as a string
     */
    String strType;

    /**
     * Type of field as a Variant type (vt)
     */
    short vt;

    /**
     * Label attached to field (if any)
     */
    Label label;

    /**
     * TextField attached to field (if any)
     */
    TextField field;

    /**
     * Attributes of field
     */
    int attributes;

    /**
     * Validation text for field
     */
    String strValidation;

    /**
     * Constructor
     * @param strName Name of field in database
     * @param strType Description of field type
     * @param vt Type of Variant (see Variant.Variant*)
     */
    public DBField(String strName, String strType, short vt)
    {
        this.strName = strName;
        this.strType = strType;
        this.vt = vt;
    }
}

/**
 * Frame class for the myfirst2 applet.
 */
class DBFrame extends Frame
{
    /**
     * The applet that brought up this frame window.
     */
    myfirst2 applet;
```

```java
    /**
     * Constructor
       * @param applet Applet to notify (via applet.stop) when the frame
         window closes.
       * @param strTitle The title of this frame window.
       */
    public DBFrame(myfirst2 appletmyfirst2, String strTitle)
    {
        // Send title to superclass and set applet member
        super(strTitle);
        this.applet = appletmyfirst2;
    }

    /**
     * This method is used to intercept the WINDOW_DESTROY event so the
     * recordset can be closed. It is accomplished by calling the
     * applet's exit() method.
     * @param evt Event description class.
     * @return True if the event was handled, false otherwise
     */
    public synchronized boolean handleEvent(Event evt)
    {
        switch (evt.id)
        {
            case Event.WINDOW_DESTROY:

            //-------------------------------------------------------------
            // DAO SUPPORT: Close database and window on WINDOW_DESTROY
            //-------------------------------------------------------------

                applet.exit();
                return true;

            default:
                return super.handleEvent(evt);
        }
    }
}


/**
 * Main myfirst2 applet/application class.
 */
public class myfirst2 extends Applet
{
    /**
     * The myfirst2 applet (if we created it in main).
     */
    static protected myfirst2 applet = null;

    /**
     * The frame window if it's currently active.
     */
    protected Frame frame;

    //---------------------------------------------------------------------
    // DAO SUPPORT: Variables used for DAO support.
    //---------------------------------------------------------------------

    protected boolean readOnly = false;
    protected String strDatabase = "C:\\My Documents\\shop.mdb";
    protected String strRecordset = "Suppliers";
    protected int recordCount;
 protected static Variant varEmpty;
 // Valid table not specified via wizard,
 // must specify table name here.
```

```
    // protected String strRecordset = "<name>";

// DAO Objects
protected _DBEngine m_IEngine;
   protected Database database;
   protected Recordset recordset;

   /**
    * Fields to include in the display and their types.
    * Any fields you didn't select will still appear here, but they will
    * be commented out.  To include a field, just uncomment it.
    */
   static DBField[] field =
   {
       new DBField( "Address",     "Text", Variant.VariantString  ),
       new DBField( "City",        "Text", Variant.VariantString  ),
       new DBField( "Country",     "Text", Variant.VariantString  ),
       new DBField( "PhoneNumber", "Text", Variant.VariantString  ),
       new DBField( "SupplierID",  "Long", Variant.VariantInt     ),
       new DBField( "SupplierName","Text", Variant.VariantString  ),
   };

   /**
    * An associative array that maps the string name of a field
    * to the DBField class associated with it.
    */
   static Hashtable hashField = new Hashtable();

   static
   {
       for (int i = 0; i < field.length; i++)
       {
           hashField.put(field[i].strName, field[i]);
       }
   }

   /**
    * The number of columns to use when laying out fields.
    * If you want to specify anthing other than a fixed number of
 * columns, you can change the initial value of this variable.
 *
 * Here is an example that will ensure that no column has more
    * than 10 rows in it.
 *
 *   protected int columns = (field.length + 9) / 10;
 *
    */
   protected int columns = 1;

   /**
    * Width of TextFields (in characters)
    */
   protected int textFieldWidth = 25;

   /**
    * Global vName variant for COM thread safety
    */
   Variant vName;

   /**
    * Global vValue variant for COM thread safety
    */
   Variant vValue;

   /**
    * Global vOriginalValue variant for COM thread safety
```

```
    */
    Variant vOriginalValue;

    // Containers of database components
    protected Panel db = new Panel();
    protected Panel dbcolumn[] = new Panel[columns * 2];

    // Toolbar with "Next", "Prev", "First" and "Last" buttons
    protected Panel tools = new Panel();
    protected Panel toolbar = new Panel();
    protected Button buttonFirst = new Button("<< First");
    protected Button buttonPrev = new Button("< Prev");
    protected Button buttonNext = new Button("Next >");
    protected Button buttonLast = new Button("Last >>");

    // Toolbar with "Save!" and "Re-read" buttons
    protected Panel updatetools = new Panel();
    protected Button buttonUpdate = new Button("Save!");
    protected Button buttonAdd = new Button("Add!");
    protected Button buttonDelete = new Button("Delete!");
    protected Button buttonReread = new Button("Re-read");
    protected Button buttonExit = new Button("Exit");

    // User feedback labels for showing current position in database.
// Need a big empty status label to allow for status string display
    protected Panel feedback = new Panel();
    protected Label labelDatabase = new Label("", Label.CENTER);
    protected Label labelRecordset = new Label("", Label.CENTER);
    protected Label labelPosition = new Label("", Label.CENTER);
    protected Label labelStatus = new Label("       ");

    /**
     * Run the frame window
     */
    protected void makeFrame()
    {
        frame = new DBFrame(this, "myfirst2");
    }

    /**
     * Entry point for applications
     * @param args Arguments to the application.
     */
    public static void main(String[] args)
    {
      applet = new myfirst2();
      applet.makeFrame();
      applet.frame.add("Center", applet);
      applet.init();
      applet.start();
      applet.frame.pack();
      applet.frame.show();
      applet.frame.setResizable(false);
    }

    /**
     * The getAppletInfo() method returns a string describing the applet's
     * author, copyright date, or miscellaneous information.
     */
    public String getAppletInfo()
    {
        return "Name: myfirst2\n" +
               "Author: Unknown\n" +
               "Created with Microsoft Visual J++ Version 1.1";
    }
```

```java
public void init()
{
  //---------------------------------------------------------------
  // DAO SUPPORT: Open the database and set up field info
  // Initialize database engine through license manager
  //---------------------------------------------------------------
   // Use a global empty variant for optional variant args
   varEmpty = new Variant();
   varEmpty.putEmpty();

     ILicenseMgr mgr = new LicenseMgr();
     m_IEngine = (_DBEngine)mgr.createWithLic
     (
      "mbmabptebkjcdlgtjmskjwtsdhjbmkmwtrak",
      "{00000010-0000-0010-8000-00AA006D2EA4}",
         null,
         ComContext.INPROC_SERVER
     );

     // Open database
     Variant vExclusive = new Variant();
     Variant vReadOnly = new Variant();
     Variant vConnect = new Variant();
     vExclusive.putBoolean(false);
     vReadOnly.putBoolean(readOnly);
     vConnect.putString("");
     database = m_IEngine.OpenDatabase(strDatabase, vExclusive,
              vReadOnly, vConnect);

     // Create a new recordset
     Variant vOpenType = new Variant();
     Variant vOptions = new Variant();
   Variant vLockType = new Variant();
     vOpenType.putShort((short)RecordsetTypeEnum.dbOpenDynaset);
     vOptions.putShort((short)0);
// NOTE: The RecordsetOptionEnum.dbReadOnly value is shared by LockTypeEnum
// There is no LockTypeEnum value denoting read only concurrency
     vLockType.putInt(readOnly ? RecordsetOptionEnum.dbReadOnly :
            LockTypeEnum.dbOptimistic);
     recordset = database.OpenRecordset(strRecordset, vOpenType, vOption
            vLockType);

     // Count records in record set
   if (recordset.getEOF())
      recordCount = 0;
   else
   {
      int nOptions = 0;
      recordset.MoveLast(nOptions);
      recordCount = recordset.getRecordCount();
      recordset.MoveFirst();
   }
     // Create COM variants
     vName = new Variant();
     vValue = new Variant();
     vOriginalValue = new Variant();

  //---------------------------------------------------------------
  // DAO SUPPORT: Create, arrange and initialize components for each field.
  //---------------------------------------------------------------

   // Create column panels
     columns *= 2;
     db.setLayout(new GridLayout(0, columns));
     for (int col = 0; col < columns; col++)
     {
```

```
        db.add(dbcolumn[col] = new Panel());
        dbcolumn[col].setLayout(new GridLayout(0, 1));
    }

    // Add new components for each field
    int col = 0;
    Fields fields = recordset.getFields();
    for (int i = 0; i < field.length; i++)
    {
        DBField df = (DBField)hashField.get(field[i].strName);
        vName.putString(field[i].strName);
        _Field thisfield = fields.getItem(vName);
        df.strValidation = thisfield.getValidationText();
        df.attributes = thisfield.getAttributes();
        String attribs = new String();
        df.field = new TextField(textFieldWidth);
        if (!readOnly && ((df.attributes &
            FieldAttributeEnum.dbUpdatableField) == 0))
        {
            attribs += " (ReadOnly)";
            df.field.disable();
        }
        if ((df.attributes & FieldAttributeEnum.dbAutoIncrField) != 0)
        {
            attribs += " (Auto)";
            df.field.disable();
        }
        df.label = new Label
        (
            df.strName + " (" + df.strType + ")" + attribs + " :",
            Label.RIGHT
        );
        if (readOnly)
        {
            df.field.disable();
        }
        dbcolumn[col++].add(df.label);
        dbcolumn[col++].add(df.field);
        col %= columns;
    }
    // Set the layout of the toolbar panel
    toolbar.setLayout(new GridLayout(1, 0));
    toolbar.add(buttonFirst);
    toolbar.add(buttonPrev);
    toolbar.add(buttonNext);
    toolbar.add(buttonLast);

    // Set the layout of the update tools panel
    updatetools.setLayout(new GridLayout(1, 0));
    updatetools.add(buttonUpdate);
    updatetools.add(buttonAdd);
    updatetools.add(buttonDelete);
    updatetools.add(buttonReread);

    // Combine the tools together
    tools.setLayout(new FlowLayout());
    tools.add(toolbar);
    if (!readOnly)
    {
        tools.add(updatetools);
    }
if (frame != null)
    tools.add(buttonExit);

    // Set layout for feedback panel
    feedback.setLayout(new GridLayout(0, 1));
```

```
        feedback.add(labelDatabase);
        feedback.add(labelRecordset);
        feedback.add(labelPosition);
      feedback.add(labelStatus);

        // Lay out the component groups vertically
        GridBagLayout gb = new GridBagLayout();
        setLayout(gb);
        GridBagConstraints c = new GridBagConstraints();
        c.insets = new Insets(20, 30, 20, 30);
        c.gridx = 0;
        add(feedback);
        gb.setConstraints(feedback, c);
        add(db);
        gb.setConstraints(db, c);
        add(tools);
        gb.setConstraints(tools, c);

        // Update fields based on current record
        updateUI();

        // TODO: Place additional initialization code here
    }

    /**
     * Destroy() is called when your applet is terminating and being unload
     */
    public void destroy()
    {
        // TODO: Place applet cleanup code here
    }

    /**
     * The start() method is called when the page containing the applet
     * first appears on the screen. The AppletWizard's initial implementati
     * of this method starts execution of the applet's thread.
     */
    public void start()
    {
        // TODO: Place applet startup code here
    }

/**
 * The stop() method is called when the page containing the applet is
 * no longer on the screen.  We get rid of our frame window here (if one
 * exists) and either exit the system (if we're an application) or
 * enable the button again (if we're an applet).
 */
    public synchronized void stop()
    {
        // If started as application, exit
        if (frame != null)
            System.exit(0);

        // TODO: Place additional applet stop code here
    }

    /**
     * This method is called when an action occurs inside this component.
     * @param evt Event class with information about the action.
     * @param o Argument object.
     * @return True if the event was handled, false otherwise
     */
    public synchronized boolean action(Event evt, Object o)
    {
```

```
//------------------------------------------------------------------
// DAO SUPPORT: Perform actions when the user presses a toolbar button
//------------------------------------------------------------------

    labelStatus.setText("");

      if (evt.target == buttonFirst)
      {
          recordset.MoveFirst();
          updateUI();
          return true;
      }
      else if (evt.target == buttonPrev)
      {
          recordset.MovePrevious();
          updateUI();
          return true;
      }
      else if (evt.target == buttonNext)
      {
          recordset.MoveNext();
          updateUI();
          return true;
      }
      else if (evt.target == buttonLast)
      {
       int nOptions = 0;
          recordset.MoveLast(nOptions);
          updateUI();
          return true;
      }
      else if (evt.target == buttonUpdate)
      {
          buttonUpdate.disable();
          buttonAdd.disable();
          buttonUpdate.disable();
          updateDatabase(EditModeEnum.dbEditInProgress);
          buttonUpdate.enable();
          buttonAdd.enable();
          buttonDelete.enable();
          return true;
      }
      else if (evt.target == buttonAdd)
      {
          buttonUpdate.disable();
          buttonAdd.disable();
          buttonUpdate.disable();
          updateDatabase(EditModeEnum.dbEditAdd);
          buttonUpdate.enable();
          buttonAdd.enable();
          buttonDelete.enable();
          return true;
      }
      else if (evt.target == buttonDelete)
      {
          buttonUpdate.disable();
          buttonAdd.disable();
          buttonUpdate.disable();
          updateDatabase(EditModeEnum.dbEditNone);
          buttonUpdate.enable();
          buttonAdd.enable();
          buttonDelete.enable();
          return true;
      }
      else if (evt.target == buttonReread)
      {
```

```
                updateUI();
                return true;
        }
        else if (evt.target == buttonExit)
        {
                exit();
        }

        // TODO: Place additional action handlers here

        return false;
}

/**
 * Close any open results and notify the applet/application to
 * close this frame window.
 */
protected void exit()
{
        // Close any open recordset
        if (recordset != null)
        {
                recordset.Close();
                recordset = null;
        }

        // Notify the application to exit by calling the
        // stop() method of the applet.
        stop();
}

//-------------------------------------------------------------------
// DAO SUPPORT: Methods to update the database and the UI
//-------------------------------------------------------------------

/**
 * Updates the contents of the TextField associated with a given field
 * using the current record.
 * @param f Field to update
 */
void updateTextField(DBField f)
{
        if (recordset != null)
        {
                String strValue;
                try
                {
                        // Get the field's value at the current record
                        vName.putString(f.strName);

                        // Attempt to get the value
                        Variant vValue;
                        vValue = recordset.getCollect(vName);

                        // We want booleans to be 'true' and 'false'
                        if (f.vt == Variant.VariantBoolean)
                        {
                                Boolean b = new Boolean(vValue.getBoolean());
                                strValue = b.toString();
                        }
                        else
                        {
                                strValue = vValue.toString();
                        }
                }
```

```
                    // Converting a variant of type VT_NULL to a String can cause
                    // this exception to be thrown.
                    catch (ClassCastException c)
                    {
                        // Choose "" as the String representation for null.
                        strValue = "";
                    }

                    // Set the text of the TextField associated with the field
                    f.field.setText(strValue);
            }
    }

    /**
     * Updates the field in the database based on the associated TextField.
     * @param df Field to update.
     */
    void updateDatabaseField(DBField df) throws Exception
    {
        if (recordset != null)
        {
            try
            {
                // Convert field value to the right variant type
                String strValue = df.field.getText();
                vValue.putString(strValue);
                vName.putString(df.strName);

                // We want booleans to be 'true' and 'false'
                if (df.vt == Variant.VariantBoolean)
                {
                    if (strValue.equals("true"))
                    {
                        vValue.putBoolean(true);
                    }
                    else
                    if (strValue.equals("false"))
                    {
                        vValue.putBoolean(false);
                    }
                    else
                    {
                        throw new Exception(df.strName +
                        " must be either 'true' or 'false' in lowercase.");
                    }
                }
                else
                {
                    // Convert to variant type
                    vValue.changeType(df.vt);
                }

                // Write to database unless the original value was null
                // and the text field is empty.
                vOriginalValue = recordset.getCollect(vName);
                if (!((vOriginalValue.getvt() == Variant.VariantNull) &&
                    (strValue.equals(""))))
                {
                    recordset.putCollect(vName, vValue);
                }
            }

            // Converting a variant of type VT_NULL can cause this exception
            catch (ClassCastException c)
            {
            }
```

```
        }
    }

/**
 * Converts an exception into a human readable string possibly involving
 * the DBField structure and the HRESULT value if it's a COM exception.
 */
    protected String getExceptionMessage(Exception e, DBField f)
    {
        if (e instanceof ComFailException)
        {
            int h = ((ComFailException)e).getHResult();
            switch (h)
            {
            case 0x800a0c5b:
                return "Field value is too long";

            case 0x800a0cf4:
                if ((f == null) || f.strValidation.equals(""))
                {
                    return "Validation rule failed";
                }
                else
                {
                    return f.strValidation;
                }

            default:
                return "DAO COM Exception " + e.getMessage();
            }
        }
        return e.getMessage();
    }
/** * Updates the database from the information in the TextFields.*/
    protected void updateDatabase(int nMode)
    {
        // Update each field
        try
        {
         // If no mode, must be a delete
         if (nMode == EditModeEnum.dbEditNone)
         {
            recordset.Delete();

            // If deleting last record, scroll back
            recordset.MoveNext();
            if (recordset.getEOF())
                recordset.MovePrevious();

            // Decrement the record count
            recordCount--;
         }
            // Go into edit/addnew mode to change the recordset
        else
        {
            if (nMode == EditModeEnum.dbEditAdd)
                recordset.AddNew();
            else
                recordset.Edit();

            int i;
            for (i = 0; i < field.length; i++)
            {
                // If the field is updatable and it is not autoincrement
                if (((field[i].attributes &
                    FieldAttributeEnum.dbUpdatableField) != 0) &&
```

```java
                    ((field[i].attributes &
                    FieldAttributeEnum.dbAutoIncrField) == 0))
            {
                try
                {
                        // Try to update the field.
                        updateDatabaseField(field[i]);
                    }
                catch (Exception e)
                {
            // If the update failed, alert the user and cancel the update
                String strError;
                strError = "Error updating " + field[i].strName + " : "+
                    getExceptionMessage(e, field[i]);
                if (frame != null)
                    new Alert(frame, "Modification Failed!", strError);
                else
                    labelStatus.setText(strError);
                recordset.CancelUpdate(UpdateTypeEnum.dbUpdateRegular);
                break;
                }
            }
        }
        if (i == field.length)
        {
            // Commit the update
            recordset.Update(UpdateTypeEnum.dbUpdateRegular, false);
            if (nMode == EditModeEnum.dbEditAdd)
            {
                // Increment the record count
                recordCount++;

    // If adding to empty recordset make sure to set currency
                if (recordset.getEOF())
                    recordset.MoveFirst();
            }
        }
    }
}
catch (ComException eCom)
{
    String strError = new String();
    Errors errs = m_IEngine.getErrors();
    Variant var = new Variant();

    for (int n = 0; n < errs.getCount(); n++)
    {
        var.putInt(n);
        dao350.Error err = errs.getItem(var);
        if (nMode == EditModeEnum.dbEditAdd)
            strError += "Error adding record: ";
        else if (nMode == EditModeEnum.dbEditInProgress)
            strError += "Error updating record: ";
        else
            strError += "Error deleting record: ";

        strError += err.getDescription();
    }

    if (frame != null)
        new Alert(frame, "Modification Failed!", strError);
    else
        labelStatus.setText(strError);
}
    catch (Exception e)
    {
```

```
            // Failed to update the table in the database
      String strError;
      strError = "Error updating record: " + getExceptionMessage(e, null);
      if (frame != null)
         new Alert(frame, "Modification Failed!", strError);
      else
         labelStatus.setText(strError);
      }
      updateUI();
   }

/**
 * Updates all TextFields using the field array.  Then updates all
 * feedback labels based on the current record.
 */
protected void updateUI()
{
   int pos = -1;
     // Update each field if there are records
   if (recordCount > 0)
   {
      for (int i = 0; i < field.length; i++)
      {
         try
         {
            updateTextField(field[i]);
         }
         catch (Exception e)
         {
         // Getting the field value failed for some reason
         String strError;
         strError = "Error retrieving field value for " +
                    field[i].strName +" : " + e.getMessage();
         if (frame != null)
            new Alert(frame, "Data Fetch Failed!", strError);
         else
            labelStatus.setText(strError);
         break;
            }
        }
       pos = recordset.getAbsolutePosition();
   }

      // Set the states of the buttons and the feedback labels
      buttonFirst.enable(pos != 0 && recordCount > 0);
      buttonPrev.enable(pos != 0 && recordCount > 0);
      buttonNext.enable(pos != (recordCount - 1));
      buttonLast.enable(pos != (recordCount - 1));
      labelDatabase.setText("Database: " + strDatabase +
                (readOnly ? " (Read Only)" : ""));
      labelRecordset.setText("Table: " + strRecordset);
      labelPosition.setText("Record: " + (pos + 1) + " of " + recordCount)
   if (recordCount == 0)
      labelStatus.setText("There are no records in the table!");
   }
// TODO: Place additional applet code here
}
```

Index

helvetica, 131, 132, 137
italic, 209, 210, 244, 245
symbol, 131
times Roman, 131, 137
For loop, 31, 33, 35, 71
Forms, 229
Fourth, 36
Fragment, 166
Fragmentation, 188
Frame, 165, 166, 182, 263, 269, 311, 315,
319, 322–325, 33–344
France, 65, 66, 171
Ftp, *see* File Transfer Protocol

Garbage collection, 40, 50
Gateway, 164–169, 173, 174
Gateways, 165, 167, 169, 173, 174, 229
Germany, 65, 66
GIF, 92, 101, 218
GMT, 136, 138
Gopher, 174
Gradient, 51
Graphics, 1, 56, 68, 69–71, 77–85, 90–
100, 104–117, 122, 127–137, 158, 179,
217, 218, 236, 238, 252, 253, 254, 259,
260, 311, 316, 318, 319, 320, 321,
324–326, 327
Graphics-based, 93, 224
GUI, 255

Hardware, 1, 8, 236
Header files, 4
Hexadecimal, 6, 9, 20, 21, 39, 155, 216,
217
Horizontal lines, 221
Hosts, 165, 169, 171, 188
HT, 8
HTML, 2, 67, 68–72, 78, 79, 82, 84, 85,
92, 95, 96, 98, 100, 187, 209–243, 307,
309, 310, 324
anchors, 224, 225
background images, 218
colours, 216
definition lists, 215, 245
displaying images, 218
hexadecimal colours, 216
horizontal lines, 221
input types, 232
links, 211
lists, 212, 245
menus, 102, 233
ordered lists, 212
tables, 226

unordered lists, 212, 214
HTML script, 67–72, 78, 79, 82, 84, 85,
92, 95, 96, 98, 100, 209–238
HTTP, 2, 56, 172–174, 183, 184, 211,
218, 222
Hubs, 237
Hypertext, 172

IBM, 237
IEEE, 58, 171
IETF, 172, 243
If statement, 24, 25, 27, 28
Images, 92, 172, 218, 219, 220, 259, 260,
262, 311, 315, 316, 318–321, 324–327
Import statements, 55
Increment, 12, 13, 90, 91, 209
Indexing, 59
Initialisation, 11, 44, 75–77, 99
Initialisation and exit methods, 75, 76
Input/output, 4
Integer division, 12, 19
Intel, 171
Intensity, 251
Interconnected networks, 165
Interconnection length, 237
Interface, 1, 6, 76
Internet, 1, 2, 67, 164–176, 235, 299
addresses, 168, 169
datagram, 166, 167
example domain addresses, 171
example, 168
Explorer, 2, 67
naming structure, 171
primary domain names, 171
IP, 1, 164–171, 176, 178, 188, 189, 196–
198, 215, 236, 237
address format, 169
address, 1, 164–171, 176, 178, 196–
198, 215, 237
addressing, 165, 169, 170
class A, 169
class B, 169
class C, 169, 310, 315, 318, 324
data frames, 166
header, 188
protocol, 165, 166, 167, 168
time-to-live, 167
IPX, 236
ISO, 165
ISO-IP, 165

J++, 306, 310, 311, 315, 319, 325, 328,
335

Java
  compiler, 2, 3, 5, 56, 69, 76, 99
  interpreter, 3, 5, 50, 119, 195
Java.exe, 3–5, 119
Javac.exe, 3–5, 69
JDK, 2–4, 55, 68
JPEG, 92, 101, 218

Key methods, 87
Keyboard, 75, 78, 84, 86
  events, 75, 86
  input, 84
KeyPress, 84–86
Keystroke, 89
Keywords, 24

LAN, 225, 236
League table, 65
Least significant, 35, 36
Length, 232
Library, 54, 57, 63, 70, 130, 331
Light, 217
Line break, 209, 210, 228, 237, 245
Links, 211
List box, 102, 120
Listeners, 80, 86, 87
  action, 106
  item, 109
Lists, 212, 245
Local Area Network, 236
Logical, 12, 14, 24
Logical operator, 14, 16
LOGIN, 189
Loops, 31
Lowercase, 145, 151, 153, 286, 295, 341

Mac, 2
MAC, 164, 165, 168, 214
  address, 164, 165, 168, 214
  layer, 165
Magnitude, 52
Math exceptions, 160
Mathematical, 26, 32, 53, 57, 59, 76, 291
Mean, 51
Memory, 7, 50, 60, 77, 174, 217, 293
Menus, 102, 113, 233
  bar, 102, 118
  multiple, 117
  pop-up, 102, 113, 115, 116, 186, 250, 265
Methods, 40, 58, 70, 75, 247–305, 340
  overloading, 40, 45
Microsoft, 118, 183, 306, 310, 311, 315,

319, 325, 335
  Windows, 118
Military, 171
MIME, 175, 235
Modem connection, 164
Modulus, 12, 13, 36, 39
Mouse, 75, 78, 80, 82, 89, 308
  events, 75, 78
  selection, 82
Moving objects, 97
MPEG, 234
Multi-dimensional arrays, 62
Multimedia, 233, 234
Multiple-line text input, 129
Multiplexing, 188
Multiplication, 13
Multi-station access unit, 237

NAK, 8
Negative, 7, 27, 94, 157–163, 285, 292, 296
Netscape, 2, 67
Network, 1, 164, 170, 225, 233, 234, 236, 237
  addresses, 171, 176
  layer, 164, 166, 188
  management, 237
  traffic, 174, 237
Newline, 9
Non-zero, 24
NT, 2, 68
Numbers, 6

Object-oriented, 1, 40
Objects, 40, 96, 102, 334
Octal, 6, 9, 20, 21, 35, 36, 155
Operating system, 224, 278
Operators, 12–19, 24, 139, 140
OR, 82
Ordered, 212, 213, 244
Organisation, 165, 172, 215, 237
OSI, 164, 165, 166, 188, 214, 238

PA, 90, 91, 256, 272
Packet, 166, 175
Paint() object, 70
Paragraph, 209, 210, 244, 245
Parallel, 11
Parameter list, 59
Parameter passing, 1
Parameters, 51, 67, 68, 70, 84, 93, 95, 221, 227, 228
Parentheses, 18, 19